Jefferson's Body

Jeffersonian America

JAN ELLEN LEWIS, PETER S. ONUF,
AND ANDREW O'SHAUGHNESSY, EDITORS

Jefferson's Body
A Corporeal Biography

MAURIZIO VALSANIA

University of Virginia Press
CHARLOTTESVILLE AND LONDON

University of Virginia Press
© 2017 by the Rector and Visitors of the University of Virginia
All rights reserved
Printed in the United States of America on acid-free paper

First published 2017

9 8 7 6 5 4 3 2 1

Library of Congress Cataloging-in-Publication Data
Names: Valsania, Maurizio, 1965–
Title: Jefferson's body : a corporeal biography / Maurizio Valsania.
Other titles: Jeffersonian America.
Description: Charlottesville ; London : University of Virginia Press, 2017. | Series:
    Jeffersonian America | Includes bibliographical references and index.
Identifiers: LCCN 2016045905| ISBN 9780813939704 (cloth : alk. paper) | ISBN
    9780813939698 (ebook)
Subjects: LCSH: Jefferson, Thomas, 1743–1826—Philosophy. | Jefferson, Thomas,
    1743–1826—Influence.
Classification: LCC B885.Z7 V345 2017 | DDC 191—dc23
LC record available at https://lccn.loc.gov/2016045905

Cover art: Full-length silhouette portrait of Thomas Jefferson by John Marshal, ink
drawing, 1800. (Library of Congress, Prints and Photographs Division, Washington,
D.C.)

To Andy and Frank

Contents

Acknowledgments

Writing a book entails sharing ideas and experiences with friends and colleagues—the more, the better. Sharing represents perhaps the most challenging and exciting part of so-called authorship. This book, in particular, made me aware that I am a citizen in a thriving Republic of Letters.

To begin with, I am honored to have collaborated with Kathleen Brown. With an amazing dedication, Kathy went again and again through my manuscript. Her comments, suggestions, and criticisms brought my original project to a new level. I have stolen ideas from her, and at times I have lifted many smart phrases she happened to pitch during our virtual and real conversations. Should I voice my debt to her one hundred times over I would not convey enough my sense of gratitude: without Kathy, *Jefferson's Body* would never exist.

The support of a group of *Amigos* has been similarly important. *Amigo* Peter Onuf has been taking me on Jeffersonian journeys for fifteen years now. His confidence has never wavered, and I only hope to be up to the task for many more years to come. A mentor, Peter read the entire manuscript and provided invaluable suggestions. But there is more here than just collaboration and professional commitment. On many occasions, he and Kristin Onuf put me up at their *Rancho de Luxe* in Charlottesville. We talked things through over wine and many beers. Kristin and Peter fed me. They know that it is no joke when I call them Mom and Dad.

Amiga Annette Gordon-Reed has been incredibly generous with her time and expertise. Over dinners, lunches, and walks, whether in Central Park or by Italian lakesides, she has discussed with me several Jeffersonian topics. Furthermore, she has read and commented on many sections of this book. I count myself very lucky to have succeeded in seeing her regularly, both in

Europe and in the United States. That this practice will continue is my biggest wish.

From *Amigo* Alan Taylor I have learned to take a much broader view on American history than I used to. Our conversations and his marvelous books have prompted me to think on a continental scale. He has literally enlarged my horizons. Getting to know Alan and Emily Albu has been a life-changing experience. It happens sometimes that people meet and immediately hit it off—in this case, more than intellectually. We not only talked history; we traveled together, we cracked many jokes, and, of course, we played pool. He and Emily have introduced my wife and me to their closest friends. Do I sound boastful if I say that I trust I have become one of these *closest*—perhaps an *Amigo* myself?

Speaking of my wife, *Amiga* Serenella Iovino: her path-breaking intellectual creativity in the field of the environmental humanities is recognized the world over. From her research I took the notion that corporeality can be a source of endless narratives. I owe her a lot more than these acknowledgments may, as a matter of fact, acknowledge. We have been living together for twenty years, but she is still new. She makes me laugh.

For more than twenty years, the Robert H. Smith International Center for Jefferson Studies (ICJS), part of the Thomas Jefferson Foundation, has been providing support to scholars interested in the age of Jefferson. Its outstanding staff and excellent facilities, first and foremost the Jefferson Library, are coveted by a growing number of fellows, both international and national. The ICJS awards generous grants, from which I have repeatedly profited. The persons who work at the Thomas Jefferson Foundation are no less generous. In particular, I have to thank Andrew Jackson O'Shaughnessy, the Saunders Director of the ICJS, and then (listed alphabetically) Anna Berkes, Lisa Francavilla, Melanie Lower, Madeleine Rhondeau, Jack Robertson, Mary Scott-Fleming, Tasha Stanton, Susan Stein, Endrina Tay, and Gaye Wilson.

Christa Dierksheide, historian at the ICJS, deserves a special mention. Without losing her temper, she underwent the ordeal of going through a very rough draft of my manuscript. Her inputs have been tremendously helpful. A first-rank historian, Christa is also gifted as a cook. She set up for me many lavish Italian meals, the best I ever had. Her friendship is dear to me.

Jefferson's Body has benefited from two grants. The first was given in 2014 by the ICJS; the second, in 2015, by the German Academic Exchange Service (DAAD). The DAAD allowed me to spend three months at the Ludwig Maximilian University of Munich under the supervision of Michael Hochgeschwender, to whom I extend my heartfelt thanks. While in Bavaria, I had the chance to give a lecture at the University of Augsburg. Hubert Zapf has been a wonderful host. He is a still more wonderful friend.

Working with the University of Virginia Press is a reward on its own. Richard Holway, for the third time, has believed in what I do. Apparently, Dick has taken up the peculiar habit of turning all my projects into books. It is always a pleasure to team up with Robert Burchfield. Bob's copyediting is impeccable.

Jefferson's Body is dedicated to Andrew Burstein and Francis D. Cogliano. Andy and Frank are two of the most refined Jefferson scholars the Republic of Letters has ever had—but everyone already knows that. For many years, they have been reading everything I put on paper. I rely on them unapologetically. I pester them because their judgment is sound. Furthermore, their conversation is deep and amiable; their bearing is always unassuming—very Jeffersonian qualities. They have become my role models. Every time I make a decision, or I undertake an action whatsoever, I ask myself the same question Thomas Jefferson used to ask himself apropos his personal role models, William Small and George Wythe: "What would Andy and Frank do in this situation? What course in it will ensure me their approbation?"

Jefferson's Body

Introduction

Over the last two centuries or so, historians have dissected Thomas Jefferson's mind. Jefferson's thoughts, tenets, and public statements have been woven together in a plausible narrative—actually many plausible narratives. Similarly, his inner self—his heart, beliefs, emotions—and secret ruminations have been analyzed, contextualized, and narrated over and over again.

However, to a large extent, Jefferson's *persona* or, in material terms, his body, still waits to be discovered. Bits and pieces about what Jefferson "looked like" are scattered throughout the archive. But do we have a coherent historical narrative about Thomas Jefferson's outer self? Perhaps more important, can a systematic analysis of Jefferson's corporeality give us new insights into his personality? Can we interpret this long-gone body to gain access to eighteenth-century challenges and limitations?

This gentle, reserved man always sought to divert attention away from himself—or so he claimed. And yet Jefferson did not escape the general rule that bodies as such exhibit an almost magical quality: they are "here" and "there" at the same time, simultaneously private and public, at once silent and eloquent. Human bodies cross boundaries. They reach out toward social spaces as they move, make gestures, have postures, dance, or put on facial expressions. They make impressions through clothes, adornment, hair, skin, sounds, and smells. And they reach out through time, by leaving clear memories and traces on other persons' experiences. (How many visitors to Monticello have had the impression that Jefferson's electrical presence seems to still hover around?) Bodies tell stories.

We are told that Jefferson's voice was unfit to reach out to large audiences. He lacked the masculine, authoritative tone devised to overawe listeners. William Wirt, the man who eulogized both Jefferson and John Adams in the House of Representatives on 19 October 1826, wrote that when Jefferson spoke in public, his voice usually sank into his throat and became unintelligible: "he wanted volume and compass of voice for a large assembly; and his voice, from the excess of his sensibility, instead of rising with his feelings and conceptions, sunk under their pressure and became guttural and inarticulate."[1]

Like everyone else's, Jefferson's corporeal self combined strong and flimsy elements. But whether or not his voice was a match for thunder, whether or not he was really reserved, we can confidently assert that his body was far from inert matter, an insignificant or ineffective mass. Jefferson's body was like every other human body, a movable field of lived experiences, of tentative performances, of eloquence made practical, and a locus of continuous revelations spanning over eighty-three years of his life.

There are a series of problems to fathom in any assessment of the body. Understandably, Thomas Jefferson as a case study raises particular concerns. But historical distance and the inaccessibility of the subject, or its accessibility only via signs and traces, do not represent the only obstacle.

The biggest problem when we speak of the body, any body, is that we are referring to a huge array of phenomena. What we call "the body" is actually a blend of style, manners, hair, skin, smiles, postures, clothes, ceremonial costumes, gestures of salutation, facial expressions, carriage, tattoos, jewelry, mechanical aids and proxies, anatomic features, physiological and medical issues, and many other elements. Sociologists and anthropologists have long launched warnings against splitting the *body system*, as they prefer to call it, into its constituent parts.[2]

Given that the body is actually a rather complex system, to interpret Thomas Jefferson's body, or any other body, we need to do much more than just opening our eyes and focusing on a selected aspect, clothes or manners, or a few well-known physical, anatomic, and physiological characteristics, like height and health. To fully grasp a human body, we would need to synthesize research on a vast array of subjects, from clothing and fashion to manners, adornment, posture, gesture, expression, visual culture, and so on. We would need to survey medical sciences, cultural anthropology, psychology, social anthropology, and gender studies. We would need to incorporate studies of education, whiteness, masculinity, and material culture, among others. In addition, to properly assess *this* body, Jefferson's body, we would also have to absorb what is known about race and slavery, to become acquainted with the American eighteenth-century elites, to gather information about the history of the Early Republic, to analyze Virginia society and its families, to delve into oratory, art history, and much more. Obviously, no one will ever be able to master all these realms of knowledge. But these difficulties notwithstanding, I believe the venture is worthwhile and should be attempted.

I think the reader will be fascinated by the ways Thomas Jefferson's body branched out in many directions, telling several interesting and, at times, harrowing stories. But in no way can we maintain that the body—his body as well as our bodies—is simply a language of which the intellect and the inner self are in full command. Our inner selves and minds do not only convey messages through our outer selves but our bodies also set our minds in motion and make us who we are. Our bodies control us at least as much as we control our bodies.

It is not only that from time to time bodies break away from our intentions and escape our plans, as everyone would agree. Bodies often betray us by delivering the wrong message; they reveal calculations, feelings, and desires that we wish to hide, subverting the ways we would like to be perceived and interpreted by other people.

Saying that bodies control us also means that, as we are increasingly aware, our consciousness, cognitive processes, deepest emotions, and beliefs are often shaped and structured by corporeality and corporeal interactions. The way individuals carry themselves, intentionally or otherwise, forces their inner selves to adjust and adapt along the lines suggested by their body systems. Physical attributes and how we "feel," manners, clothes, postures, and in general our corporeality, make us who we are at least as much as the other way around. We choose our clothes and manners, we decide to put on stage a certain *persona*, at times a revolutionary one, but clothes and manners, traits and behaviors, also make the person. The body makes the person.[3]

The trajectory of this book goes from Jefferson's self (part 1) to his interaction with others (part 2).

Part 1 deals with Jefferson telling us about his outer, material, embodied self. Testimonies and firsthand characterizations of Jefferson's physicality provide fundamental clues to better understand this late eighteenth-century postmartial, postaristocratic philosopher and "deeply conflicted" slave owner. However, since "body" means many things—behaviors, habits, deliberate performances, strategies of self-presentation, anatomical characteristics, styles, and so on—I did not make as my premise a too rigid, a priori definition of corporeality. I let Jefferson's body system speak for itself, often through the words of others, depending on the context and the moment of my narrative.

As the reader is about to see, Jefferson's corporeality took its cue from a cluster of basic principles. Throughout his life, and each time he could, Jefferson aimed at what for him were naturalness and simplicity. The "invention of naturalness," as we may also call the strategy Jefferson devised, and by which *he* was devised, gave direction to his life.

Part 2 expands the discourse on Jefferson's corporeality along the only other possible direction. After "Jefferson on himself," part 2 examines Jefferson's interactions with, and reactions to, others' bodies. It is more than reviewing what he thought about other human groups. It gets more physical than just a repertoire of ideas. After having situated Jefferson in his body, I then situate the embodied Jefferson in the world of other men, white women, and enslaved people. Whether male or female; free or slave; black, red, or just an "odd" shade of white, these "others" helped this eighteenth-century Virginian to define himself and his own place in the world.

Although this book is not an example of comparative biography (Jefferson and Adams, Jefferson and Sally Hemings, and so on), I do delve into specific, unique interactions between Jefferson and other people, his daughters being a notable example. On the whole, however, rather than analyzing relationships between Jefferson and his family or lovers or political enemies or allies about which other biographers have had much to say, I try to stick to Jefferson's reactions to typical, generic bodies, "natural" specimens belonging to "natural" classes. While in part 1 the discourse is to a certain extent biographical (an attempt at *corporeal* biography), in part 2 the argument is necessarily somewhat more theoretical—anthropological and ethnological—but my goal in structuring the book in this way is to arrive at a conclusion about Jefferson that has perhaps eluded other writers.

Through the comparison between the two parts of the book a clear pattern emerges. Jefferson presented himself as a simple "nature's man." But when Jefferson applied "nature" to his body, such a strategy was in no way an obstacle to a process of liberation and especially modernization. His Enlightenment principles led him to a very modern perspective, that he could perfect his own corporeality. On the other hand, each time Jefferson deployed "nature" to make sense of "others"—African Americans, for example—he imagined that nature was a constraining and limiting force. "Nature," this time, decreed that the "other" was *determined*, that those groups of people were unfortunate. The consequence is that as long as Jefferson's body became more dynamic and flexible, the other's body remained, for him, significantly rigid and unable to change.

It is perhaps no mystery that such an "invention of the other" enhances an individual's sense of possibility and control, while providing some kind of reassurance about personal status or capabilities. Such a static definition of the body of the "other" provides its inventor with an excuse for indulging in self-aggrandizement.

Through this journey into the discovery of what is perhaps the most interesting example of an eighteenth-century American body system, I draw on quotes and excerpts from Jefferson's writings that will be familiar to many. However, I ask readers to bear with me and to read these familiar quotes from a different angle—one that reveals complex dynamics concerning corporeality. I hope that my different approach will allow these quotes and other notorious facts about Jefferson's life to be read anew. Through the writing of this book, I have come to believe that they will show us that Jefferson, a "nature's man," freed himself (and to a lesser extent the selves of others) from many traditional strictures. But he did not, could not, become "one of us."

PART 1

Self

A Mild and Pleasing Countenance

Contemporaries recognized Thomas Jefferson as an extraordinary man. It was Jefferson's mind, his erudition and character, that struck them in the first place. The philosopher who drafted the Declaration of Independence made an impression. Congress appointed him minister plenipotentiary to France on 7 May 1784, because almost everyone was convinced of his intellectual merits. The years he spent in Paris (from late August 1784 to October 1789) added to his fame. Furthermore, those years broadened and strengthened his mind and refined his character.

But even before setting sail for Europe, Jefferson was already widely admired. Ezra Stiles, president of Yale College and celebrated theologian and author, called him "a most ingenuous Naturalist and Philosopher, a truly scientific and learned Man, and every way excellent." Jefferson's friend John Adams agreed with Stiles. Adams and Jefferson had worked together "at many a knotty Problem," and Adams trusted his "Abilities and Steadiness."[1]

Marquis de Chastellux, the French officer who brilliantly served during the War of Independence, got to know Jefferson well. He visited Monticello in April 1782 and was glad to see him again in Paris. Chastellux bequeathed one of the most famous characterizations of the young man: "Let me describe to you a man, not yet forty, tall, and with a mild and pleasing countenance, but whose mind and understanding are ample substitutes for every exterior grace." Chastellux saw Jefferson as an accomplished musician, a geometrician, an astronomer, a legislator, and a statesman, a philosopher who voluntarily retired from the world "because he loves the world." "No object had escaped Mr. Jefferson," he concluded, "and it seemed as if from his youth he had placed his mind, as he has done his house, on an elevated situation, from which he might contemplate the universe."[2]

Offering a personal view rather than an impartial description, Chastellux focused his attention upon the topic of "mind and understanding." Jefferson was skilled and reserved; he was effective enough as a governor of Virginia during troublesome times, but, possibly, such effectiveness was played against his natural temper. On the whole, for Chastellux, Jefferson was an "elevated mind" almost without body, happy to contemplate the world, and eager to improve it. A philosopher or an ideologue (as Jefferson's foes would prefer to label him) rather than an embodied man of action and a ruthless operator, Jefferson, according to Chastellux, would have fully realized his natural destiny if he could set himself apart from the public arena, literally and materially.

Modern-day biographers and historians have added many more facets to Jefferson-the-philosopher. The latest research shows that this leader was far from timid or idealistic when he had to put up with harsh reality and expedients—even though the "leadership he sought," as Henry Adams wrote, may have been "one of sympathy and love, not of command." Jefferson kept jumping into the arena. Regardless of many famous disclaimers and utterances about early retirement, he never seriously sought to stay away from the world and achieve disembodiment. As he eloquently wrote to his daughter Mary, "I am convinced our own happiness requires that we should continue to mix with the world, & to keep pace with it as it goes."[3]

Wrong as Chastellux may have been in missing the physically proactive aspects of Jefferson's *persona,* he was right to emphasize that his corporeality communicated mildness. Jefferson was tall, Chastellux said. But his masculinity, as he made very clear, relied more on a "mild and pleasing" countenance than on the self-possessed bearing and the "exterior grace" expected from a military hero (but his "mind and understanding," Chastellux acknowledged, counterbalanced this shortcoming). Chastellux was himself a military man and an aristocrat, and he had a precise notion of what a truly "gracious" man should look like. And yet Jefferson's bodily mildness makes a lot of sense. We will see Jefferson's mildness unfolding throughout the first part of the book, its components analyzed.

Almost Femininely Soft and Gentle

Firsthand descriptions of corporeal Thomas Jefferson insist on his excellence. Many witnesses, family and acquaintances, depicted Jefferson as "right square-shouldered" and "a tall, straight-bodied man" (Isaac Jefferson, slave at Monticello). He was "like a fine horse," which means a "well proportioned [man] and straight as a gun barrel" (Edmund Bacon, overseer at Monticello). Sir Augustus John Foster, a British diplomat, described his "appearance being very much like that of a large-boned farmer . . . very tall and bony." "Mr. Jefferson's figure was rather majestic: tall (over six feet), thin, and rather high-shouldered" (George Flower, upon his visit to Poplar Forest). Everyone agreed on Jefferson being "tall and very straight" (Samuel Whitcomb Jr., itinerant bookseller).[4]

Jefferson was in fact tall, six feet two-and-a-half inches, as his grandson Thomas Jefferson Randolph tells us. This means that he was conspicuously tall, but not a giant. He must have impressed his contemporaries in the way a man over six feet four inches would impress us today. More than height per se, harmonious bearing, mildness, and natural agility were the features of his *persona* that contemporaries invariably noticed. Samuel Harrison Smith, a lifelong supporter of Jefferson and the founder of the Washington *National Intelligencer,* described him, not surprisingly, as "lofty and erect." But he also mentioned that Jefferson was remarkably "flexible and easy" in his motions, even as he aged: "such were his strength and agility, that he was accustomed in the society of children, of which he was fond, to practise feats that few could imitate." "Mr. Jefferson's large person," Reverend Theodore Dehon wrote upon visiting Monticello in May 1814, "moved with great ease and more rapidity, than one unaccustomed to it could have done, over his well-waxed, tesselated mahogany-floor." Frances (Fanny) Wright, the feminist writer and social reformer who accompanied General Lafayette on his 1824 trip to the United States, agreed that Jefferson's "tall well-moulded figure remains erect as at the age of 20, and his step is as light and springy as tho it cd. bear him without effort up the steepest sides of his favourite mountains."[5]

Despite the fact that Jefferson was slightly taller than George Washington, who almost certainly measured six feet two inches, we do not perceive him, or remember him in our collective national memory, as the prototypical imposing hero. Jefferson did not want to be seen that way, as primarily tall and imposing. He cared about other features. It was for him more important being perceived as flexible, adaptable, limber, harmonious, inviting, and to a wide extent seductive. He capitalized on his "light and springy" step.

And he succeeded, at least up to the moment when age took its revenge. Nature and deliberate choices crafted Jefferson's body into a more than just commanding specimen of eighteenth-century heroic masculinity. He had limbs "uncommonly long; his hands and feet very large, and his wrists of an extraordinary size." He was a lanky figure, as Daniel Webster, the famous orator and senator from Massachusetts, pointed out in this last characterization. In his gait, Webster wrote, Jefferson was "not precise and military, but easy and swinging. . . . His general appearance indicates an extraordinary degree of health, vivacity, and spirit." Thomas Jefferson Randolph agreed with this characterization. Jefferson, he wrote, was "well formed, indicating strength, activity, and robust health; his carriage, erect; step firm and elastic, which he preserved to his death." Many comments on Jefferson, even as a slightly stooped old man, emphasize elasticity and what we may call a *magnetic mildness:* "Mr. Jefferson—a tall, straight, sandy-complexioned man," the American author Daniel Pierce Thompson wrote upon meeting him sometime between June and July 1821, "advanced with an elastic step and serene countenance." Thompson was greeted with a "sweet, winning smile." Doubtless, this was "one of the secrets of his great personal popularity and magnetic power over all whom he would conciliate."[6]

Not a martial, but a musical, mild, swinging, and inviting masculinity seemed to emanate from Jefferson's body. In his celebrated *Life of Thomas Jefferson: Third President of the United States* (1874), James Parton evoked the iconic larger-than-life hero, an ideal hovering above history. More than other interpreters, Parton shaped the understanding of subsequent generations. He represented an exceptionally masculine and yet musical and gracious idol, harmoniously gesturing, dancing, and felicitously engaging with his own corporeality. Which American public figure, Parton rhetorically asked, could "calculate an eclipse, survey an estate, tie an artery, plan an edifice, try a cause, break a horse, dance a minuet, and play the violin"?[7]

Another famous analogous description comes to mind. Parton's Jefferson, pursuing harmony and embodying mildness, resembles Margaret Bayard Smith's romanticized characterization of him as "almost femininely soft and gentle." Late in her life, Smith, the wife of Samuel Harrison Smith and a regular visitor at the White House during Jefferson's presidency, discovered a talent for writing novels. She also recorded her recollections, which were eventually published in 1906. An interesting mixture of speculation

and reportage, *The First Forty Years of Washington Society,* as her reminiscences and notebooks were called, is an important document. It contains the
suggestive, if perhaps extravagant sketch of Jefferson as so mild as to be at
odds with the average male identity: "With a manner and voice almost femininely soft and gentle," she wrote remembering her first impressions of the
man, Jefferson "entered into conversation on the commonplace topics of the
day. . . . I know not how it was, but there was something in his manner, his
countenance and voice, that at once unlocked my heart." "Extravagant" does
not mean "mistaken." Despite her overloaded nineteenth-century language,
Margaret Bayard Smith spotted a trait of Jefferson's engaging corporeality
that appeared in many other accounts of the man.[8]

Habituate Yourself to Walk Very Far

Mild, harmonious, flexible, engaging, maybe also "feminine," and not only
during the episode recalled by Margaret Bayard Smith, Jefferson had an
unconventional corporeality. With body, Jefferson reached out mildly, gently,
never violently, but with appropriate vigor. This idealist and dreamer was very
much present in the world. He attached extraordinary importance to the principle of keeping his body fit, *mens sana in corpore sano,* as Latin poet Juvenal
put it. Exercising and movement were obviously important for his health.
Sex, it has been argued, was also part of a healthy regimen, which included
diet, horse-riding, gaming, conversation, and especially walking: "Give about
two . . . [hours] every day to exercise," Jefferson wrote programmatically to
Peter Carr. "A strong body makes the mind strong." Exercise should always
be moderate, never "too violent for the body." Walking was definitely the best:
"Habituate yourself to walk very far. The Europeans value themselves on having subdued the horse to the uses of man. But I doubt whether we have not
lost more than we have gained by the use of this animal."[9]

More than good health was at stake in Jefferson's plea for "moderate" exercise. A trim, healthy, mild, and balanced body, wary of any excess, molded
upon precise routines and regimens, is at once the cause and the effect of an
increased sense of one's potential, or what we would call a sense of "agency."
Self-representation and self-image have much to gain from a hale and harmonious body. For almost all his life, Jefferson was blessed with the capabil-
ity of experiencing his body as entirely his own, occupying a virtuous middle
ground between the extremes of slothful softness and brutal force. He cultivated his body in order to reach mildness, and he came to know that this

vehicle was some kind of reliable machine over which he could exert full control.

Jefferson felt he was in command of his body—not quite so, as we will see, when he reached old age. For most of the time, he could envision himself as strong *enough* and not weak, limber *enough* and not rigid. Because of these enoughs and middle grounds, he could sense he was ultimately free and not in shackles. Consequently, the belief in his personal ability to generate, to beget, to produce was reinforced by the fact that his corporeality became much what he wanted it to become: mild and harmonious, a perfect middle ground. Jefferson's Enlightenment optimism, his sanguine trust in the future, even his confidence in his unwavering mental performances, were conditional on a tamed and trained bodily frame that complemented a gentle and welcoming character, an ally and not a hindrance.

Consciousness, intellectual life, capacity for knowledge, lucidity, or memory cannot be held apart from a certain kind of "successful" body. As Maurice Merleau-Ponty, the French philosopher, appropriately wrote, "consciousness is in the first place not a matter of 'I think that' but of 'I can.'" And Jefferson definitely sensed he could carry out plans, execute missions, and implement many projects. During almost all his life, he remained confident in his capacity to control his physical motility, while achieving what for him was a harmonious Aristotelian middle ground between two extremes.[10]

If the Body Be Feeble, the Mind Will Not Be Strong

There are more than medical issues at play in Jefferson's saying that "if the body be feeble, the mind will not be strong." Jefferson presented and represented his body as achieving the middle ground and his mind, consequently, as "strong." When the body is too feeble, or hungry, deprived, displaced, slothful, or in shackles, unfree, taken by a bout of rage and violence, or under the spell of unrestrained passions, the mind is affected and knowledge or wisdom cannot be gained.[11]

This eighteenth-century man, evidently, never theorized about the process of embodiment, as Merleau-Ponty would do about two centuries later. But the reader who sifts through Jefferson's writings will realize that they are articulating the basic concepts of such a process. It is not an arbitrary choice to read him along these lines because Jefferson himself repeatedly described his personal way of envisioning an *optimal* process of embodiment. Corporeal presence in terms of flexibility, moderation, harmony, and equilibrium, and those other "mild" characteristics we have already encountered, was for him the necessary condition for a healthy and balanced inner life.

Jefferson knew how to direct this process of embodiment. Exercise was not intended to nurture sheer force, a harsh display of prowess, and an athletic performance for its own sake. Jefferson did not aim at a brutally masculine, explosive body, fraught with aggressiveness or unchecked animality. The metaphor appearing in this letter to Thomas Mann Randolph of "brute animals . . . the most healthy" may work as a regulative principle, or simply a theoretical limit, but Jefferson was seeking a more civilized, virtuous version of bodily activity. The type of body he had cultivated during a big part of his life, for himself and others, had to be trained, and had to convey a message of equilibrium, a "golden mean," or *controlled* strength.[12]

We should take Jefferson's love of walking very seriously. Jefferson never did or said things haphazardly. If he focused his attention on walking, and if he wanted to be recognized as a committed walker, it was because walking, of many other physical activities, enhances a sense of mildness and control. It does not make you ruffled, or sweaty, or unattractive, or inurbane. Walking dictates a vertical and straight bearing. In addition, being so distinctively recursive, formalized, and musical, walking is similar to a prayer, a ritual, and may lead the walker into a state of trance. Walking is essential to the construction of a person's sense of humanness: it is cathartic. Moreover, it draws a clear line between humans and nonhumans. We need no leap of fantasy to picture Jefferson, when he was at the peak of his personal *bildungsroman*, taking endless strolls in Paris. He certainly reconstituted his corporeal self by means of many experiences, and one of the most important, for him, was walking hours on end to buy books or furniture, to visit shops or friends, or just for the intrinsic pleasure of (self-)discovery. Back home, he could have taken part in more traditionally "masculine" and typically Virginian "sports," such as cockfighting, horse racing, wrestling, drinking, and gambling. But he preferred mildness and walking.[13]

I Am on Horseback Three or Four Hours of Every Day

Beginning a sought-after retirement from public office, Jefferson pretended to read not very much, only "one or two newspapers a week." Whether true or (probably) false, the fact remains that neighbors and slaves often saw the aging man constantly on horseback, but still taking strolls. He wanted to be seen in constant movement. Reading may have been somewhat neglected, but he actually gave "more time to exercise of the body than of the mind, believing it wholesome to both." God forbid he had to give up his composed and dignified physical activity or be portrayed as sedentary: "The loss of the power of taking exercise would be a sore affliction to me," he wrote to his friend the physician Benjamin Rush. "It has been the delight of my retirement to be in constant bodily activity, looking after my affairs. it was never damped, as the pleasures of reading are, by the question of cui bono? for what object? . . . the sedentary character of my public occupations sapped a constitution naturally sound and vigorous, and draws it to an earlier close."[14]

When biology waged its revenge, as we will see better later on, and Jefferson was forced to slow down, he reverted full-time to horse riding. Starting from 1812, walking had for him become painful: "I walk little," he wrote to John Adams, "a single mile being too much for me." And yet his pursuit of mildness took other forms. He spent considerable time on his steed: "I am on horseback 3. or 4. hours of every day; visit 3. or 4. times a year a possession I have 90 miles distant, performing the winter journey on horseback."[15]

At seventy-six, Jefferson was frequently seen on horseback, "too feeble, indeed, to walk much, but riding without fatigue six or eight miles a day, and sometimes thirty or forty." "I can walk but little," he wrote again to John Adams one year later, "but I ride 6. or 8. miles a day without fatigue. . . . Our University, 4. miles distant, gives me frequent exercise." In November 1820, Edmund Bacon, Jefferson's overseer, bought "Eagle," an especially good-natured and reliable "fine bay." Jefferson trusted this new four-legged friend without reserve, likely his last riding horse. In 1824, Jefferson wrote to painter Charles Willson Peale: "I ride every day from 3. or 4. to 8. or 10. miles without fatigue, but I am little able to walk, and never further than my garden." Still, Jefferson continued the habit of riding up to the moment when, as Sarah Randolph tells us, he "was so weak that he could only get into the saddle by stepping down from the terrace."[16]

Horse riding has always carried a symbolic appeal, thus bringing the human figure to a mythical completion. A useful, necessary tool, for sure, the horse has for centuries, perhaps millennia, uplifted the horseman, imaginatively, physically, and socially: the horseman could become, literally, a cavalier. But for Jefferson the horse retained few of the traditional meanings that Virginians had customarily attached to it. Virginians carried on endless conversations about their horses. Virginia tradition had that a horse, as one historian has eloquently put it, "was an extension of its owner; indeed, a man was only as good as his horse." For the elder Jefferson, it was no longer such a direct surrogate of manly prowess and aristocratic martiality, but he kept his interest in horses alive well into the 1820s, as we can see from his Memorandum Books. He relied on his horses to reach mildness. He cared for his horses, and gave them names: "The General," "Jacobin," "Le Fleur," "Powhatan," or "Tecumseh." Ossianic names are even more stylish and tongue-in-cheek: "Fingal," "Ryno," or "Cuthona." In this way, he could perhaps imagine himself dressed in the garb of a mythical hero.[17]

Always Singing When Ridin' or Walkin'

Horse riding requires coordination, equilibrium, containment, bodily discipline, strength, and a sense of rhythm. Many of these qualities are also engaged by playing and listening to music. Jefferson's lifelong talent for music, including an enduring interest for dance, is narrated in every biography. Music, he once famously confessed to the Florentine polymath Giovanni Fabbroni, was "the favorite passion of my soul." Unfortunately, Jefferson was not much of a public performer. He actually had performed with his beloved violin, at the Governor's Palace in Williamsburg, when he was a young student. Throughout his life he continued to buy violins, harpsichords for his daughters, and guitars for his daughters and granddaughters. But as the years flew by, Jefferson-the-musician and Jefferson-the-dancer were consigned to the sequestered space of the parlor, at Monticello, where he could amuse himself with his wife first, and his daughters later. Music was no longer a characteristic of his public *persona*, even though his intellectual curiosity never dwindled.[18]

In a way, however, music kept entering the field of Jefferson's mild and civilized public performances. Ellen, Jefferson's beloved granddaughter, gives us an eloquent sketch of what had become an enduring habit: "his voice, though *he never sang except in the retirement of his own rooms*, was sweet and clear and continued unbroken to a very late period of his life." Ellen's chamber at Monticello was directly over Jefferson's. During the intervals of his occupations, the granddaughter recalls, "*I used not unfrequently to hear him humming* old tunes, generally Scotch songs but sometimes Italian airs or hymns." Jefferson-the-musician, including Jefferson-the-singer, never left the "retirement" of his own rooms, but his humming did become widely known to his acquaintances. Jefferson, Edmund Bacon observed, "was nearly always humming some tune, or singing in a low tone to himself." Isaac Jefferson writes in his memoirs that Jefferson was a hummer, "always singing when ridin' or walkin'."[19]

The mature Jefferson sang almost incessantly, but in a contained, controlled, semiprivate, and measured way. The singing and humming Jefferson did was simultaneously controlled and uncontrolled. It was controlled in that Jefferson never embarrassed himself or his friends. Jefferson did not suffer from a syndrome, and he could stop if he wanted or when circumstances dictated. But the constant humming was also an involuntary reflex, a leak of instinct, the signal of a deep passion of his soul, a useful discharge of psychological energy, so to speak, occurring in an otherwise highly controlled and harmonious personality. Humming is self-stimulating, recursive, ritualized, cathartic. Not really a mannerism or a pathological stereotyped behavior, humming nonetheless revealed Jefferson's bubbling interiority.

In a certain sense, Jefferson performed music publicly, by presenting himself, intentionally or unintentionally, not only as a hummer but as a man craving order, regularity, the "golden mean," and rhythm. Jay Fliegelman, the scholar who studied the Declaration as a specimen belonging to a larger "culture of performance," insists that Jefferson-the-musician, together with Jefferson-the-hummer, must be tied to Jefferson-the-counter: Jefferson's penchant for accounting, scientific measurement, and "a lifetime habit of dividing virtually everything into mathematical units" had much to do with his musical disposition, and vice versa. "Jefferson's interest in music had as much to do with *measure* as with *expression*."[20]

Music is more than an audible experience or, as Fliegelman says, "expression." Jefferson performed music and *was* musical, especially in the sense that he presented himself as taken by measure. Jefferson let other people see him as a *persona* in search of measure, mildness, and perfect equilibrium. An older Jefferson restated in a sublimated form what he had long before confessed to Giovanni Fabbroni, that music was his favorite passion. Mathematics, which is a form of music before it becomes audible expression, was similarly able to capture his soul. As he said to his friend Benjamin Rush in 1811, mathematics was "ever my favorite" study. In mathematics, "all is demonstration & satisfaction." Jefferson did not change his mind, and both music and mathematics gave him the same amount of satisfaction. The passion of his soul was at once music and, on the other hand, equations, charts, diagrams, graphics, tables, or lists. These things are essentially the same.[21]

Agreeable Society Is the First Essential

In music, as in public speaking, dressing, declaiming poetry, or any other expression, the virtue consists in attaining measure, control, and the "middle ground." Measure enhances the effect and adds to the beauty of the performance. Good manners do precisely the same with the body; they are a sort of music for the body. The corollary is that a human body endowed with manners and seeking mildness and refinement is better than an instinctive one, be it a feeble or, at the opposite, a brutally strong body. Manners have been defined as the "rule-bound and symbolic behaviors that we perform in the presence of others." Manners intersect with, or are tantamount to, etiquette, ceremonial behaviors, social and rituals of interaction, politeness, refinement, and many practices of consumption. Through our manners, we always differentiate between what is admissible or inadmissible, appropriate or taboo.[22]

The general trend of manners in America, as historians have highlighted, goes from a minus to a plus. The refinement of America began around 1690, Richard Bushman argues. "With the houses went new modes of speech, dress, body carriage, and manners." However, as Bushman insists, "it would be an error to conclude that by the Revolution most Americans were genteel. . . . Gentility was the proper style of the gentry alone in the eighteenth century, as earlier it belonged to courtiers."[23]

Manners vary greatly and not only, obviously, across cultures and time. They vary, as Bushman makes clear, within a given social setting: even when individuals share a community, the measure of refinement that is commendable for one may not be permissible or even thinkable for another. Gender, ethnicity, age, and especially class create differences. The obvious fact that manners in eighteenth-century Virginia society were in many ways different from those into which we are immersed today does not need further discussion. Much more interesting to underscore is that, within a given social setting, manners create distinctions. Refinement and good manners may have swept the American continent. But manners and refinement kept performing an important social function, "that of communicating a person's place in a social group." In other terms, they "served one common purpose—that of regulating and reinforcing inequality." The tension between, on the one hand, good manners and, on the other hand, class inequality and exclusion is precisely what this section analyzes.[24]

White southerners, and Jefferson in particular, were legendary for their good manners and refinement, including hospitality. Stories go that, especially after Jefferson retired from the presidency, there were flocks of visitors going uphill to pay him homage, with sometimes up to fifty guests dining and staying overnight. First of all, Jefferson was such a generous, refined host because the material burden of hospitality fell upon the shoulders of slaves and women. These are obvious darker sides of Jefferson's mildness, good manners, and gentility, and this is what "regulating and reinforcing inequality" means in its most brutal and concrete form. That slaves and women had to materially provide the hospitability that Jefferson took credit for is the first, most apparent type of inequality upheld by the practices of refinement and good manners.

Let me insist on this first form of inequality. A famous letter Jefferson sent from Paris to his friend the physician George Gilmer helps make the point very clear. Pining for a quick return to his refined, harmonious, simple, and pleasing society, Jefferson reveals *to us* the extent of his unawareness—first of all about the burden carried by his women and his slaves: "I am as happy no where else and in no other society," he wrote "and all my wishes end, where I hope my days will end, at Monticello. Too many scenes of happiness mingle themselves with all the recollections of my native woods and feilds, to suffer them to be supplanted in my affection by any other."[25]

In the same geographical locations where he experienced happiness, harmony, mildness, refinement, friendship, and rural simplicity, we see brutality. We see, just like Comte de Volney saw, *"corps brun sale plutôt que noirs"* (dirty-brown bodies rather than black) disgraced by a *"demi-nudité misérable et hideuse"* (seminakedness wretched and hideous), and, like him, we are seized by *"un premier sentiment de tristesse et de terreur"* (a primeval feeling of sadness and terror). Jefferson knew he had not to raise his voice in anger; he knew he had not to lift the whip to inflict punishment. But what he took for the proper measure of refinement was simply the separation of authority, hierarchy, and power from physical coercion. Under the magic spell of Jefferson's flexible, musical masculinity and friendly good manners, as Kathleen Brown has written, "self-mastery and harmonious, if not affectionate, familial relations thus went hand in hand, swathing the violent history of planter power in an insulating layer of emotional serenity." Relinquishing violence while retaining intact the structure of authority and hierarchy, refinement and good manners communicated to everyone the impression that the relationships of which the master was the artificial center were normal and natural.[26]

Good manners and "agreeable" society were inseparable. But as long as Jefferson worshipped refinement and gentility, as long as he kept being an exquisite host, as long as he worked to build up Monticello, he begot consequences. Jefferson's manners, no matter how mild and refined, were never a private and personal choice of preference. They led to specific practices that defended a given social order, with women and slaves at the bottom.

A second form of inequality existed as well. Entertaining guests and giving public proof of one's refinement had long been a sign of gentility, honor, and domestic authority. What was new, as the sociologist Thorstein Veblen would have put it, was the level reached by "conspicuous consumption" in America, particularly in the South. Recent research shows that almost everyone in Virginia, rich, poor, or enslaved, started to pursue some form of refinement. Everyone bought "into the world of goods." For sure, backcountry simple Virginians, women and men, hit rather low targets. Their "refinement" was limited, and these lesser people, when they wanted to enhance their good manners, had to stick to inexpensive items, like ribbons or hats. Planters, on the other hand, set for themselves a much higher standard. They bought furniture, fine china, and fancy tablecloths. Each time they wanted directions, they had access to specialized literature. In this way they separated themselves from less prosperous neighbors. Since good manners improved and almost everybody underwent a process of refinement, the planter felt an increasing pressure to show off to neighbors and foreign visitors the visible symbols of his achievement and class distinction. The prospect of falling into debt did not discourage this practice.[27]

Planters had to differentiate themselves not only from enslaved persons and coerced women but also from less refined white neighbors. And in order to strengthen the distinction between superiors and inferiors, they had to enhance in-group cohesion. This means that Jefferson's attainment of good manners and refinement, including his gentility and mildness, his generosity and hospitability, was not an inconsequential choice for other whites as well. At the same time that he honestly desired to democratize American society, he also fostered in-group cohesion and many forms of out-group exclusion. Jefferson's cult of "friendship" is a good case study because it allows us to appreciate what refinement and good manners meant for inferior whites. Jefferson was gentle and friendly to everyone, usually welcoming and approachable. In this sense he put his good manners into practice. But the terms "friendly" and "friendship" do not overlap.

The circle of friends provided, and still provides, the best setting where refinement and good manners could be staged. However, when we come to class, Jefferson's idea of friendship was exclusive or, more exactly, exclusionary. Despite his clear democratic targets, like his famous abolition of entail and primogeniture, Jefferson lived by the idea that only peers could enjoy the type of friendship he *personally* cared for. While Jefferson was trying to convince Madison to buy land on which to settle down near Monticello, he made clear that "agreeable society is the first essential in constituting the happiness and of course the value of our existence." He was not praising metropolitan life in which individuals intermingle on so many levels, while showing *generic* good manners. Urban, modern life thrives on contaminations, "commerce," continuous negotiations, and nonspecific acts of kindness. Jefferson preferred agreeable society instead. "Agreeable" is a key term for every aristocrat, no matter how mild and harmonious. Not society per se, but a selected guild elicited Jefferson's refined, pleasing, and harmonious manners.[28]

In a previous letter to Madison, Jefferson had already made the remark that "with such a society I could once more venture home and lay myself up for the residue of life." In this way, he had already clearly referred to his peers—bodies looking visually and behaving more or less like his own. Not society in general—for example, the company of workmen and white lesser classes—but "such a society" gave him inspiration. Jefferson selected "such a society" as the main stage where his refinement and good manners took place. Modern though he was, his ideal was to live in aristocratic retirement and what he thought was rural simplicity. What he wanted was to have *these* friends over for dinner and a few glasses of wine; he wished to engage in agreeable, polite conversation while sundry furniture, art, exquisite silverware, and fine china embellished the surroundings.[29]

That Honest Simplicity Now Prevailing in America

Jefferson carried himself with confidence along the pathways leading to mildness, refinement, good manners, and genteel society. He felt he belonged to an American avant-garde and gave generous advice to other fathers and to younger peers about the *appropriate* measure of refinement, neither excessive nor insufficient. Ralph Izard, the U.S. senator and president *pro tempore* of the Senate during the Third Congress, asked for Jefferson's opinion about the intention to send his eldest son to study at the College of William and Mary. Not surprisingly, Jefferson was enthusiastic: "Williamsburg is a remarkeably healthy situation, reasonably cheap, and affords very genteel society." He was convinced young Izard could make good contacts and learn manners. Jefferson wrote from Paris, where he had grown accustomed to the excesses, artificiality, and decadence of courtly society. He thought that American society, in comparison, was simpler and relatively not constructed—but, because of this, perhaps even classier. Jefferson's "Hints to Americans Travelling in Europe," jotted down to help Thomas Lee Shippen and John Rutledge Jr. find their way during their Grand Tour, puts into words his preoccupation with the appropriate and modern form of gentility his American peers should pursue:

8. Courts. To be seen as you would see the tower of London or Menagerie of Versailles with their Lions, tygers, hyaenas and other beasts of prey, standing in the same relation to their fellows. A slight acquaintance with them will suffice to shew you that, under the most imposing exterior, they are the weakest and worst part of mankind. Their manners, could you ape them, would not make you beloved in your own country, nor would they improve it could you introduce them there to the exclusion of that honest simplicity now prevailing in America, and worthy of being cherished.[30]

It is difficult to quarrel with Jefferson's statement that European courts were generally worse than American high society. But Jefferson's "honest simplicity" was in turn imagined, constructed, and artificial in its own terms. In essence, it was not so dissimilar from courtly sophistication. It was parasitic on the bodies and labor of many "others." And yet Jefferson's imagination remained closed, and what he kept seeing in America was happiness and simplicity and, often, more updated ways to embody real elegance and real class: "Of all the errors which can possibly be committed in the education of youth," he had written shortly after he had set foot in Paris, "that of sending them to Europe is the most fatal. I see [clearly] that no American should come to Europe under 30 years of age: and [he who] does, will lose in science, in virtue, in health and in happiness, for which manners are a poor compensation, were we even to admit the hollow, unmeaning manners of Europe to be preferable to the simplicity and sincerity of our own country."[31]

Jefferson could not come to an ultimate decision about whether to despise or approve of European manners and refinement. Depending on how he interpreted these notions, he could embrace either of these options. Manners were generally good and signaled progress: "It is the happiness of modern times," Jefferson had written in 1776, in an effort to ease the lot fallen on Ethan Allen, who had been taken prisoner by the British and lay in irons on board a vessel, "that the evils of necessary war are softened by refinement of manners and sentiment, and that an enemy is an object of vengeance, in arms and in the feild only."[32]

All in all, manners had to be cultivated, although Americans did not have to renounce their modernity and exceed a proper amount of "simplicity": "With respect to what are termed polite manners," Jefferson wrote to Charles Bellini in 1785, "I would wish [my] countrymen to adopt just so much of European politeness as to be ready [to] make all those little sacrifices of self which really render European manners amiable, and relieve society from the disagreeable scenes to which rudeness often exposes it." A self-styled "savage of the mountains of America," he found "the general fate of humanity here [in Europe] most deplorable." He could not help assessing it against "that degree of happiness which is enjoyed in America by every class of people." Even so, Jefferson was convinced that Americans had something to learn from Europe: "Here it seems that a man might pass a life without encountering a single rudeness. In the pleasures of the table they are far before us, because with good taste they unite temperance. They do not terminate the most sociable meals by transforming themselves into brutes. I have never yet seen a man drunk in France, even among the lowest of the people."[33]

When manners are presented this way, as an abstract regulative ideal and a basic philosophical principle, it becomes almost impossible to disagree with Jefferson. But he seemed oblivious precisely to the fact that the "simple" American manners he was channeling by means of advice and personal example were not only an ideal and a principle; they were discourses and performances endowed with material agency. This means that they existed materially, not only as ideas, and not only as verbal elements within a given system of philosophy. Manners and refinement invited inclusion and elicited exclusion at once. To those who were excluded, manners appeared rather violent.

Jefferson overlooked that *his* "simpler," more "modern," more "appropriate," and possibly classier version of manners and sociability excluded and exploited many people—precisely what those of corrupt European courts had been doing for centuries. He did not see this dynamic precisely because he lingered insistently over *discourses* on simplicity, friendship, and an American happiness encompassing "every class of people." While in Washington, at the beginning of 1801, the soon-to-be president was again on the theme of

American simplicity, lack of sophistication, and social harmony. He saw himself as a castaway, a man robbed of the exclusive and happy environment in which he could exert his "simple" and yet highly refined manners: "I pant for that society where all is peace and harmony," Jefferson wrote to his daughter Martha, "where we love & are beloved by every object we see."[34]

Among peers, dynamics of inclusion and exclusion that brought about *certain* material practices, including *certain* manners, could well not be acknowledged as real social dynamics. These dynamics could hide themselves in talks about good manners, the best of gentility and modernity, taste, civilization, friendship, virtue, honest simplicity, refinement, elegance, politeness, and natural aristocracy. Under certain conditions, moored in the midst of his affections, Jefferson-the-philosopher could understandably agree with John Adams about the hypothesis of a natural, nonconstructed aristocracy: "I agree with you that there is a natural aristocracy among men. the grounds of this are virtue & talents. formerly bodily powers gave place among the aristoi. but since the invention of gunpowder has armed the weak as well as the strong with missile death, bodily strength, like beauty, good humor, politeness and other accomplishments, has become but an auxiliary ground of distinction."[35]

At home, within the exclusionary circle of friendship, Jefferson could miss that slave labor, female labor, and poor whites' labor, not virtue and talent, had "armed" the natural aristocrat and made it possible for him to refine, modernize, and "simplify" his manners. The "other" had made it possible for the natural aristocrat to become refined, graceful, dignified, and unruffled. This eighteenth-century "aristocrat" categorized the use of bodily strength as a mere *auxiliary* ground for distinction. This natural aristocrat had successfully become "almost femininely soft and gentle," despite the possible negative consequences. He had discarded the excesses of the court, as well as transcended the outdated forms of masculinity (military, aristocratic, patriarchal); but, again, such an accomplishment was not neutral. He could well *seem* to be a creature of the mind, a contemplator ("he had placed his mind . . . on an elevated situation, from which he might contemplate the universe"), but in fact his body, a crucial asset in the accomplishment of natural aristocracy, had simply won the battle.

May We Ever Be What We Wish to Appear

Not everyone in America could hope to achieve "appropriate" and "modern" forms of gentility—not even every white male. Not everyone could be educated to style and politeness, to sincerity and honest "simplicity." Jefferson bowed to every (white) person he met, and talked with his arms folded at his chest. But not everyone had the luxury of appearing mild and pleasant, nonviolent, postmilitary, and unquarrelsome. Jefferson, this anomalous "savage of the mountains of America," had been lucky to attend college and to join good society: Williamsburg first, and then Paris, Philadelphia, New York, and Washington. Moreover, as a reader and collector of books, Jefferson had bought and perused, among other items, the bible of eighteenth-century refinement and good manners, Lord Chesterfield's *Letters* to his son (1774).[36]

Chesterfield's *Letters* belong to a precise literary genre, very popular in the eighteenth century. Something in-between the modern, quasi-scientific treatises on education and the more traditional, religious moralistic guidebooks, Chesterfield's *Letters* are a masterpiece of conduct literature. Moralistic Christian literature had for centuries taught young men and women how to properly carry themselves. But these booklets and manuals had put emphasis on virtue interpreted as an act of piety leading to submission to God. Still popular in the eighteenth century, they centered on religion as both a spiritual and a corporeal practice. On the other hand, conduct literature developed from books written expressly for Italian courtiers, aristocrats, and high clerics, the most popular being Baldassarre Castiglione's *Cortegiano* (1528) and Giovanni Della Casa's *Galateo* (1558). Conduct literature translated many principles and ideas of courtesy literature into a vocabulary more adapted to a society that was becoming increasingly individualistic, bourgeois, refined, consumerist, and middle class. "The appeal of Chesterfield's work," Dallett Hemphill writes, "lay in the fact that more than any of its predecessors his was a manual for strivers. His chief message to his son was that he should work to appear a certain way, regardless of his true character, natural endowments, or inner state. His advice was thus to cultivate appearances—even, when necessary, to dissimulate."[37]

Conduct literature focused on the process of construction of these "simple," genteel manners. "The Graces, the Graces, Remember the Graces," Chesterfield had thundered, coining one of the most famous eighteenth-century mottos about manners and ideals of refinement. Gracefulness was for him an end to attain and the epitome of more updated versions of gentility. The challenge was all about making gracefulness appear simple, unconstructed, effortless, and natural. Nothing especially new, since Castiglione had already directed courtiers toward practicing in all things "a certain sprezzatura [nonchalance], so as to conceal all art and make whatever is done or said appear to be without effort and almost without any thought about it." Over time, sprezzatura, such a staple of southern European style in carriage and manners, gained international success. Many modern men of style wanted to *appear,* but not to appear constructed, sophisticated, and rigid. Many men wanted to appear "natural," either Italian or French.[38]

I am not postulating that Jefferson must have been influenced by Chesterfield or, let alone, that he was educated to become a disingenuous trickster and a middle-class striver. I would rather say that Jefferson's mild manners and refinement were largely a product of a culture, in which he was immersed, that was influenced by Chesterfield and others like him: "May we outlive our enemies," a twenty-nine-year-old Jefferson had entered in his Memorandum Books, "May we ever be *what we wish to appear.*"[39]

Chesterfield, among other authors, had elevated appearances over what John Locke, the famous philosopher and another influential author of conduct literature, had called "natural roughness." In *Some Thoughts Concerning Education* (1693), for example, Locke had applied himself to overthrow "natural *roughness* which makes a man uncomplaisant to others." The interesting thing, as we will see better in a moment, is that Jefferson, like many others who sought to perform "simplicity," relied heavily on the worship of naturalness. Impossible to hide is the fact that "natural" in the period could simultaneously mean something good and something bad; nature had to be emulated and defeated at the same time.[40]

Locke's *Some Thoughts* was not just about the education of the mind and intellect, not just about perfecting morality, but also about how to properly lead the body. Education was about how to maintain clean teeth, regulate bowels, or keep nails short. Locke was authoritative on similar issues, and Chesterfield referred to him generously: "I send you," Chesterfield wrote to his son, "the famous Mr. Locke's book upon education; in which you will find the stress that he lays upon the Graces, which he calls (and very truly) good-breeding." Good breeding was definitely not, according to Locke, a condition into which an individual was born. A well-directed, well-engineered process of self-fashioning, good breeding was the art to please, or simply "complaisance." In Locke's words, good breeding made a person *"well-fashioned,"* "that decency and gracefulness of looks, voice, words, motions, gestures, and of all the whole outward demeanor which takes in company and makes those with whom we converse easy and well pleased."[41]

Jefferson's legendary aversion for quarreling, direct confrontation, entering into polemics, or engaging in verbal arguments can be easily accommodated to the Lockean and Chesterfieldian principle of complaisance and their campaign waged against natural roughness. Being genteel and forthcoming, simple and harmony seeking, and thus in command of good manners, ranked higher than just fighting for personal opinion or success: "It is a charming thing," Jefferson wrote to his grandchildren, "to be loved by every body: and the way to obtain it is, never quarrel or be angry with any body."[42]

In the battle of opinions as well Jefferson refused to antagonize the opponent: "It does me no injury for my neighbor to say there are twenty gods, or no god," Jefferson wrote in *Notes*. "It neither picks my pocket nor breaks my leg." Years later, he was still upon the same concept of refined sociability as superior to the instinct to defeat the opponent: "When I hear another express an opinion which is not mine, I say to myself, he has a right to his opinion, as I to mine." In good society, the other should never be openly questioned: "His error does me no injury, and shall I become a Don Quixote, to bring all men by force of argument to one opinion?" Locke could not have agreed more. He had long before grasped the rationale beneath Jefferson's mildness: "He that knows how to make those he converses with easy without debasing himself to low and servile flattery has found the true art of living in the world and being both welcome and valued everywhere."[43]

Let the Sublimated Philosopher Grasp Visionary Happiness

Sociability gets more physical than just conversation. Like every other human being, Jefferson made use of his body to produce either distance or proximity. Anthropologists, sociologists, and behavioral psychologists usually refer to it as proxemic behavior, or simply proxemics, notably, the analysis of the organization of space in interpersonal relationships. I will only touch upon such a complex topic, and I do not want to attempt a psychological or psychoanalytical analysis-at-a-distance of Jefferson's personality. By addressing proximity, my only purpose is to recap well-known Jeffersonian themes in order to show that bodily proximity was for him real and important—a decisive ingredient within his understanding of simple and proper manners. Unquarrelsome, soft, refined, flexible, controlled, and gracious, Jefferson was at the same time generous with his own body—at least generous *enough*.

To begin with, his quirks and anxieties about staying too close are well known. Take his aversion against cities, for example: "I view great cities as pestilential to the morals, the health and the liberties of man," he wrote to Benjamin Rush. In an age of epidemics and doubtful hygienic practices, to set oneself apart and especially to stay away from foreigners were sensible prophylaxes. To draw boundaries, to dissociate oneself, to build fences, to mistrust fellow human beings, while trying not to breathe each other's air, were often wise options. Bodily distance was necessary, on occasion, but distance and philosophical aloofness were not the defining features of Jefferson's corporeality. For him, drawing oneself physically close to a fellow human being was conducive to happiness.[44]

There is at least one instance of the famous letter to Maria Cosway, the "Dialogue between My Head and My Heart," that we should take seriously and literally. The "Head" could well admonish that real happiness was negative, "avoiding pain," and that the goal of life was "to retire within ourselves, and to suffice for our own happiness." But to such a cautionary advice the "Heart" knew how to reply. Just like Jefferson did all his life, the Heart emphasized sharing, amiability, and sociability in a very corporeal sense: "friendship is precious not only in the shade but in the sunshine of life. . . . Let the gloomy Monk, sequestered from the world, seek unsocial pleasures in the bottom of his cell! Let the sublimated philosopher grasp visionary happiness while pursuing phantoms dressed in the garb of truth! Their supreme wisdom is supreme folly."[45]

All his life Jefferson had been unwavering on the doctrine that happiness does not come out of isolation and individual separateness—bodies standing apart from each other. Happiness was not an egotistic, individualistic, and self-interested drive. Happiness involved virtue, and virtue, in turn, needed other human beings. When Jefferson first drafted the Declaration he had hastily philosophized about individual beings "created equal & independant." But he dropped "& independant" before submitting the draft to Congress. The independence that the Revolution secured and *his* Declaration advocated must not be confused with what today libertarians would identify as a worship of privateness, separateness, or the promotion of mutual distrust and antisocial indifference. Jefferson was, indeed, an aristocrat, no matter how modern and natural. He was refined, very high-end, and exclusionary; but the other fellow, for him, was not by definition a hindrance or a threat. Society, which in the most concrete form meant his exclusive circle of friends and family, was all too real for him. Jefferson was a communitarian, on the whole, and not only because he smuggled a few ideas from the Scottish philosophers.[46]

Immersed in a "culture of sensibility," there is no doubt that Jefferson, the adversary of this wrong kind of "independence," adopted the eighteenth-century vocabulary of love. Many studies have emphasized Jefferson's indebtedness to the Scottish School, Francis Hutcheson in particular. They have underscored his reliance on the philosophy and physiology of the moral sense and on literary themes such as "compassion," "feeling," and "sympathy." Moreover, his letters to family and female friends, especially to the English-Italian painter Maria Cosway, often reveal him as romantic, even a little flirtatious. Experiments in a literary genre, or simply an amusement, these letters contain interesting elements in favor of human sharing and happiness as body approaching body.[47]

We will never know if Jefferson actually fell in love with Maria Cosway during those two intense weeks devoted to roaming Paris and its environs—or if the two ever consummated their "love." His letters to her, including the "My Head and My Heart" letter, if read through the lens of the dominant "culture of sensibility," appear rather innocent: these letters hide more than disclosing. Maybe in Paris Jefferson made love to Maria. Maybe he had other lovers. Maybe Jefferson spent the rest of his days ruminating about the sex he enjoyed in France. Maybe the parental advice he gave to younger Americans to restrain from European "luxury and dissipation" and to thwart the "passion for whores" was based on firsthand experience. But conclusive evidence is missing.[48]

Not in the Habit of Showing Partiality or Fatherly Affection

Central to Jefferson's vision of republicanism were two complementary tenets. The first was that government should foster an organic link among individuals and between generations (via circles and families), thus making the "Spirit of the American People" effective—what Brian Steele has recently identified as Jefferson's specific version of "nationhood." The second was that government should permit as many citizens as possible the time and resources—financial, intellectual, or otherwise—to cultivate themselves. Reading, studying classical authors, or endeavoring scientific investigations represented only the intellectual aspects of his notion of the pursuit of happiness. In addition, happiness was associated with the possibility to enjoy proximity: to draw close to another fellow human being, to actually touch him or her, and not only to get pleasure from emotional sharing, were part of Jefferson's republican vision.[49]

While Jefferson-the-philosopher-of-the-heart advocated emotional and physical sharing, and Jefferson-the-lover *maybe* experienced it, Jefferson-the-family-man, a more mature *persona,* actually lived by the anticipation of real intimacy and corporeal proximity. This was his most personal happiness: "An only daughter and numerous family of grandchildren," Jefferson wrote on the eve of retirement, "will furnish me great resources of happiness."[50]

Even though few persons were allowed into his private quarters at Monticello, his study or "sanctum sanctorum," Jefferson let several individuals enter his intimate spaces. More than his "love letters" and his vocabulary of love, other facts tell us that Jefferson let others enter his personal space to help him build his happiness. The Hemings family, as Annette Gordon-Reed has shown, and Sally in particular, contributed to Jefferson's happiness. Sally and Maria were not analogous cases. With no doubt, Sally and many of her relatives were an enduring intimate presence in Jefferson's daily routine: they had access to Jefferson's actual, private physical body; they were more than a literary dalliance.[51]

Madison Hemings, the son of Sally Hemings and Thomas Jefferson, has left us a devastating document that touches directly upon Jefferson's engaging with corporeal proximity. "His general temperament was smooth and even," Madison Hemings said in his memoirs, "he was very undemonstrative." And then Hemings goes directly to the question currently at stake: "He was uniformly kind to all about him. He was not in the habit of showing partiality or fatherly affection to us [black] children. We were the only children of his by a slave woman. He was affectionate toward his white grandchildren."[52]

True as it is that not being "in the habit" does not mean that Jefferson never showed affection to his black children, Madison Hemings voices nonetheless a certain tension. Blinded by an ominous institution, Jefferson was unable to see the arbitrariness of his choice to allow himself the "habit" to bestow fatherly, unconditional affection to some while denying himself this very "habit" when others were concerned. Jefferson would have been happier had he realized he could do more with his "habit" and bestow bodily proximity upon many other persons belonging to the circle of his family. Maybe he loved his black progeny, but he certainly did not turn such a secret love into a corporeal public performance, let alone a "habit."

He eventually freed his black children, and that was it: a lot, but not enough. The narrative of Jefferson's life, his mildness, his good manners and refinement, his philosophy of the heart, his language of love and feeling, and the legacy of his concept of an American nationhood, would have been richer had he been habitually more generous—at least with his own body. Such a postpatriarch, a considerate father and mentor of so many children, had left some of *his* children to forage for intellectual experiences: "I learned to read," Madison Hemings wrote, "by *inducing* the white children to teach me the letters and something more." Jefferson's reading lists for boys and girls are legendary, and yet Madison had to pilfer: "what else I know of books I have picked up here and there till now I can read and write."[53]

Jefferson was generous not only while giving spiritual and intellectual support. He was customarily generous with his body or, better, as just said, he was selectively generous. A postmartial, relatively modern male who nurtured "simplicity" and conceived of happiness in corporeal terms, he could not help throwing himself into real proximity, just like a mother would do. Jefferson's mildness, complaisance, gentle and genteel manners, and many other facets of his body we have already encountered were not only expressed as amiable conversation, intellectual mentoring, and paternal advice. They were physical and maternal. The caring, playful presence of his flexible body was there, especially when, after 1809, he was relieved from office and had regained control of his time. His body was there, definitely, for his white daughters and white grandchildren. Jefferson knew how to perform both the typical, detached masculinity expressing itself through patronage, offering advice, or even punishing, and a nondetached masculinity attuned to caring and touching as its main feats. Jefferson had already cared, in this very corporeal sense, for his dying wife, and likely he had cared on many other occasions. While tradition has allowed only women's bodies to be touchable and accessible, Jefferson's body, often touchable and accessible, was quite a modern and atypical father's body.[54]

He Often Joined Them in Games

Jefferson had the habit of playing games with his grandchildren, both on the West Lawn and inside the house. In the parlor, board games occurred, of course, from the Game of the Goose, to word games, to chess. But Jefferson was not only interested in intellectual games. He engaged himself physically by organizing races and rewarding the winner with dried fruits. The corporeal proximity he created while reading with his grandchildren, for example, was paired by the proximity he experienced by playing with them. Proximity should foster self-confidence and autonomy in the younger generations, the virtues of a mature citizenry. Virginia J. Randolph Trist tells us that "when it grew too dark to read . . . as we all sat round the fire, he taught us several childish games, and would play them with us. . . . When the candles were brought, all was quiet immediately, for he took up his book to read, and we would not speak out of a whisper lest we should disturb him . . . and I have seen him raise his eyes from his own book and look round on the little circle of readers, and smile and make some remark to mamma about it." Martha J. Trist Burke confirms the story and adds other details as well:

> My mother (Mrs N. P. Trist) the "Virginia" [Virginia J. Randolph Trist] of the Monticello family, and my two aunts Cornelia & Mary, who made their home mostly with my mother, (after the breaking up of the family) have often told me of their childish games such as "Puss in the corner" played among the trees on the edge of the lawn, or "Hide & seek" up in the 3^d Story, where under the large roof, there was ample room, for lofts & "Cuddies," affording admirable places for hiding, there on rainy days, or in wintry weather the "children" could play, & make as much noise as they liked, without danger of annoying the grown members of the family, or of disturbing "Grandpapa" which the youngest child was careful not to do. In the winter evenings, sitting around the fire at dusk, the children were encouraged by "Grandpapa" to play games suitable to the hour & to the place, & he often joined them in games such as "Hunt the Slipper."[55]

Not only did Jefferson not seem disturbed by this hoard wreaking havoc; he took pleasure in partaking of the children's playful corporeality. Jefferson wanted intervals of silence and noise to be woven together, democratically, keeping as his sole aim that of increasing his proximity to the younger generations. He approved, for example, of eight-year-old grandson Francis Wayles Eppes's misbehavior: "He is at this moment running about with his cousins bawling out 'a merry christmas' 'a christmas gift' Etc." Overseer Edmund Bacon confirms Jefferson's physical "devotion" to his grandchildren: "They delighted to follow him about over the grounds and garden, and he took great pleasure in talking with them, and giving them advice, and directing their sports." And: "He took great pleasure in the sports and plays of his grandchildren. I have often seen him direct them and enjoy them greatly. The large lawn back of the house was a fine place for their plays. They very often ran races, and he would give the word for them to start, and decide who was the winner. Another play was stealing goods. They would divide into two parties, and lay down their coats, hats, knives, and other things, and each party would try to get all that the other had. If they were caught in the attempt to

Fig. 1. Parlor at Monticello. (©Thomas Jefferson Foundation at Monticello, photograph by Walter Smalling)

steal they were made prisoners. I have seen Mr. Jefferson laugh heartily to see this play go on."[56]

What we see here is concrete, material republicanism unfolding via corporeal performances. These performances were neither presocial nor apolitical nor, let alone, antipolitical: Jefferson was actually strengthening a sense of self-confidence and self-government, thus implementing a specific process of embodiment. This kind of proximity had direct republican significance for the nation. It is far from an exaggeration to claim that nationhood happened, according to Jefferson, not only by means of daring political visions and effective institutions. At the same time, it happened through playing, laughing, touching, running, and other seemingly "private" corporeal activities. Playing with his grandchildren, and doing it corporeally, was a form of republican education. It was no other thing from Jefferson's ambitious philosophical vision of an American nationhood for which generations had to be close to one another, and caring after one another. Close, and yet not too close in a way that fathers put shackles on their sons' wrists (just like it happened in Europe). At an early stage in his life, Jefferson had realized that upcoming generations could not thrive unless the present generation acted as caring parents. The "biological" language of fathers and sons, including grandfathers and grandsons, and especially *mothers* and their progenies, encompasses Jefferson's entire vision of nationhood.[57]

He Sits in a Lounging Manner on One Hip

Beneath one of the most characteristic defining traits of Jefferson's corporeality, his being "straight," several dimensions and interesting anthropological issues are hidden. When we come to a postural analysis we have to agree that Jefferson was undeniably posturally straight, as seen in the opening sections. But being straight should not be taken as something actually without history and, in a word, unconstructed. It opens up more dimensions than one may at first suspect.

The first component we have to emphasize is that human bodies, typically, are *not* straight and vertical. "The posture we regard," has written one anthropologist, "as typical of the body in all societies is upright. This is to contradict experience: during most of the time we are, even in very physically active societies, as a matter of fact slouched, twisted and recumbent in sleep or rest, or crouched or seated or bent in action. Yet being upright seems a general convention of thought about being human."[58]

When we imagine a human body, verticality and straightness come to mind as obvious, despite the fact that we should regard them as momentary conditions or episodes. Moreover, we fill verticality with significance because humans, during their evolutionary history, have learned how to straighten themselves up in order to better deal with space manipulatively and organizationally. The human species has undeniably succeeded by means of verticality, and, retrospectively, we read it as a value—verticality evokes uprightness, fortitude, success, or nobility. But there was nothing predetermined in that: *it has happened* that we have learned to model our body with this unnatural form, but verticality is far from the realization of our primeval essence. It is not a posture that happens without effort; it is not what humans were from the outset, but what they have evolutionarily become.

Straightness and verticality, especially conspicuous ones, like Jefferson's, give the illusion that the human body was designed in compliance with classical canons: a magnificent warrior, a noble statue, an imposing hero. Furthermore, straightness and verticality, especially conspicuous ones, give the impression that certain body types are more valuable than others. We have to remember that European elite people, the aristocracy, came to define themselves through the straight, elegant, martial posture and taller-than-average stature that distinguished them from those individuals *they themselves* defined as "crooked" and unworthy. Consequently, interpreters, biographers, and admirers will always be tricked by the equation "verticality=nobility" and supply Jefferson's body type with a connotation of nobility, worth, and natural dignity. Historic figures, heroes, and Founding Fathers in particular seem "true to character" when they are visually represented as straight and tall, with feet on the pedestal to reach up to the sky.

In fact, most of the time human bodies, even "noble" ones, do other things than imitating Greek or Roman statues: "from sunset till noon I am chained to the writing table. at that hour I ride of necessity for health as well as recreation. and even after dinner I must often return to the writing table." Like everyone else's, Jefferson's straight figure was usually bent in the act of writing or poised to begin many other activities: riding horses, singing and humming, caring, drawing closer to other human beings, playing, or laughing.[59]

The second component is that straightness, more than a posture, is in itself a complex series of performances. Straightness and verticality, just like remaining "chained" at the writing desk, are the outcome of elaborate decisions and actions that humans take. As a species, we have educated ourselves to execute straightness, or seatedness, a certain way. These actions are more than a neutral, nonmuscular, and ahistorical "standing still." In principle, there is no rigid opposition between posture (a structured arrangement of the body in space) and gesture (a structured movement of a part of the body). The fact that we consider "postures" such as standing straight or seated as effortless and neutral is only because our vocabulary does not allow us to see more gradations. "English postural vocabulary is mediocre," anthropologists have realized. "Quite the opposite is true of the languages of India, where the yoga system has developed an elaborate postural terminology and rationale, perhaps the world's richest."[60]

Posture requires training and effort. Eighteenth-century higher classes, these persons in particular over workmen and poorer people, were anxious about the rules concerning the most up-to-date execution of verticality. Conduct literature, and Chesterfield better than other authors, taught them how to struggle to achieve the "appropriate" version of verticality. It was far from simple, just like "simple" good manners and the proper dose of refinement were far from easy to achieve. Artistic control was needed, as Bushman writes, "to keep the line from the base of the spine through the neck to the back of the head as straight as possible. . . . the chin was held up. . . . shoulders were kept down and back with the chest and abdomen protruding. . . . the genteel stance resembled the positions of formal ballet." A lot of effort and education were exerted here. Elite young men and women had to be taught the methods for not letting their shoulders slump awkwardly or their heads hang. The late eighteenth century allowed a retreat from the more martial erect formality of previous aristocratic times, but the straight back line was still taken as a sign of nobility.[61]

Straightness was both an ideal and a value. It was good when someone could be described as straight, albeit "easy" rather than ridiculously "stiff and bolt upright." When they were not blessed by stature or a suitable body structure, well-heeled people relied on mechanical proxies, like stays. But the goal was to learn to perform straightness along modern-day standards and to avoid overstatement.[62]

For its part, remaining seated properly was no less an ensemble of elaborate performances. Chesterfield has an eloquent, often reprinted and paraphrased passage on the topic of modern gentlemanly sitting—which Jefferson must have absorbed via the genteel, postmartial culture to which he belonged. "Ashamed and confused, the awkward man sits in his chair stiff and bolt upright, whereas the man of fashion, is easy in every position; instead of lolling or lounging as he sits, he leans with elegance, and by varying his attitudes, shews that he has been used to good company. Let it be one part of your study, then, to learn to sit genteely in different companies, to loll gracefully where you are authorized to take that liberty, and to sit up respectfully, where that freedom is not allowable."[63]

Playful easiness and lolling were within the reach of Jefferson's modern corporeality. William Maclay, a senator from rural Pennsylvania, met Jefferson on 24 May 1790. Jefferson had just returned from Paris and had assumed the position of secretary of state. Maclay wrote in his *Journal* that Jefferson "sits in a lounging Manner on one hip, commonly, and with one of his shoulders elevated much above the other." This way of sitting, of course, gives us a sprinkle of the sprezzatura of which Jefferson was capable and that he absorbed in Europe. Maclay could not make sense of the spectacle of refinement and updated, postaristocratic good manners he was seeing, and the only conclusion he reached was that this "dandy" Jefferson "had been long enough abroad to catch the tone of European folly."[64]

His Hair Which Has Been Red Is Now Grey

Nothing about the body is neutral, meaningless, and without history. In particular, for an eighteenth-century cultured and forward-looking individual like Jefferson, it was essential to convey easiness, simplicity, refinement, and modern gentility—whether this happened through gestures and postures or through the appropriate proximity or distance. Clothing as well, this singularly complex topic, conveyed easiness and good manners. Before examining it, we need to consider a few threshold zones: hair, skin, and faces.

Clothes do not cover the entire body; they have hardly ever done that. The face, to begin with, stays visible although only rarely totally deprived of adornment and makeup. Skin and hair set up a negotiation with clothes to gain their proper space. To some extent, skin and hair may remain visible. The acceptable extension of such a visibility varies across cultures and over time within a given culture. When Jefferson was a boy, for example, men of high rank used to wear wigs. Wigs were taken as symbols of economic self-reliance and success. By the late eighteenth century, the situation had changed, and, on the American continent, the wig had for obvious reasons taken up the meaning of an ungainly declaration of dependence on the British courtier style and aristocratic fashion. It became an excess of manners, analogous to a posture "stiff and bolt upright," and an example of improper refinement. Either powdered or unpowdered hair, combed and dressed in more or less complicated styles, had eventually become fashionable and "simple."[65]

We know with precision what Jefferson's hair looked like. Thomas Jefferson Randolph writes that "Mr. Jefferson's hair, when young, was of a reddish cast, sandy as he advanced in years." In the early 1770s, Jefferson bought wigs and accessories, including pomades and hair powder, but we do not know if he ever actually wore wigs—maybe he did so in his early career when he practiced law. While in Europe, as Mather Brown's portrait clearly indicates, Jefferson chose to have his own hair dressed according to the fashion required at the Court. He sat for Brown during a trip to London, in March and April 1786. The aim of this trip was to negotiate a commercial treaty with Britain, to meet with emissaries sent from Tripoli and Portugal, and to take part in a levee at the presence of the queen and king. But on this occasion, even amid such a bounty of aristocratic sophistication, artificiality, and protocol, he did not put on a wig. In the late 1780s and early 1790s, Jefferson took up the habit of avoiding more elaborate styles. John Trumbull's re-creation of the famous scene in Philadelphia, for example, depicts Jefferson's hair in its

Fig. 2. Portrait of Thomas Jefferson by Mather Brown, 1786. (National Portrait Gallery, Smithsonian Institution; bequest of Charles Francis Adams; frame conserved with funds from the Smithsonian Women's Committee)

natural reddish color. Charles Willson Peale, similarly, gives us a secretary of state with reddish hair unpowdered and without side curls.[66]

In this embrace of "simplicity" and "naturalness," Jefferson was, however, *à la mode,* and the way he gently tampered with his hair, occasionally by applying powder and other accessories, instead of relying on wigs and heavier

Fig. 3. *Declaration of Independence* by John Trumbull, 1819, with Thomas Jefferson at right center. (Architect of the Capitol)

adornment, demonstrates that he tended toward what was then "modern." By 1802, most likely, Jefferson cut off his hair, again an interesting indication of his embrace of an incipient bourgeois flexible practicality. The pencil drawing by Benjamin Henry Latrobe together with Gilbert Stuart's "medallion portrait" show that Jefferson cut his hair rather short and kept it curled at the hairline and over the forehead. More elaborate French hairdressings had long gone, even though Jefferson continued to use hair powder later in his life. From Monticello, in 1809, he wrote to Thomas Jefferson Randolph about his impending necessity: "I must pray you to put half a dozen pounds of scented hair powder into the same box. none is to be had here, & it is almost a necessary of life with me." However, later portraits, like Thomas Sully's, suggest that Jefferson was not afraid to let visitors see his aging natural red hair mixed with gray.[67]

These few examples allow us to conclude that, by and large, Jefferson did not conceal his hair and was not embarrassed by it, not even when he was in office. He believed he did not have to increase his authority this way. William Dunlap, the American painter, actor, producer, and playwright, wrote in

Fig. 4. Portrait of Thomas Jefferson by Charles Willson Peale, 1791. (Courtesy of Independence National Historical Park)

his diary after he had met the president that graciousness and style did not abandon Jefferson's head: "His hair which has been red is now grey & is worn in negligent disorder, tho not ungracefully." "Negligent" could either mean ruffled or, more likely, unpowdered, naturally aged, postmartial, postaristocratic, and modern.[68]

Fig. 5. Pencil sketch of Thomas Jefferson by Benjamin Henry Latrobe, 1802. (Maryland Historical Society, 1953.73.2)

Hair, or lack thereof, can be a source of embarrassment, and this is one of the reasons why men began donning wigs in the first place. There is a ritual, social function performed by wigs (barristers and judges in courts, for instance), but wigs also conceal baldness or skin diseases. Jefferson was lucky, as to his hair. Not so much when we come to his skin.

Fig. 6. "Medallion Portrait" of Thomas Jefferson by Gilbert Stuart, 1805. (Harvard Art Museums/Fogg Museum, Gift of Mrs. T. Jefferson Newbold and family, in memory of Thomas Jefferson Newbold, Class of 1910, 1960.156; Photo: Imaging Department © President and Fellows of Harvard College)

His Skin, Thin, Peeling from His Face

Not affected by any serious disease, Jefferson's skin was nonetheless delicate. A gentleman affecting some of the southern European biases like a certain way of lolling, a degree of flexibility, easiness, and a cultivated sprezzatura, as we have seen, Jefferson could not have lived comfortably under the sun of Rome. His Welsh or English lineage did not help him by providing rich pigmentation. Especially with age, his sensitive skin peeled easily, giving him a "tattered" appearance. Thomas Jefferson Randolph describes Jefferson's skin as "thin, peeling from his face on exposure to the sun, and giving him a tet-

Fig. 7. Large full-length portrait of Thomas Jefferson by Thomas Sully, 1822. (Courtesy of the West Point Museum Collection, United States Military Academy)

tered appearance; the superficial veins so weak, as upon the slightest blow, to cause extensive suffusions of blood, in early life, upon standing to write for any length of time, bursting beneath the skin: it, however, gave him no inconvenience." The 1805 portrait by Rembrandt Peale shows in all details such a fragility.[69]

Fig. 8. Portrait of Thomas Jefferson by Rembrandt Peale, 1805; oil on canvas, 28 × 23½ inches. (New-York Historical Society, gift of Thomas Jefferson Bryan, negative #6103, object #1867.306)

Fig. 9. Engraving of Thomas Jefferson by Charles Fevret de Saint-Mémin, drawn with the help of a physionotrace, 1804. (©Thomas Jefferson Foundation at Monticello)

Jefferson was not unique in experiencing the skin as a sort of weakness and embarrassment, not a good tool for enhancing social connections. Understandably, letting their fellows see too much of the body's surface has never been a popular option among Europeans. No simple theory can be ventured here about why and when Europeans came to refuse the nude: excessively cold or hot weather, highly differentiated social hierarchies and professions, rituals more and more complex, or perhaps an endemic "tattered" and weak skin. Additionally, from early on, Christians as well as Jews and Muslims have insisted on virtues such as physical modesty and discretion. The nude, and nakedness in particular, was offensive. The Bible's vision of an original sin and the notion of a resulting sense of disgrace about being naked, as in Genesis 3:7, turned the skin—not only the genitals—into a taboo. Whatever the reason, Europeans became a clothed people, and yet, ironically, a clothed people bestowing such a weight upon the color of the skin.

He Can See Himself Only by Reflection

The portraits presented so far, as well as those I introduce later on, open many more questions than just a discussion of Jefferson's skin and hair: they tell us about the apparel, of course. But a portrait, by definition, also offers a person's face, the air and countenance. And by watching these portraits, the temptation to ask the obvious is strong: What did Jefferson "actually" look like in a strict visual sense? By coincidence, this man died the very summer when the oldest surviving camera photograph, *View from the Window at Le Gras,* was created by Nicéphore Niépce at Sait-Loup-de-Varennes, France. Thomas Jefferson missed the art of photography by a few years. Consequently, we are left with a handful of portraits—and some are even copies of lost originals. Unfortunately, or rather fortunately, as art historians would say, portraits are works of theory, imagination, and interpretation. They conjure a *persona* radiating allure and communicating achievement. They ennoble the subject. They do not passively reproduce a surface, but they go down to the "essential."

Stuart's "medallion portrait" (see fig. 6) was the one preferred by Jefferson's family and friends. But it is hard to tell whether their liking was based on the profile's "realism" and a particular graphic loyalty to the original. More probably, this profile succeeded in meeting the expectations, loaded with moral and cultural biases, of those persons who already knew him—or thought they did. It gave them *their* Thomas Jefferson. Jefferson himself wanted to have it reproduced, but what he thought of this particular image, or other images of him, is difficult to say. In May 1813, Jefferson wrote to the Philadelphia publisher Joseph Delaplaine expressing skepticism about exercises in self-assessment and self-interpretation, especially when applied to art: "of the merit of these [portraits] I am not a judge, there being nothing to

Fig. 10. Bust of Thomas Jefferson by John Henri Isaac Browere, cast 15 October 1825 at Monticello. (Fenimore Art Museum, Cooperstown, New York, Gift of Stephen C. Clark, No209.1961, photograph by Richard Walker)

Fig. 11. Bust of Thomas Jefferson by Jean-Antoine Houdon, 1789. (Museum of Fine Arts, Boston, George Nixon Black Fund, photograph © 2017 Museum of Fine Arts, Boston)

which a man is so incompetent as to judge of his own likeness. He can see himself only by reflection, and that of necessity full-face or nearly so." Individuals can see themselves by "reflection" only, both materially, because the image is reversed by the mirror, and allegorically, because our self always eludes our self-representations.[70]

Another successful likeness, cherished by some of Jefferson's descendants, was Saint-Mémin's portrait, drawn with the help of a physionotrace (a device to capture the silhouette) in November 1804 in Washington. John Henri Isaac Browere's plaster cast, from the life mask the artist molded from Jefferson's head on 15 October 1825, at Monticello, has been repeatedly deemed a "perfect facsimile." "Perfect likenesses" were also Jean-Antoine Houdon's 1789 bust and Giuseppe Ceracchi's larger than life marble bust from a terra-cotta model that the artist had modeled from life, regrettably destroyed in the Library of Congress fire of 1851. Again, what these testimonies saw in similar representations was hardly the same explicit thing that excites our curiosity. Our camera-renderings of the subject, capturing a surface, a grin, a twitch, a shade, would maybe please us. We would swear that *this* snapshot was the actual Jefferson. But eighteenth-century onlookers were in the hunt for other, less fleeting, less graphic elements.[71]

The Negligence of His Dress a Little Surprised Me

Portraits give us Jefferson groomed and dressed in many studied ways. On the whole, however, his attire has stirred controversies, and allegations of negligence have been made over and over again. In the forthcoming sections, I try to disentangle the complex topic of Jefferson's multifaceted relationship to dress. Readers must be aware that this man adhered to more than one standard, doing more than one thing with the apparel he donned. Depending on the situation, the office he held, and especially the message he deemed appropriate for the moment, he could alternatively perform negligence or fastidiousness; he could show to the general public that he was either outmoded, and cared nothing for fashion, or that he was keenly fashionable. Most important, I argue that he was never simply negligent or indifferent. Sections will unfold thematically, first, and chronologically, second.[72]

William Dunlap, as we have seen, held that Jefferson's hair was in "negligent disorder." But many other testimonies have drawn attention to elements other than the "negligence" of Jefferson's hair. Frances Few, the niece of Hannah Nicholson Gallatin, wife of Secretary of the Treasury Albert Gallatin, upon dining with the president in 1808, could not help noticing the "shabbiness of his dress." Joseph Story, a law professor at Harvard and a Supreme Court justice from 1811 to his death in 1845, had a similar experience. He met Jefferson in 1807, and wrote to a friend: "the negligence of his dress a little surprised me. He received us in his slippers, and wore old-fashioned clothes, which were not in the nicest order, or of the most elegant kind; a blue coat, white worked cassimere waistcoat and corduroy breeches . . . constituted his dress. You know Virginians have some pride in appearing in simple habiliments, and are willing to rest their claim to attention upon their force of mind and suavity of manners."[73]

When Jefferson entered office, the legend of his overall "lack of decorum" was already in the public domain. William Maclay, for example, was struck by the fact that the secretary of state "had a rambling, vacant look, and nothing of that firm, collected deportment which I expected would dignify the presence of a secretary or minister. I looked for gravity, but a laxity of manner seemed shed about him." It was not only Jefferson's general deportment that stirred up controversies. The fact that he deliberately overlooked formalities when in office was perhaps sill more upsetting. Robert Troup, the friend of Alexander Hamilton and a judge in the District of New York, wrote to Rufus King, another famous Federalist, that Jefferson "has no levee days—observes no ceremony—often sees company in an undress, sometimes with his slippers on—always accessible to, and very familiar with, the sovereign people." Troup was evidently confirming King in his prejudices against the enemy, the prototypical anti-Federalist. The historian Henry Adams, on his part, produced similar accounts. He described President Jefferson greeting British ambassadors and diplomats, like Baronet Augustus John Foster and Anthony Merry, in far from crisp underclothes and worn-out slippers, "down at the heel." Jefferson, according to Adams, wanted to show his visceral hostility toward Britain.[74]

Allegations of Jefferson's "negligence" should not be taken at face value. First of all, the fact that Anthony Merry and his wife had made no secret of their disgust for "barbarous" America should put us on guard. Conceivably, upon meeting Foster and Merry, Jefferson broke the protocol, and he did it intentionally; plausibly, in these few cases at least, he tried (successfully) to be rude, and to perform an act of bravado. Biographers have excused Jefferson by pointing out, correctly, that he wished to convey the democratic message that *this* president dressed the same for all. Along these lines, Henry Adams wrote that "Jefferson, at moments of some interest in his career as President, seemed to regard his peculiar style of dress as a matter of political importance, while the Federalist newspapers never ceased ridiculing the corduroy small-clothes, red-plush waistcoat, and sharp-toed boots with which he expressed his contempt for fashion."[75]

Instead of embracing the postulate of negligence, readers should start from Henry Adams's *main* point. Adams was right to emphasize that Jefferson-the-officeholder acted deliberately—although maybe not because of a "contempt for fashion." Adams is right to invite us to avoid the conclusion that Jefferson acted randomly, and that his apparel had no political significance whatsoever. Jefferson never acted randomly, especially when he was in office. So, was he negligent? Did he actually hold elegant dresses, refinement, and high style in contempt? Was he merely uninterested in fashion? Did his "simplicity" and postaristocratic stances turn him into a bumpkin?

In principle, what is negligent and sloppy for one (a high Federalist, a British baronet, or a rich merchant and his prissy wife, for instance) may be, for another, nifty and appropriate, even urgent and necessary. In matter of refinement, Jefferson was cultured and deliberate. American preferences, including quirks, may have been different from those with which British merchants and baronets were familiar. But an American taste was developing. Americans were becoming more and more self-aware, more exigent and knowledgeable about the meanings and values of their outfits and manners. In America, Kathleen Brown writes, "the widespread self-consciousness about public appearance, especially the body's visible, clothed surface is especially striking." By the end of the eighteenth century, almost everyone, not only the elite, participated in the commodity market and bought into the world of goods. In particular, the president who allegedly held fashion in contempt had been schooled in Williamsburg and Paris: he may have, on occasion, affected simplicity and exaggerated his aversion for aristocratic conventions, but this affectation came from a man who knew what he was doing. His Memorandum Books, among other texts, allow the conclusion that he was extremely experienced in matters of refinement, fabrics, accessories, furniture, gadgets, and the up-to-date European styles generally.[76]

Jefferson had won the "Revolution of 1800," as years later he labeled his victory over John Adams in the contest for the presidency. Consequently, he was convinced, the style of his office had to bear a visible mark of the "Spirit of 1776." In this sense, he deployed his administration as a tool to rejuvenate that spirit. Revolutionaries, among other things, had gone through the appalling spectacle of British uniforms and Loyalists wearing British insignia. Especially as president, Jefferson thought he had the chance to offset the spell of antirepublicanism by reenacting homespun virtue and American simplicity. He wanted to signify that the American people had entered the presidency. It was neither negligence nor a whim, and definitely more than an instinctive visceral hatred for the British.[77]

Our Slavish Obsequiousness to British Fashions

We may laugh at Jefferson's anxiety, but this president was actually convinced that Britishness was still corroding the American character. He was not hostile to Britain, as Henry Adams surmised; he rather had a far-reaching program in mind. George Washington's levees together with John Adams's pomposity appeared to many as ominous signs. The Revolution had been won, for sure. But despite such a dramatic change in the administrative and institutional framework, Jefferson knew that British America was still in many ways *British* America, "an integral part of a larger British cultural and social world." France or Italy may have elicited curiosity and sincere interest as to their styles, manners, and refinement, but the language of poets, rhetoricians, and jurists, the cultural routes of everyday life in America (including objects), were assets those individuals had in common with their British counterparts. "Seeking approval of the high arbiters in England" was embedded in American Britishness, no matter the independence.[78]

Jefferson was neither joking nor exaggerating when, at the beginning of 1815, he complained about "our slavish obsequiousness to British fashions." He was serious, and not simply repeating well-worn slogans about the degeneracy of European aristocracy: "this is a great evil" and, Jefferson feared, "an irremediable one. it is the particular domain in which the fools have usurped dominion over the wise, and as they are a majority they hold to the fundamental law of the majority." The infamous embargo, in his mind, should have worked as an effective incentive to restrain Britishness in America. The embargo was more than just an occasional expedient to strike British interests. It was an intensive program of education. Jefferson's aim of cutting importation by half should have helped American citizens to learn the virtue of economic self-sufficiency. Styles, desires, modes of self-representation, an entire culture and corresponding processes of embodiment should have emerged as reenergized, simplified, and Americanized.[79]

But it did not work as he imagined. In a fit of pessimism, Jefferson wrote to Cesar Rodney that "the cities, I suppose, will still affect English fashions, & of course English manufactures." Jefferson's hope rested on two factors. On the one hand, it hinged on the Weberian notion that ideas, desires, and other intellectual attributes may change economic structures—although he was aware that only jurisdictional measures, like the embargo, and material institutions, like schools and universities, may change the people. On the other hand, Jefferson's hope underscored a flimsy and problematic dualism between the city and the country: "but the cities are not the people of America. the country will be clothed in homespun."[80]

Implementing such a general program of mass Americanization was his priority during the presidency, and he soon realized that *his own* apparel could work as a valuable tool. He did not want simply to be rude to some British baronets—although rude he was. Jefferson was anti-British at least as much as he was pro-American. Analogously, he did not intend just to build a noticeable style for his presidency, to be promptly recognized as a certain type of leader in order to gain consensus. Jefferson had a plan in mind that was more than a self-serving "branding strategy." He did not reenact republican simplicity only for self-serving personal objectives. In Paris, Jefferson had witnessed Benjamin Franklin acting out Americanness both strategically and pedagogically. Louis Philippe, Comte de Ségur, the "grand master of the ceremonies," among the many titles this man held, the soldier who had served during the American War of Independence, did not fail to notice the strategy below Franklin's "rustic apparel, the plain but firm demeanor, the free and direct language." Franklin, he said, communicated "antique simplicity of dress and appearance" and "seemed to have introduced into our walls, in the midst of the effeminate and servile refinement of the 18th century," a distinctive figure, "contemporary with Plato, or . . . of the age of Cato and of Fabius." Franklin's "provincial presence" fired the popular imagination in France. His long brown coat and beaver hat did not go unremarked.[81]

Jefferson's sartorial performances as a revolutionary president were the chosen complement of the political theory, operative strategy, and economic measures he had in mind. The first factor cannot be considered apart from the second: in that case, we would have an old cranky man acting with rudeness and only showing frustration and contempt. Jefferson's sartorial preferences need to be put in a broader context.

In his mind, transatlantic, large-scale trade conducive to "dependence" had to be replaced by a small-scale household manufacture that would give a sense to words such as "independence," "democracy," and "self-government." In his retirement years, after the embargo had clearly proved ineffective, Jefferson continued to dress up or down *and* to draft his economic visions of equilibrium and self-sufficiency. Raising merino sheep or buying carding machines and looms, for example, became a favorite of his. In a letter to John Adams of 1812, Jefferson gives a clear synopsis of his economic vision: "Every family in the country is a manufactory within itself, and is very generally able to make within itself all the stouter and midling stuffs for it's own cloathing

& houshold use. . . . for fine stuff we shall depend on your Northern manufactures." Relying on New England for finer clothing and other luxuries was part of his notion of an American integrated and dynamic nationhood. This kind of specialization had the scope to rule out the gruesome dependence on Britain.[82]

Jefferson-the-officeholder thought he could educate Americans via both his republican sartorial performances and his reckless economic measures. A third factor upon which he relied to implement this program was what we may call the spectacularization of his unassuming democratic habits. Just like the spectacle of his "negligent" outfits, Jefferson's refusal to have an attending servant accompany him when he took his daily rides, even in Washington, while he was president, was aimed at serving a larger educational purpose. As a matter of fact, it gave occasion to many anecdotes about citizens failing to recognize the famous man. Probably a mixture of truth and legend, such accounts of Jefferson being mistaken for a common man indicate that he succeeded in conveying his republican message. Within the President's House as well, analogous stories go, he took extreme care to go unnoticed, a fit compendium to his overall "negligence." William Plumer, for example, the New Hampshire senator, thought Jefferson a servant upon meeting him: "He was drest, or rather undrest, with an old brown coat, red waistcoat, old corduroy small clothes, much soild-woolen hose-and slippers without heels. . . . I thought this man was a servant."[83]

Gatherings and dinners at the President's House were often disarmingly, ostentatiously unceremonious and "simple"—hard-core republicanism. Frances Few chronicles an especially compelling description in her diary: "The President made his appearance he bowed and the strangers present were named to him—he then took a seat himself and his example was followed by the gentlemen who since his entrance had all been standing—he joined in the conversation but did not monopolize it—in about half an hour dinner was announced and we were handed into another room-with-out the least ceremony he seated himself at the head of the table and immediately began to help himself and those around him." No British lord would have ever consented to such a bourgeois habit, but more than just humiliating the British, Jefferson wanted to educate Americans.[84]

Jefferson's shows were studied. In particular, they have to be interpreted within their proper context. Jefferson's corporeality, especially at the beginning of this new century, was intended to support an economic, educational, and political vision. His anti-Britishness was not a momentary whim, not even an instinctual aversion. His "negligence," in turn, was not an unmotivated eccentricity, a flaw in his otherwise measured, harmony-seeking, and mild personality.

Virginians Have Some Pride in Appearing in Simple Habiliments

Jefferson's nineteenth-century performances in "simplicity" were not strategies he invented from scratch; performances such as these have a longer history. Before the Revolution broke out, Americans commenced the so-called age of homespun, an imaginative reenactment of a mythical republican simplicity meant to counteract European aristocracy and its inlays of corruption. Jefferson, obviously, had gone through this. In the late 1760s, as the crisis with Britain intensified, rebellious colonists made the decision to forego British luxuries. Aversion against fashionable living was mostly felt in New England, where religious restraint was conceived as a desirable feature of a yet-to-build American character. Consequently, ostentation of elegance was frowned upon as a moral evil.[85]

In Virginia, religious sentiments played a lesser role. Ideologically at ease with British luxuries, Tidewater planters had customarily imported clothing and fostered refinement. Especially when the price of tobacco was high, big planters gave themselves the illusion that they were not incurring excessive debt. Importing fabrics from Scottish merchants was an easier option to conceive and a cheaper practice to attain than striving with experiments in self-sufficiency.

Nonetheless, in May 1769, when Jefferson sat as a member of the House of Burgesses, a majority of Virginia leaders took on a nonimportation agreement: eleven types of clothes, including stockings and hats, "Upholstery of all Sorts," and "Ribbon and Millinery of all Sorts," were boycotted, but coarse fabric for slaves did not enter into the agreement. Backcountry householders who did not produce for export experimented with domestic production of homespun. Their surplus slaves helped them out in this project for "independence." Predictably, demand was not satisfied by home production, and the Nonimportation Resolutions only resulted in shortages. Besides considerations of practicality, however, planters thought this was the right moment to try to reconnect with lesser citizens by public display of republican dress. For a short while, planters dropped fancier dress and donned hemp, flax, osnaburg, and deerskin, just like frontiersmen. By 1775, the hunting shirt, sometimes with a tomahawk by one's side, had become fashionable. The historian Rhys Isaac has underlined "a readiness among the gentry to identify with the woodsmen."[86]

Upon meeting President Jefferson, Joseph Story, as noted above, could not overlook that "Virginians have some pride in appearing in simple habiliments." Story was definitely right, and Jefferson was not the first member among the Virginia gentry class to carry out similar "democratic" assertions. Other upper-class Americans, even before the "age of homespun," had attempted shows in democracy, seeking to combine refinement and good manners with "pre-genteel practicality." In the late seventeenth and early eighteenth centuries, away from European urban centers, many Americans, including many big planters from Virginia, thought they could improvise and recast aristocratic entrenched paradigms. Not only did they often dress down; they also sensed they could lessen the typical bodily distance characterizing European social space—with the aristocracy and the "third estate" cast physically far apart. Sudden shows of collective participation, sociability, and fraternization—for example, during games or at the inn—had been considered unacceptable by the British high culture; but, even before the "age of homespun," these demonstrations had become commendable in the southern colonies, almost a ritual. Kathleen Brown writes that American men "were expected to get a little grimy as they pursued farming and public life." The embrace of rural wholesomeness, at its peak during the crisis in the 1760s and early 1770s, was far from a novelty.[87]

From what we have just seen, we can infer that Jefferson-the-cultured-Virginian was well trained to perform simplicity. The social world into which he was reared knew, in turn, how to become "simple" without renouncing refinement and good manners. Jefferson had been "simple" decades before entering high office. The famous juvenile letter to his friend John Page, of December 1762, gives us an early example of Jefferson's well-known ability to pitch literary hyperboles. Jefferson was able to turn himself not only into a simple farmer but also into a young bohemian confined in a garret, while "cursed rats" ate up his pocketbook and his "Jemmy worked silk garters."[88]

And yet Jefferson bought clothes and accessories throughout the period of the "age of homespun." Never negligent or ignorant, his choices reveal an enduring tension between a long-lasting American and Virginian tradition of "simplicity" and the reality made of widespread practices of consumption. In 1771, for example, with the boycott on British luxuries about to be lifted, Jefferson wrote to his agent in London and urged him to comply with his former order for, among other items, "India cotton stockings for myself," a forte-piano, "a large Umbrella with brass ribs covered with green silk, and neatly finished," shoes, and "other prohibited articles." Should the committee decide not to take off the restrictions, "I can store, or otherwise dispose of them."[89]

The Memorandum Books provide extra information on Jefferson's consumption habits and sartorial expertise during the crisis of 1769. On 16 March, besides orders for osnaburg, coarse striped woolen blankets for his slaves, and coarse linen fabric for his coachman, Jupiter, Jefferson requested cotton stockings, silk, buckskin gloves, and scarlet cloth for waistcoats. Interestingly, besides orders, figures, and notes for payments, Jefferson also recorded verses and maxims, some possibly of his own invention. There are several maxims for 16 March. The first maxim, "Moderation in all respect [is] best," acts as an explicit self-warning. He probably took the maxim from Greek poet Cleobulus, knowing that he had to contain himself by curtailing unnecessary purchase. "Simplicity" did not come natural for him, despite its popularity in Revolutionary-era discourse.[90]

Jefferson was not alone in his quest for republican simplicity. Actually, "few colonists bought the new American modes in any sustained manner," Kate Haulman writes. "Homespun, however fine, was not high style, which resurged in the early 1770s." By the early 1780s, then, it was clear that many Americans would have "continued to look to Europe for la mode." When the war was over, imported goods swamped port cities, and Americans could again satisfy their hunger for consumption, refinement, and good manners. The 1780s abound of warnings against "fondness for European luxury and dissipation" conducive to "contempt for the simplicity" of America, to borrow from a letter Jefferson wrote to John Bannister; but no serious legislative measure was taken.[91]

It Was the First Time I Saw Him since His Return from France

The tension between Jefferson's performances in "simplicity," or "appropriate" manners, and his passion for high style and refinement is now under analysis. Actually, as said, Jefferson's enthusiasm for luxurious goods, or simply for quality, was nurtured by firsthand knowledge and dire application.

Studies of Jefferson's Paris years have recounted in detail this most significant phase of his process of personal refinement. Already knowledgeable before setting foot in France, Jefferson-the-minister-plenipotentiary picked up a unique opportunity to purify his competence, taste, and entire personality. For five years he bought and learned. Learning and buying were not, are not, mutually exclusive. From the moment he arrived in Paris, Jefferson had adjusted himself to the French "informal," "simpler," more casual elegance. Elegance and postaristocratic *beau monde* were everywhere to be seen.

It was difficult to remain untouched by such a whirlwind of style and modernity. "In society," Jefferson explained to David Humphreys, former aide-de-camp to General Washington and member of the famous commission to negotiate treaties of commerce with European nations, "the habit habillé [the coat *de grande toilette*] is almost banished, and they begin to go even to great suppers in frock [the more casual coat]: the court and diplomatic corps however must always be excepted. They are too high to be reached by any improvement. They are the last refuge from which etiquette, formality and folly will be driven." Paris was obviously the seat of the Court, the city of conservative high clerics and mummified aristocrats, a repository of absurd protocols, including archaic Catholic rituals and ceremonies. But Jefferson and the entire American diplomatic circle had entered a Parisian "Old World" that was at the same time new, dynamic, tolerant, playful, an avant-garde fraught with philosophy, daring in its studied shows of tasteful simplicity and nonchalance, and extremely seductive.[92]

With no doubts, Jefferson picked up such a quality, seductiveness. Thomas Lee Shippen, a young man from Philadelphia, was a lucky boy. He was introduced at the Court of Versailles and had Jefferson himself as his patron. "I observed," Shippen wrote, "that although Mr. Jefferson was the plainest man in the room, and the most destitute of ribbands crosses and other insignia of rank that he was most courted and most attended to (even by the Courtiers themselves) of the whole Diplomatic corps."[93]

Jefferson soon cracked the code of French casual elegance and added a personal, American flavor to it. French society liked Jefferson almost without reserve because, among other qualities, he followed Franklin's American "simplicity." Jefferson did not wear a beaver hat in Paris, but he was similarly noticeable. The fact that Jefferson "was original not only in his thinking but also in his manners and slightly *outré* appearance," William Howard Adams writes in his study of Jefferson's Paris years, "may have been part of his appeal to jaded Parisians." At ease both at the French court and at the postaristocratic salons, cradles of the Enlightenment culture, Jefferson cracked the code of the emerging bourgeoisie. "There was an aura of self-confidence about him, a historical fascination, that gave him the stamp of legend." His relatively plain appearance, without ribbons or other symbols of rank, stuck out as a statement of distinction in its own way. For his part, Jefferson may have despised European courts, but he liked the French style with no reserve: "I am much pleased with the people of this country. The roughnesses of the human mind are so thoroughly rubbed off with them that it seems as if one might glide thro' a whole life among them without a justle."[94]

When Jefferson returned to the United States to take up the position of secretary of state, on 21 March 1790, his friends feared he might have turned into a man of fashion: a boor, a fop, a dandy, a sophisticated "molly," and a courtier irremediably spoiled by the Parisian aristocratic life. After all, was it not Jefferson himself who had thundered against the "fatal" error of sending young Americans to Europe? Benjamin Rush, whom Jefferson befriended when they met during the Congress of 1775, was eventually relieved: "It was the first time I saw him since his return from France," Rush wrote in his *Autobiography*. "He was plain in his dress and unchanged in his manners. He still professed himself attached to republican forms of government." Jefferson did not lose his Americanness and "simplicity," but his taste for Frenchness and modernity was similarly unequivocal.[95]

You Know the Importance of a Good Maitre d'Hotel

Jefferson did not lose his Americanness, including his homespun "simplicity," but he incorporated a dose of Frenchness—both in his *persona* and within his houses. In other words, Jefferson's "negligence" as president was at once studied, part of a broad educational plan, and affected. We will see that such "negligence" did not derive from a man who had forgotten everything, who had lost his passions and knowledge, and who had actually become oblivious of himself. Luxurious furniture, lavish French cuisine, and expensive French wines were actually an endowment of the President's House, and, during his retirement, Monticello became the venue for luxurious settings and lavish meals in "half Virginian, half French style."[96]

Those who visited the president in Washington could easily see that Jefferson had successfully joined republican "plainness" with French style. Jefferson kept pursuing "simplicity" with a French twist. In the very moment he was pushing his program of education in republican values, Jefferson felt he needed some kind of director of ceremonies, a choreographer, or, more precisely, a majordomo: "You know the importance of a good maitre d'hotel, in a large house, and the impossibility of finding one among the natives of our country," Jefferson wrote to the French envoy in Philadelphia, Philippe Létombe. Jefferson asked Létombe to help him find the right *French* person for the job. Létombe helped Jefferson out by providing Joseph Rapin and, six months later, the faultless Etienne Lemaire. It was Lemaire, more and better than the rest of the numerous staff, who successfully instated French style at the President's House. "Negligent" Jefferson had his domestics (slaves), especially higher-rank servants, wear sumptuous liveries with a daring sprinkle of bourgeois modernity: velvet or corduroy pantaloons had replaced more old-fashioned breeches. Blue broadcloth coats with plated buttons and a silver livery lace, crimson or scarlet cuffs and collars, and red waistcoats must have necessarily gained the favor of Jefferson's guests.[97]

His Cloaths Seem Too Small for Him

But Frenchness was also visible in a typical feature of Jefferson's clothing, allegedly too small. This famous myth about Jefferson's peculiarly "negligent" style needs to be historicized. The individual who originated the contention was probably William Maclay. We have already met this senator from rural Pennsylvania because of his comments on Jefferson's "laxity of manner" and his way of sitting—lounging on one hip, and with one of his shoulders elevated above the other. Jefferson was then a freshly appointed secretary of state, and the style and manners of the French *philosophes* and the avant-garde with whom he spent his time were both vivid in his memory and appealing to his taste. In his *Journal*, Maclay also wrote that Jefferson's "face has a scrany [scrawny] Aspect. His whole figure has a loose shackling Air." Furthermore, he added, his "cloaths seem too small for him."[98]

Recently arrived from Paris, Jefferson may have absorbed vices and mannerisms with which the provincial senator, a farmer from rural western Pennsylvania, was not familiar. Gaye Wilson, better than other historians so far, has analyzed this issue. She has also grasped the striking contradiction between, for example, Benjamin Rush's memory of Jefferson as being "plain in his dress" and Maclay's censorious attitude. The two characterizations were jotted down at about the same time, and yet they are so different in their substance.

Wilson notes that the observation that Jefferson's clothes looked rather small "could be an indication that Maclay did not keep up with the latest in fashion, which inevitably came to America from Europe." Wilson makes very clear that "throughout the eighteenth century, the fashionable cut of the man's coat had continued toward a slimmer shape. By the beginning of the 1790s, the cut of the back of the coat was very narrow, with the midline of the front curving more toward the back, and therefore producing much narrower skirts. Even the sleeves fit more closely to the arm, and if a cuff was attached, it was no more than four inches wide." The apparent contradiction between the two observations would be only the consequence of the fact that Benjamin Rush was from Philadelphia, the most cosmopolitan American city at the time, and William Maclay came from the deep province. "American provincialism," Wilson concludes, "was always unevenly distributed."[99]

Jefferson's clothes were probably not too small for him. They neither conveyed an aristocratic or military pomp, with ribbons, crosses, and other insignia of rank that would have probably appealed to those who wanted a less "negligent" president; nor did his clothes "hang" on the body with the larger cut still popular in America. Maclay's comment, however, was spot on about a degree of fastidiousness, the "tone of European folly" that Jefferson caught in Europe."[100]

Upon his return to America, Jefferson's apparel did not become larger again. In New York, where the capital was provisionally located when the young secretary of state entered the Washington administration, Jefferson usually wore the clothing he brought back from France. He actually bought gloves, shirts, and other accessories right away, but the first payment to Christian Baehr, his tailor on Wall Street, was only made in mid-July, a couple of months after Maclay had seen him. We have here Jefferson at his peak as a "well-bred Frenchman," as Henry Randall eventually said.[101]

He Paid Little Attention to Fashion

Thomas Jefferson Randolph wrote about Jefferson undergoing a transformation: "In early life, his dress, equipage, and appointments were fastidiously appropriate to his rank. As he grew old, although preserving his extreme neatness, his dress was plainer, and he was more indifferent to the appearance of his equipage." Similarly, levees, this powerful symbol of rank, were not a favorite of his, but his entourage thought the president should continue the custom: "On the first levee day," Thomas Jefferson Randolph wrote, "he rode out at his usual hour of one o'clock, returning at three, and on entering the President's house, booted, whip in hand, soiled with his ride, found himself in a crowd of ladies and gentlemen, fashionably dressed for the occasion.

He greeted them with all the ease and courtesy of expected guests that he had been prepared to receive, exhibiting not the slightest indication of annoyance. They never again tried the experiment."[102]

Thomas Jefferson Randolph may have invented or sentimentalized a few details (the soiled boots, the whip in hand), but the substance of his narrative is correct. He is only wrong when he says that Jefferson had become "indifferent to the appearance." On the contrary, the green and brown of his inaugural suit, his corduroy breeches, plainer than the already plain garments he wore in New York and, later, in Philadelphia, had to elicit the ambitious educational plan he had in mind, as we have seen. Randolph is right to point out the overall trajectory: a first phase during which Jefferson tried to abide by his rank and official position yielded to a more mature effort at breaking (as said, stylistically more than substantially) the barriers of rank and conventions and exploiting his official position and, later on, his fame and popularity, in order to reach out with a powerful republican message. Negligence and indifference never entered this picture.

Even when we take as a case study the most outer aspects of Jefferson's *persona*, like the textures, cuts, and especially the colors of the garments he wore, we have to conclude that he definitely remained cognizant about what was going on upon his skin. Like Thomas Jefferson Randolph, Ellen Wayles Randolph Coolidge was right, but not completely, when she wrote that Jefferson's dress was "simple, and adapted to his ideas of neatness and comfort. He paid little attention to fashion, wearing whatever he liked best, and sometimes blending the fashions of several different periods." Jefferson, as Coolidge claimed, "did nothing to be in conformity with the fashion of the day." She was correct to stress Jefferson's preference for simplicity and comfort; but simplicity and comfort need to be defined according to Jefferson's complex priorities and personal standards, not hers, not even ours. Jefferson did not let others become his master: he wore "whatever he liked best" not randomly, but in the sense that, just like for so many other dimensions of his life, he remained consistently the master of his own decisions. On many levels, he actually kept paying close attention to style, good manners, and refinement.[103]

It is always worth repeating that Jefferson was reared in a fashionable society and, moreover, that he kept buying fashionable items almost compulsorily throughout his life. Young Jefferson was admitted to the houses of Governor Fauquier and George Wythe, in Williamsburg, and was on familiar terms with the scions of the great Tidewater plantations, the Pages, Burwells, Lewises, Willises, and Harrisons. In the mid-1770s and 1780s, when the "age

Fig. 12. Miniature of Thomas Jefferson by John Trumbull, 1788. (© Thomas Jefferson Foundation at Monticello)

of homespun" was but a memory, Jefferson was not wary of appearing fastidious, appropriate to his rank and, especially in Europe, maybe also a little showy. Painter Mather Brown (fig. 2) gives us this dandy. John Trumbull also, above all in the two miniatures, insists on flashy details, like the buttons "as big as a half a dollar."

Fig. 13. Miniature of Thomas Jefferson by John Trumbull, 1788. (Metropolitan Museum of Art, www.metmuseum.org, bequest of Cornelia Cruger, 1923, 24.19.1)

It is probable, almost certain, as Isaac Jefferson pointed out, that Jefferson kept wearing showy apparel in Virginia well into the nineteenth century: "He brought a great many clothes from France with him: a coat of blue cloth trimmed with gold lace; cloak trimmed so too. Dar say it weighed fifty pounds. Large buttons on the coat as big as a half a dollar; cloth set in the button; edge shine like gold. In summer he war silk coat, pearl buttons." Pearl buttons, gold laces, and silk coats expressed Jefferson's preferences and, as often, went along with his standards of "simplicity," comfort, and appropriateness. In this respect, his Memorandum Books chronicle an accomplished man who cultivated enduring relationships with tailors and who kept buying fancy accessories.[104]

When we discard the unlikely hypothesis of an emerging negligence, we discover the reality that Jefferson, on occasion, could dress up or down. Like many other men of his rank, Jefferson made many experiments. Any eighteenth- and nineteenth-century gentleman could choose red, scarlet, and bright hues. At least in western Europe, as a general rule, red and scarlet have been traditionally associated with royalty and aristocracy, including the high clergy. In general, bright colors and elaborate designs signified wealth and birth. Smoothness, by the same token, was almost universally acknowledged as a sign of gentility. Not surprisingly, showing clean, fine linen at one's throat and wrists was almost mandatory. The gentry did not necessarily choose brilliant colors, but they could. They had a very large margin of freedom. At the lower end of the spectrum, working-class people and slaves had a very limited range of options. They were expected to wear homespun clothing, coarse osnaburgs and fustians in dull whites or browns and greens obtained by vegetable dyes reminiscent of the natural world. Genteel refined men could dress down, but for their social inferiors, above all slaves, it was either economically impossible or against the law to mimic higher styles and act above one's station—unless, as runaways, they covered up their former identity and tried to "pass."[105]

His Supposed Predilection for Red Breeches

Jefferson was deliberate, first of all, about the colors of his garments. Even after the "dandy phase" of the 1770s and 1780s was gone, Jefferson did not rebuff bright colors. "His supposed predilection for red breeches," as nineteenth-century biographer George Tucker contended, had become a theme of "party wit." Certainly there were accounts of the mature Jefferson resplendent in red. Sir Augustus John Foster, the British diplomat who met the "tall and bony" president, substantially approved of him wearing "a blue coat, a thick grey-coloured hairy waistcoat with a red under-waistcoat lapped over it, green velveteen breeches with pearl buttons." Red waistcoats had fallen out of favor with the nineteenth-century American gentleman—as Isaac Jefferson notices, "all the gentlemen wore red waistcoats *in dem days*." As a consequence, Boston educator and scholar George Ticknor saw it as progress that Jefferson eventually gave up the "red plush waistcoat." Such bright waistcoats, elegant enough but out of date, "have been laughed at till he [Jefferson] might perhaps wisely have dismissed them."[106]

Rather than a sign of indifference or negligence, Jefferson's commitment to outmoded red waistcoats and red breeches sounds like another statement: at times at least, he wanted to stress that he was an old specimen, a survivor, and that he belonged to a bygone world. Implicitly, he was asking his guests to look back in time. In this regard, Gaye Wilson discusses another example of Jefferson performing with passé colors, his preference for blue coats and buff (that is, pale yellow) waistcoats. During the Revolution, Washington and his soldiers were clad in these colors, and Jefferson conjured this visual memory frequently, even at a late time.[107]

By performing style and shabbiness at once, or carrying about a peculiar mixture of tasteful and coarse details, he analogously made his guests notice that he gauged his bodily self against a temporal dimension longer than *la mode*. Upon meeting Jefferson in 1814, for example, young Harvard graduate Francis Calley Gray could not make sense of the weird spectacle he was beholding. The horn buttons of Jefferson's coat and the precious red velvet bounding his flannel under-waistcoat contrasted sharply with "grey worsted stockings, corduroy small clothes, blue waistcoat and coat, of stiff thick cloth made of the wool of his own merinoes and badly manufactured." In her 1808–9 diary, Frances Few, the young woman who had stressed the "shabbiness" of Jefferson's dress, tells that she was puzzled by an "old fringed dimmity jacket that he bought with him from France which reached down to his hips." Nonetheless, Jefferson's "worsted stockings nicely drawn up & a clean pair of leather shoes" made a certain positive impression upon her.[108]

We can register an analogous perplexed reaction about the simultaneous presence of stylish and problematic details in what William Plumer, for example, wrote in 1804: "I found the President dressed better than I ever saw him at any time when I called him on a morning visit. Though his coat was old & thread bare, his scarlet vest, his corduroy small cloths, & his white cotton hose, were new & clean—but his linnen was much soiled, & his slippers old."[109]

Jefferson had a sweeping educational plan in mind, a strategy concerning the future, as I have argued in the preceding sections. For him, by means of his *persona*, republicanism had to be made visible. Furthermore, especially as a mature famous man, he also wanted to give the impression that he belonged to a different era, somehow representing a link with a more or less imagined past. Testimonies have grasped Jefferson being to some extent *archaic*. In 1822, upon spotting Jefferson riding his elegant horse, for example, Reverend S. A. Bumstead, from Maryland, noticed that he "had every appearance of antiquity about him." Whatever precise meaning Bumstead had in mind, it is unquestionable that future and past, ambitious educational plans and memories of a bygone time, were both entrenched in Jefferson's corporeal present. Jefferson crafted effective strategies to build this public perception: this Enlightenment devotee was modern and yet antique at the same time.[110]

Since he deployed his apparel, among others tools, to convey more than one message, the actual Jefferson could simultaneously rely on coarse Virginia clothing, including worn-out and maybe less-than-clean complements, while keeping with his orders for superfine French cloth: "If either now or at any time hence," Jefferson wrote to Christian Baehr, his tailor in New York, "you can find a superfine French cloth, of the very dark blue which you know I wear, I will be obliged to you to make and send me a coat of it." This was Jefferson in the early 1790s, but expenditures for "superfine" fabrics are repeatedly annotated in his Memorandum Books. He could adopt many strategies to better convey his messages: he could shock his guests when he wanted, positively impress them, inspire them, or, through his unheard-of mixtures of styles and elements, just invite them to think about the inexorability of time passing. But we should never misinterpret Jefferson's dressing down as a sign of indifference, passivity, and negligence. He paid attention to fashion throughout his life.[111]

His Pantaloons Are Very Long

Both Thomas Jefferson Randolph and Ellen Wayles Randolph Coolidge were right: Jefferson's style evolved toward actual "middle-class" simplicity. However, such a transformation was by and large historical and collective, not only biographical and personal. Style itself was evolving toward a standard of simplicity and sobriety—including slimmer cuts, pantaloons instead of breeches, and strings instead of buckles—that we, inheritors of the bourgeois culture, would promptly acknowledge as such.

Jefferson's body, eventually, underwent a bourgeois revolution. Descriptions of and comments about Jefferson in the 1820s emphasized his emerging bourgeois attires. Ellen Wayles Randolph Coolidge, for example, writes that Jefferson "adopted the pantaloon very late in life, because he found it more comfortable and convenient, and cut off his queue for the same reason." Bourgeois practicality, or maybe just the bourgeois aesthetic that decreed the disappearance of breeches, hair with queues, and shoes with buckles, eventually took hold in America. Daniel Webster depicts Jefferson in 1824 wearing "a grey surtout coat, kerseymere stuff waistcoat, with an under one faced with some material of a dingy red. His Pantaloons are very long, loose, & of the same colour as his coat. His stockings are woollen, either white or grey, & his shoes of the kind that bear his name. His whole dress is neglected but not slovenly."[112]

Jefferson's gray pantaloons together with his laced booties, the "shoes of the kind that bear his name," made him into a quite modern figure. Not that we have to conceive of this transformation as a sudden break with eighteenth-century standards. Thomas Sully's 1822 portrait (fig. 7) still gives us breeches, for example; but it also gives us booties and, most important, a distinctively black-garmented figure. The blue and buff reminiscent of the Revolutionary period are gone. The dingy red waistcoats and white stockings, of which Italian Renaissance *signors* would have approved, are absent. There are no country greens and browns. In their place, we behold a professional, an austere middle-class man who oozes respectability and competence. No longer an eighteenth-century eccentric polymath, peculiar and old-fashioned, Jefferson at the end of his life could on occasion take up an aura of marketable efficiency and progress.

The black jacket and its complement, the white shirt, had been slowly but steadily emerging for at least a couple of decades. The two most iconic portraits of Jefferson, by Rembrandt Peale, 1800, and Gilbert Stuart, 1805, the "Edgehill portrait," presented a figure in black and white. In Western culture, black has long been associated with death and mourning. But it also became associated with sobriety and austerity: ecclesiasts and academics, among others, had sported black for centuries. The Dutch, in the seventeenth century, envisioned black as the color most suitable for merchants and burghers, and by the end of the eighteenth century France also took it as the

Fig. 14. Portrait of Thomas Jefferson by Rembrandt Peale, 1800. (©2017 White House Historical Association)

standard attire for middle-class professionals. In the early nineteenth century, black had become *the* bourgeois color for lawyers, merchants, financiers, politicians, and public figures regardless of their social rank. Men dressed in black imparted individualistic ethos, professionalism, efficiency, and practicality, rather than republican values, revolutionary aspirations, and optimistic philosophical visions. Jefferson's "simplicity," good manners, and refinement, indeed, embodied more than one standard and crossed more than one historical phase.[113]

Fig. 15. "Edgehill Portrait" of Thomas Jefferson by Gilbert Stuart, 1805. (©National Portrait Gallery, Smithsonian Institution, and Thomas Jefferson Foundation at Monticello)

I Was Not Provided with the Enchanted Arms of the Knight

Besides clothing, other dimensions of Jefferson's corporeality are similarly revealing and complex. I have already hinted at his being "almost femininely soft and gentle"; his being limber, mild, and approachable, postmilitary and postaristocratic; his lounging French attitudes; and his aversion to conflict.

It is now time to take these notions to a new level. We are ready to ask more abstract questions about softness and femininity: Was he *really* feminine? Was he masculine? What did these features mean to the people who knew him and described him this way?

By the late eighteenth and early nineteenth centuries, American cultured men, like Jefferson, moved within intellectual and social spaces whose canons and limits we, twenty-first-century interpreters, would maybe censor as blurred and excessively porous. These men were polymaths, professionals and beginners at once, simultaneously cool and passionate, "simple" and cultivated, natural and highly artificial. They may have sensed the importance of the rising professionalism and competence, but, among other things, they also kept praising virtue as conducive to personal and communitarian happiness, not to economic or academic success. Furthermore, their masculinity included many elements that many of us today might consider obviously female. Apparently, "masculinity" and "femininity" are not fixed qualities or attributes a given person either has or does not have.

All the whirlwind and excitement, for example, coming from buying silk, gloves, stockings, superfine French fabrics, tablecloths, ribbons, furniture, and so on, are often timelessly attributed to women or to an apolitical female love of fashion. Jefferson, as I have noted, took exception to this prejudice. Despite his black dress and, late in life, his habit of "wearing the pants in the house," he relied on studied sartorial styles (whether we like them or not) whose function was to educate American citizens and, as important, to keep personal distance from other eighteenth-century images of masculinity.[114]

Jefferson knew what he was doing not only because he wanted to educate the public to "appropriate" manners and a "simple" republican style but also because he desired to differentiate himself from other types of men that he found around him. Tight coats with a feminine silhouette were tools that helped Jefferson to revile the style of the Federalist administration, their taste for cockades, their ceremonial swords, their aristocratic pomp, and their hairstyle. Many Federalists had interpreted military costumes as both a statement of their aristocratic class identity and an ideal of masculinity. They found a gendered meaning in war and military performances. But Jefferson had become postaristocratic and postmilitary at once—modern, at least when he wanted to be. For sure, he never positioned himself in competition with George Washington's heroic military masculinity, for example, or Alexander Hamilton's unbounded ambition and, in turn, military talent. Jefferson was not a warrior, a hero in this sense. Despite his service as colonel of the Virginia militia during the Revolutionary War, from 1770 to 1779, his military career was far from illustrious. More important, he never used his military title and did little to encourage his fellows to perceive him as a warrior.[115]

At least in Europe, warriors were traditionally aristocrats, pompous and antirepublican *personae*, rigid, as to their bearing, and overawing, as to their apparel. As to their character, on both sides of the ocean, most of these men clung to specific passions and traits, like resentfulness, furiousness, bluntness, and peevishness. Their temperament lacked irony: they wanted to seduce women, they craved distinction, they sought glory and flirted with heroic death either on the battlefield or through "affairs of honor." And they had "ambitions," just like Hamilton. They made shows of "courage" and put on stage their loathing of "cowardice."[116]

Allegations of cowardice have been regularly tossed at Jefferson, at least since he fled on horseback, the morning of 4 June 1781, right in time before the British detachment led by Banastre Tarleton reached Monticello with the aim of handcuffing the governor—actually, the ex-governor by two days. While the episode has been the subject of extensive studies, more pressing questions arise: Was Jefferson really postmartial and postmilitary or, more simply, just an example of a coward and a wimpy man? Was his "femininity" and his public disrespect for aristocratic codes only a mask hiding "effeminacy"?[117]

Calling him effeminate and especially a "coward" as partisan literature as well as political opponents have done to diminish his stature is both unfair and theoretically obscure. First of all, it is problematic from a theoretical point of view: under which circumstances can we be sure that a person is a coward? Is there a specific action that an individual must perform in order to be acknowledged and classified as a coward?

Psychology has persistently failed to support the intuition that individuals are characterized by broad dispositions and by persisting traits resulting in extensive cross-situational consistency. This means that persons are variable entities changing from one situation to another more profoundly than many would expect. Character traits, such as courage, altruism, glamorousness, industriousness, or even egotism, clumsiness, laziness, and cowardice, fluctuate considerably both longitudinally over time and from one situation to another. As a matter of fact, it is very difficult to categorize a person as a coward, although on occasion one may behave cowardly, unless a consistent habit of cowardly behavior is acquired—but this last case is definitely not Jefferson's.[118]

Whether or not Jefferson's behavior on this occasion, and only on this occasion, was cowardly, what is certain is that cowardice was in the period usually deployed as a predicate adjective, "coward!" It was an "honorary" title with no precise basis, a currency by means of which people repaid their adversaries or persons they disliked. Jefferson's enemies, including General Henry "Light-Horse Harry" Lee, labeled him a coward. In 1812, Lee published his *Memoirs of the War in the Southern Department*. Allegations of the governor's effeminacy, incapacity, fear of military action, and "timidity and impotence" were thrown in Jefferson's face. Ironically enough, Jefferson himself had labeled Hamilton a coward: "A man as timid as he is on the water," he had wondered in a letter to his friend James Madison, "as timid on horseback, as timid in sickness, would be a phaenomenon if the courage of which he has the reputation in military occasions were genuine." As an adjective, "coward" was always generously distributed.[119]

"Coward" does not help us to understand Jefferson as a postmilitary man. Honor and reputation mattered to him. And this is why he entered the debate to defend himself against Henry Lee, despite a habit of trying to avoid personal exposure. Jefferson was obviously wounded by Lee. When Philadelphia publisher Joseph Delaplaine informed him about his idea of a multivolume project on distinguished Americans, Jefferson picked up the opportunity. In his correspondence with Delaplaine, Jefferson was not very generous with information, but he sent him precious material on his governorship. Jefferson wanted to make clear that, when circumstances dictated, he could advocate "action." At the same time, as important, he wanted to spell out that among the habits of behavior he picked up, he had never acted like a Don Quixote, a warrior engaging in sensational shows of courage. "I went thro' the woods," we read in the enclosure he sent to Delaplaine in 1816, "and joined my family at the house of a friend where we dined." What could he do? His guilt was that he forgot "the noble example of the hero of La Mancha, and his windmills." Jefferson declined the combat: "I was not provided with the enchanted arms of the knight, nor even with his helmet of Mambrino. These closet heroes forsooth would have disdained the shelter of a wood, even singly and unarmed, against a legion of armed enemies."[120]

Jefferson's "escape" was just the perfect example of what a postaristocratic, postmilitary man was expected to do in an analogous circumstance. Possibly, other public figures would have chosen behaviors centered on "honor" and unconditional "sacrifice." But this quite young Jefferson had already understood he had to subordinate his momentary passions, feelings, desires, and even personal honor to superior republican goods. This man was an achiever, a consistent strategist—perhaps even one slightly keen on "dissimulation" and "intrigue," as partisan libels called his style. Jefferson's mindset was teleologically oriented toward results and superior goods, and his body adjusted accordingly. On this occasion, just like on many others, he made his shrewd calculations. He was clear, in his mind and body alike, that military force and military behaviors were only means to a republican end—and definitely more than just the platform from where to show, single-handedly, one's bravery. As to his personal conduct, there was no point of reversing means and ends. At least at the time, he felt he could not sacrifice everything to the altar of a "courageous" type of masculinity, and certainly not his life.

His postmilitary *persona* exemplified a "male softness," not an unknown characteristic among Enlightenment devotees. This was not the style designed to gain the approval of French high aristocrats or of eighteenth-century American heroic males (Lafayette, Washington, Hamilton, and many others). Jefferson blended masculinity and femininity, but he was not feminine according to the then prevalent derogatory meaning of the term: weak, effeminate, and cowardly. Jefferson was feminine only in the sense that he pervaded certain popular types of masculinity with different qualities. He came up with a studied blend of calculation and reliability, authority and empathy, rationality and prudence.[121]

"Clearly," Andrew Burstein writes, "Jefferson used his body, his corporeal style, to convey an aversion to conflict. In a sense, he cheated those who expected (and might have preferred) the directness of a political battler, which Jefferson's pen proved him to be many times over during his career in government." His pen may have been lethal and uncompromising, weaponlike, but through his sartorial performances, conciliatory attitudes, and many other bodily strategies, Jefferson transmitted postmilitary softness. The main source of the many legends narrating Jefferson going unnoticed and unrecognized ("I thought this man was a servant") was Jefferson's corporeality itself. Through their more or less credible cameos, narrators invariably suggest that Jefferson was welcoming, forthcoming, and clearly feminine: "In every such vignette," Burstein concludes, "Jefferson is unruffled, even playful, offering no resistance. . . . Jefferson did not appear imposing and formidable, as one might expect a lordly southerner to appear." It is not happenstance that admirers transfigured Jefferson into a caring, maternal soul, almost a Christlike character: "His look," Randall wrote apropos these sketches, "fell benignantly and lovingly upon the weak, the simple, and the lowly, and they at once felt and returned the sympathy. They never feared him, they never presumed upon him." Randall, of course, overlooked the reality of slavery.[122]

I Have Lived Temperately Eating Little Animal Food

The American people felt, and still feel, the need to transfigure this eighteenth-century man. Jefferson, for sure, did nothing to disprove these narratives of him as a Christ-like, quintessentially humble and pious man. What he did was to popularize other dimensions related to his feminine softness.

His version of masculinity, for example, involved temperance; he curbed the desire for "fullness." Eating lightly was a typical Jeffersonian signifier, and it was performative and educational, a choice prompting more than medical implications. It was opposed to the choice many men made, and still make, to appear robust and brawny. Jefferson invited his contemporaries to visualize his male body as malleable, limber, refined instead of imposing, or formidable, or militaresque, or uncompromisingly strong. Military characters may have preferred being acknowledged as imposing and strong, but his ideal type conveyed refinement and self-mastery, and offered a different kind of virility. Overindulgence in food may have enhanced one's physical presence, an emphasis put on quantity, but it also threatened the attainment of quality and more modern ideals of beauty and middle-class simplicity.[123]

No human behavior, including how and what we eat, is completely natural, outside of history, or lacking social implications. Through his dietary habits, Jefferson educated Americans to seek for moderation. Moderation, for Jefferson, bespoke of synchronization with the soothing rhythms of nature: harmony and reconciliation instead of a titanic victory and a unilateral self-imposition. The process of embodiment that Jefferson advocated was all about simplicity and "naturalness." Nature was a caring mother, inspiring human trust. Consequently, training one's body to better abide by "her" care, just like achieving postmilitary softness, was an ideal of masculinity.

If moderation, as pursued by Jefferson, meant coming closer to the caring energy of nature, this also entailed downplaying other seemingly "universal" characteristics of masculinity, such as ferociousness, aggressive behavior, and the hunger for blood. Implicit in Jefferson's plea for moderation was his refusal to consider animal meat as the bottom line of male dietary regimen, at once the goal and evidence of a successful masculinity. "I have lived temperately," old Jefferson explained to Dr. Vine Utley, "eating little animal food, and that not as an aliment, so much as a condiment for the vegetables, which constitute my principal diet." Since, in many patriarchal cultures, vegetables have almost invariably represented second-class food, more likely to be cultivated and consumed by women, Jefferson's preference for vegetables was thus a political act. By means of the example he gave, he was inviting men to repudiate one of their allegedly essential masculine privileges.[124]

Jefferson's dietary choices were public acts. Many people could see him eating moderately, and avoiding meat consistently. Those who did not witness him eating might have encountered descriptions of the famous man's legendary temperance. By eschewing meat as the primary nutrient, Jefferson established a clear-cut difference between himself, a civilized and modern man, and those who were trapped into an inferior, almost *grotesque* stage. "I fancy it must be the quantity of animal food eaten by the English," Jefferson wrote playfully to Abigail Adams, "which renders their character insusceptible of civilisation. I suspect it is in their kitchens and not in their churches that their reformation must be worked." Playful though he may have been on this occasion, the joke alludes to a condition of superior civilization, and a finer ideal of masculinity and compassion that Jefferson actually tried to approach.[125]

Jefferson did not undergo any transformation in this respect. Occasional acts of bravado he may have performed do not disprove the truth that he had coherently tried to represent to himself and other people: his male identity as an attempt to reach some kind of equilibrium and harmony. The ideal type of male identity did not emerge, for him, through processes of conflict and victory, battle and the final defeat of the antagonist—despite the brutal fact that the patriarchal, slave-owning society of which he was a member was antagonistic to women and literally ate up the flesh of black bodies. From the point of view of his conceptual representations and conscious objectives, he sought to define his male identity via the rejection of the logic of the annihilation of the other. The nonhuman other, which had been considered edible for centuries, was not to be eaten.[126]

Rambling About the Mountain

Seeking harmony with the natural world was a serious affair with Jefferson. Nature was not, for him, the evil other—to be either eaten or destroyed. Nature was the norm and gave canons and norms in the largest sense possible. Nature was the Truth. Jefferson imagined that all humanity, not only certain types of males, should live their lives with a clear target in mind, regaining nature. He conceived of himself largely as a nature's man and a man of love.[127]

"Becoming natural" was an eighteenth-century obsession. Obviously, the nature that poets, artists, and philosophers wanted to emulate was an abstraction, an idea, the antonym of another nature counteridealized as brutality. From nature sprung moral dispositions, but from nature, at the same time, came what John Locke dubbed the "natural *roughness* which makes a man uncomplaisant to others." In the period, "nature" and "natural" could refer to positive and negative qualities alike. Jean-Jacques Rousseau's *Émile* (1762) or Henry Mackenzie's hero, Harley, whose story is told in *The Man of Feeling* (1771), popularized convincing characters that had successfully made peace with a good, positive, friendly nature, and had thus freed their "true and natural" feelings.[128]

Jefferson definitely sought to impress upon friends, admirers, and younger generations the image of himself as a nature's man. He was "but a son of nature," the young *flaneur* had joked merrily with Maria Cosway, "loving what I see and feel, without being able to give a reason, nor caring much whether there be one." He jested, many years later, about his mind having still remained uncorrupted by artificial canons: "I have always very much despised the artificial canons of criticism," Jefferson wrote to William Wirt. "When I have read a work in prose or poetry, or seen a painting, a statue, etc., I have only asked myself whether it gives me pleasure, whether it is animating, interesting, attaching? if it is, it is good for these reasons." Then, obviously, all his life he spent considerable amounts of time studying ancient and modern architecture, classical languages, literary criticism, and canons of all sort. Although he claimed the contrary, he was always in a position to "give a reason" for his personal preferences.[129]

I am alluding here to the *style* that Jefferson skillfully crafted. "Jefferson's style" is a phrase that we should not interpret only *sensu stricto,* technically and precisely, as referring to the design of his furniture, clothing, shoes, or hair. By means of all that he did and said, he fashioned a *persona*—and this is more than just a mind—whose natural style was immediately recognizable. In several senses, according to Jefferson, nature rejuvenated and restored the energy escaping from us. When Jefferson's hapless wife died, for example, he discovered that ramblings in the woods, on horseback, could operate as an effective recovery from dejection. He had attended his dying wife for days on end. When the ominous event took place, Jefferson collapsed. He fainted, his daughter Martha tells us. "He kept his room three weeks," she writes in her recollections. "When at least he left his room, he rode out, and from that time he was incessantly on horseback, rambling about the mountain, in the least frequented roads, and just as often through the woods."[130]

Woods and mountains acted upon Jefferson as a secret spring of "metaphysical" energy. "Metaphysical" is just a metaphor, of course. Nonetheless, *real* nature, intended as land, woods, mountains, landscapes, and so on, was more than just rhetoric and a trope occasionally deployed to make a point. Nature was a reality that shaped the style he constantly nurtured throughout his life. The point to which I am alluding is that, by making himself a public *persona* with a recognizable style in which nature loomed so large— not a stiff military hero, let alone a mannered aristocrat, but a limber, flexible, approachable, simple, and "feminine" figure aiming at reconciliation—he intended to bless Americans with an inexhaustible source of energy. This is no longer a metaphor, but rather a precise indication of the nationalistic plan Jefferson had in mind.

And Seem to Have Grown Out of this Land, as You Have Done

The Louisiana Purchase awoke many Americans to the possibilities that come from "owning" such a vast and rich natural world. But Jefferson, more than any other founder, had long sought to train Americans and make them capable of appreciating an identification with their land. Their land, which means the American woods, mountains, landscapes, territories, and so on, was a spring of energy and a buttress to a certain precise vision of nationalism. Jefferson was aware that this "nature's nation" needed to develop a spontaneous, immediate, prereflexive identification with the continent. Jefferson offered the political community, including future generations, just the right language and the right examples to follow. More effective than a poet, more poetic than most politicians, Jefferson built a recognizable image of American nationhood by means of his rambling in the woods, or each time he spoke about Shadwell, his birthplace, or Monticello: "our own dear Monticello, where has nature spread so rich a mantle under the eye? mountains, forests, rocks, rivers. With what majesty do we there ride above the storms!"[131]

Jefferson drew heavily on American nature as the most important source of pride and nationalism. The lesson he taught was that this powerful American nature could bring about humans' regeneration. Europe was rotten, polluted, overcrowded, artificial, and corrupted, but the American nature imparted a purifying strength. In his view, human beings were like plants and, as a famous historian has written, "to see this virgin terrain" would be tantamount to absorbing "the rudiments of a new consciousness." A virgin, powerful, and infinite land called for splendid possibilities of amelioration and hopefulness.[132]

In *Notes*, Query 6, even before jumping into the rhetoric of "our own dear Monticello," Jefferson had striven to rescue the American continent from the "imputation of impotence." The French naturalist Buffon made the obnoxious claim that in this continent nature would be "less energetic" and could produce only feeble beings. But Jefferson firmly disagreed. His opinion about the aboriginal people of the North American continent was fraught with nationalistic pride. Far from being weak, as we will see better later on, such a native product of the American land was a perfect model for American citizens to follow. In the same way, Europeans transplanted to this side of the Atlantic grew like a superb fruit. "Of the geniuses which adorn the present age, America contributes its full share." There was more eloquence than sound reasoning in Buffon's allegations, Jefferson concluded, because nature had not "enlisted herself as a Cis- or Transatlantic partisan." Jefferson believed that "men are like plants," as the poet Crèvecoeur used to say, and "the goodness and flavour of the fruit proceeds from the peculiar soil and exposition in which they grow."[133]

When, with the new century, the Louisiana Purchase unexpectedly was sealed, Jefferson had already perfected his multifaceted natural language and taught Americans about a nature-centered nationalism. Jefferson understood the kind of transformation, almost a religious redemption, that the Louisiana Purchase would eventually beget. He realized what the new nation needed: "It is so long," he wrote to the Osage nation in 1804, at the height of a sweeping, nationwide frenzy about the Louisiana Purchase, "since our forefathers came from beyond the great water, that we have lost the memory of it, and *seem to have grown out of this land, as you have done.*" Jefferson succeeded unconditionally on a philosophical, linguistic, and stylistic level, and Americans therefore believed, and still believe, that their communitarian identity did not come from questionable choices and fortuitous circumstances but was both necessary and natural, given in nature, not made by a group of white men.[134]

The image of an American man coming out directly from the land, and respecting nature's laws, is at once consoling and empowering. Jefferson's style was just like that, both consoling and empowering. He reconnected American citizens to their land, woods, and mountains, and yet made them an example for the entire humankind to follow. Cosmopolitan internationalism mixed perfectly with an American sense of rootedness. This synthesis of abstract and concrete, cosmopolitanism and rootedness, internationalism and nationalism, makes it possible for present-day Americans still to care so much for the third president. We know Jefferson's shortcomings (historians have contextualized him so well) and yet we must admit the magnetic power of his nature-inspired, refined, postmilitary, flexible *persona*.[135]

Which of Two Courses Would Be in Character for Them

Above and beyond his tenets and memorable quotes, Jefferson's educational proclivity appeared through this style he consciously fostered. He meant to be publicly acknowledged as a soft, gentle, harmonious, and simple nature's man, a product of his land. Even though he knew he would be chosen as an example for others to imitate, Jefferson never wavered. On occasion deemed an "inconsistent" and "sphinxlike" character, he did not betray qualms about either his specific version of masculinity or the reliability or efficacy of his performances.

Jefferson was never really seized by self-doubts. When he was twenty years old, according to his own admission, he was involved in an "incident." He wanted to declare his love to Rebecca Burwell, but it did not work out. His mind and body did not assist him: "I was prepared to say a great deal: I had dressed up in my own mind, such thoughts as occurred to me, in as moving language as I knew how, and expected to have performed in a tolerably creditable manner. But, good God! When I had an opportunity of venting them, a few broken sentences, uttered in great disorder, and interrupted with pauses of uncommon length, were the too visible marks of my strange confusion!" The clumsy hunter unable to catch his prey was a comedy Jefferson deliberately played to entertain his friend. It was literature. It does not inform us about Jefferson's personal cowardice, self-doubts, or a certain degree of discomfort while performing with his corporeality. Jefferson striving to achieve a goal and then accidentally revealed by the "disorder" of his shivering body is a successful storyline, one of his many characteristic hyperboles, but nothing more than that.[136]

As an adult, he might have not been a powerful orator or a remarkable military figure, he might have longed for escaping into an early "retirement,"

but Jefferson never shivered with self-doubt. Self-doubt was not his problem. Jefferson was a conscious, deliberate performer throughout his life. The
psychiatrist Ronald David Laing would have agreed that Jefferson was not
affected by an "ontological insecurity," a phrase that explains itself in opposition to its double, "ontological security." Ontologically insecure persons,
Laing claimed, lack a "a centrally firm sense of [one's] own and other people's
reality and identity." On the other hand, ontologically secure persons experience their "presence in the world as a real, alive, whole, and . . . [temporally]
continuous" substance. A quick perusal of his letters and other famous documents is enough to grasp the sense of wholeness, reality, and continuity that
characterized his entire philosophy. Moreover, he was able (at least in his
plans) to turn his very personal and private life into a consistent and coherent
public example. Had he seriously desired "retirement," he would have ended
his public career when the occasion came, and before becoming president.
For sure, he would have not founded a university in Virginia.[137]

There is no shivering and self-doubt in Jefferson's corporeality, even
though twenty-first-century readers might prefer a more candid character—a
man willing to admit of his ambiguities. An experienced public educator, Jefferson knew that his examples would be imitated. Consequently, he could not
allow himself any ambiguity or hesitancy. John Locke had written that "you
must do nothing before him [the child] which you would not have him imitate." From early on, Jefferson realized the paramount significance of such a
tenet. In *Notes*, for instance, he had denounced the mystifying "commerce"
between master and slave as an exercise of "unremitting despotism" on the
one side and "degrading submission" on the other. "Our children see this,
and learn to imitate it; for man is an imitative animal. This quality is the
germ of all education in him. From his cradle to his grave he is learning to
do what he sees others do." Imitativeness accounts for the basic mechanism
of the human mind—a fact that produces especially troubling effects in a
slave-owning society. "The parent storms, the child looks on, catches the lin-
eaments of wrath, puts on the same airs in the circle of smaller slaves, gives a
loose to his worst of passions, and thus nursed, educated, and daily exercised
in tyranny, cannot but be stamped by it with odious peculiarities."[138]

Jefferson's enlightened century put examples before precepts and abstract
rules. It was common sense that "example is more prevalent than Precepts,"
as George Washington's famous "Rules of Civility" (rule #48) asserted. Polite
conversation and exchange of opinions may have been praised as a mark
of civilization, but many people realized that examples counted more than

words and ideas. More than words do, examples, obviously, elicit imitation. In his *Discourses on Davila* (1790–91), for instance, John Adams ranked "emulation" at the level of an instinct, something natural and universal more than cultural and particular: "Emulation next to self-preservation will forever be the great spring of human actions," he declared.[139]

Precepts, rules, doctrines, opinions, and ideas counted, evidently, but at the same time Jefferson understood that he was living in a world where persons could not help but imitate other persons, literally and materially. People sought their fellows' approval. In a famous letter to his grandson Thomas Jefferson Randolph, he confessed he had repeatedly mimicked the *style* of those individuals whom he admired. "Under temptations & difficulties" Jefferson asked himself: "what would Dr. [William] Small, Mr. [George] Wythe, Peyton Randolph do in this situation? What course in it will ensure me their approbation?" To picture these examples, to imagine them in action, corporeally, was more effective than reasoning about the issue at stake: "I could never doubt for a moment which of two courses would be in character for them." Many human types exist, Jefferson allowed, "horse racers, card players, fox hunters, scientific & professional men," and, of course, "dignified men." But "many a time" he had only asked one question: "which of these kinds of reputation should I prefer? That of a horse jockey? a fox hunter? an orator? or the honest advocate of my country's rights?"[140]

The bottom line, as Jefferson admitted, was not to ask "what would my models say?" or "which way would they lead their reason?" Much more important, at least in cases like these, was behaving like these models would have behaved, gaining their approbation, carrying oneself in the way they would have carried themselves. Insisting on the "course" that would be "in character" for these models, in order to set oneself upon a preferred "reputation," means to outline education like a nonverbal set of performances, carried through the instructor's body—which takes up a distinct normative value. This explanation may sound a little academic at first, but the discovery of the body's potential for education, and in general its normativity, is precisely what happened during the long eighteenth century.

Jay Fliegelman has written extensively about the "period's preoccupation with performative elocution." The phrase "performative elocution" alludes not only to rhetorical expedients but also to the discovery of the body as a language, its normativity and its potential for education. "If actions," Fliegelman says, "are a language more influential than words (especially in the case of parents literally creating the character of a future generation) then the performing body rather than verbal language becomes the instrument of communication, and thus the site of constant inspection."[141]

Jefferson grasped that rationality, discourses, ideas, opinions, and mental performances in general do not entirely define a human being. As the powers of his mind were concerned, he did not nurture self-doubts. But humans, he would have concurred, are more than their psyche and more than a spiritual essence made of the continuous acts performed by the superior faculty we call reason. Stated otherwise, to become the "honest advocate of my country's rights," to borrow from Jefferson's own words, he had to be self-confident but not only about his mental powers. As a mind, Jefferson was certainly powerful and unwavering. But his body was no less important a factor. The bodily performances he mimicked, the gestures he assimilated, the products he consumed, the positions he assumed, the rituals he executed, the postures he incarnated, and so on, played a pivotal role as well. Much more than his unwavering mind made Jefferson into the founding father we still admire.

Till at Length It Becomes Habitual

Nineteenth-century romantics brought to an extreme the idea of authorship. They thought that humans were truer to themselves when they expressed their egos unconditionally, through the power and originality of their inventions, and when their selves acted unhampered. Jefferson did not share this enthusiasm for originality and unhampered selves. And, in fact, intellectual productions that we may judge as marred by conformism and an unforgivable lack of originality were for him a supreme achievement.

The Declaration, to take the most famous example, only mirrored the "American mind." In questions without importance, Jefferson approved of venting one's biases for novelty, originality, uniqueness. Expressing the ego was not taboo. Nonetheless, when he came to consider important subjects like politics, morals, and religion, Jefferson embraced quite an opposite attitude. Of course, reason must be followed fearlessly, and servility and prejudices must be shaken off. But just as important, for him, was to renounce every passion for singularity, originality, and novelty: "In the first place," Jefferson wrote to Peter Carr, "divest yourself of all bias in favour of novelty and singularity of opinion. Indulge them in any other subject rather than that of religion. It is too important, and the consequences of error may be too serious."[142]

According to Jefferson, those who chase novelty and express their egos without restrictions run the risk of making mistakes. Probably worse, they can shatter good manners. Benjamin Franklin's motto, "never to contradict anybody," gave voice to Jefferson's softness and deep aversion to enter into conflicts. He analyzed this motto, in fact, in the 1808 letter to Thomas Jefferson Randolph we have seen before. In his first inaugural address, Jefferson had already notoriously insisted on reconciliation: "We are all republicans: we are all federalists." In 1816, he again declared his "wish to avoid all collisions of opinion with all mankind." Jefferson was sure that if he had simply praised his unmatched achievements, his originality, his uniqueness, his geniality, and similar, he would have only antagonized his friends and peers. There is more than hypocrisy in Jefferson's famous exercises in self-effacement: "I was," he wrote in 1822, "one only of a band devoted to the cause of independance, all of whom exerted equally their best endeavors for it's success . . . so also in the civil revolution of 1801." More than disingenuous provisos, assertions like these reveal his deep belief that originality and personal "triumph" had always to be gauged against a communitarian ideal. Success, for him, was not the high peak of a solitary voice, but rather the mark of one's capacity to master the habit of social adaptability and flexibility.[143]

Jefferson actually saw himself as a member of a band, not a genial and solitary mind. He started with a strong communitarian vision; he began with the representation of fellow bodily creatures sharing in a social space, performing together, and asking for "simplicity" and harmony—although not necessarily for the abolition of hierarchies. Had he seen himself in spiritualistic terms, as a mind encapsulated in a brain, in turn confined in a head, he would have *obviously* asked for unconditional liberation. He would have *necessarily* made a case for the unhampered flowing of his spiritual energy, as if from inside out. But he never advised such an unchecked stream of consciousness and artistic creativity. Quite the contrary, the guidance he gave to both himself and others always insisted on developing the proper habit.

"Habit" is a crucial philosophical term, as we are about to see, almost a link between the spiritual and the material realms, between the psychological and the corporeal domains. If we, by which term I mean our *selves*, were the simple outcome of a given set of intellectual, psychological, or spiritual acts, our bodies would be obstructions rather than creative resources in their own ways. We should, in turn, explain away society, the collective made of the individual's material body in relation to the bodies of others, as a second-order impediment. Not a self-conscious theoretician, Jefferson nonetheless had a clear notion that we, our selves, are made of ideas, which we own, plus corporeal performances that take place in society, like buying things, wearing certain clothing, riding a horse, sitting a particular way, attending concerts, and so on. Besides ideas, bodily performances and social events as well make us who we are. Expressed in a shorter formulation, Jefferson knew that humans are not pure interiorities.

Instead of advocating unfettered expression, unheard-of novelties, or some form of geniality sprouting out from the spirit, Jefferson took care to always recommend the proper habit. Every materialist philosopher would do the same. For example, Jefferson instructed Robert Skipwith, the brother-in-law of his future wife, to fix by training his habit of virtue: "the entertainments of fiction are useful as well as pleasant. . . . But wherein is it's utility? . . . I answer every thing is useful which contributes to fix us in the principles and practice of virtue." In the famous letter to Peter Carr that we have already encountered ("Encourage all your virtuous dispositions, and exercise them whenever an opportunity arises . . . exercise will make them habitual. . . . Habituate yourself to walk very far. . . . There is no habit you will value so much"), Jefferson elaborated extensively on the significance of habits: "It is of great importance to set a resolution, not to be shaken, never to tell an untruth. There is no vice so mean, so pitiful, so contemptible and he who permits himself to tell a lie once, finds it much easier to do it a second and third time, till at length it becomes habitual, he tells lies without attending to it, and truths without the world's beleiving him. This falshood of the tongue leads to that of the heart, and in time depraves all it's good dispositions."[144]

There is much more at stake here than just the moralist's jeremiad against lying. Jefferson's subtext is more interesting. Dangerous performances or behaviors that have become habitual, he claims, undermine our sociability and maim our integrity. Commendable acts, conversely, enhance our integrity, including social worth. In this letter, Jefferson was pointing at a movement that goes from the external, a practical act and a bodily experience, to the internal: a forked "tongue" would mar Carr's "heart," which means his morality, and would turn him into a depraved being. The act, Jefferson-the-materialist was saying, could become habitual and impress upon the inner self a certain character.

Terms like "habit" and "habitual," including recommendations to "learn yourself the habit of adhering vigorously to the rules you lay down for yourself," appear regularly in Jefferson's letters and other writings. The reason is that, in the period, it was commonsensical to refer to a simplified version of Locke's sensationalism—the notion that ideas reach the mind, or spirit, via the five senses and thus that the spiritual self, which we deem we are, does not invent, but rather receives its content, *a posteriori* and by means of empirical interactions. In Federalist #27, Alexander Hamilton, for one, relied on this precise tenet: "Man is very much a creature of habit. A thing that rarely strikes his senses will generally have but little influence upon his mind." Lockean epistemology, popular in the eighteenth century, accepted as true that the most enduring meanings are those created *through* the body. Jefferson, naturally, agreed with his archenemy's Lockeanism. He endorsed the thesis that creatures at the same time material and spiritual need habits to develop stable patterns through which perceiving and interpreting the world. Angels, gods, or noncorporeal and spiritual beings would not have habits. But Jefferson was aware that humans, half-spiritual and half-material beings, needed to train their bodies as well as their minds.[145]

High Respect for Your Character as a Man and Citizen

Through the habit, a bodily act becomes a stable endowment of the mind. Through the interpenetration of socially driven habits, a character is formed: good habits form a character, as they would have said in the eighteenth century. Just like "habit," "character" was another technical term, and a pivotal one, at that. Historians have clearly pointed out that, like many other eighteenth-century figures, founders attempted to establish a character for themselves. They could not agree with the vision of a society in which every individual would pursue "novelty and singularity of opinion," in which men and women of every walk of life would simply seek to unfetter their creativity and express themselves without limit. No society of competing interests would do for them. In Federalist #11, Hamilton, again, had warned against men without character, against the "little arts of the little politicians," as he wrote.[146]

In the period, character was less a quality of an inner spirit—specific personality traits that a psychologist may describe, we would say—and more a public feature. Character did not principally belong to the sphere of one's private life, as would be the case from the nineteenth century on. Eighteenth-century men and women, rather, had to *acquire a character*. They had to train their mind and their body alike in order to gain the approval of other people, and thus become fit for a certain role. "Having long borne high respect for *your character as a man and citizen,"* to borrow from Jefferson's own words, was a typical epistolary formula. Characters were seen as patterns of behavior and, once again, were tied to corporeal performances. In the Declaration, for instance, we read that "a Prince, whose character is thus marked by every act which may define a Tyrant, is unfit to be the ruler of a free people." Good and talented though this particular person may be in herself or himself, when in private, character primarily appeared through and as actions, through and as public behaviors. Character took exception of personal, secret, inner qualities. It was something half spiritual and half material, visible and, consequently, social.[147]

Other people were beneficiaries and, consequently, judges of an individual's character. Entering society with a certain character entailed making sure these others would approve of one's performances. To our twenty-first-century sensibility all this may look like social conformism, but eighteenth-century men and women, especially of higher rank, watched themselves constantly through the eyes of others.

When someone is brought into society, Adam Smith had claimed, "he is immediately provided with the mirror which he wanted before. It is placed in the countenance and behaviour of those he lives with, which always mark when they enter into, and when they disapprove of his sentiments." Jefferson echoed Smith, for example, when he insisted with Thomas Jefferson Randolph that identifying with men of superior character, instead of emulating horse racers, card players, or fox hunters, led to a "prudent selection & steady pursuit of what is right." In his 1793 Opinion on the Treaties with France, to take another example, Jefferson explicitly praised those writers and authors who "happen to have feelings and a reason coincident with those of the wise and honest part of mankind, [and] are respected and quoted as witnesses of what is morally right or wrong in particular cases." In the letter to Peter Carr of August 1785, to end this list, he had urged his nephew to seek the approval even of generic others: "Whenever you are to do a thing tho' it can never be known but to yourself, ask yourself how you would act were all the world looking at you, and act accordingly."[148]

We see in other people's countenance the sign of approval or disapproval of our opinions and behaviors. People respond to our statements and deeds, and we try to adjust accordingly. Most of the time, there was no need for the magistrate to prosecute unorthodoxy or odd behavior, Jefferson was confident, even when these conducts could put in jeopardy good morals or peace and order. In cases like these, the magistrate and the state did not need to be "troubled," he wrote. "If a sect arises," we read in *Notes*, "whose tenets would subvert morals, good sense has fair play, and reasons and laughs it out of doors, without suffering the state to be troubled with it." An effective power thus existed upon which humans could rely. The good sense of the people would laugh unorthodoxy "out of doors" and would act as a natural equalizer. The desire of being approved and the fear of being ridiculed by a majority, Jefferson believed, would act as the main motive for heretics to amend their character.[149]

The side effect of such an eighteenth-century socialization and politicization of character is that many of those who tried hard either to acquire or to conserve their character were often stricken by bouts of anxiety—many of them, although not all of them. Possibly because Jefferson sensed he had largely succeeded in training his body-mind according to the precepts of nature, good sense, and good manners (limber, soft, gentle, simple, modern, postmilitary, postaristocratic, and so on), or possibly because he knew his origins and birth, he did not seem to be especially anxious at the prospect of being laughed out of doors.

Anxious, certainly, he was. But his anxiety took aim at particular aspects of the new nation: "I tremble for my country when I reflect that God is just: that his justice cannot sleep for ever"; "We have the wolf by the ear, and we can neither hold him, nor safely let him go"; "You and I, and Congress, and Assemblies, judges and governors shall all become wolves"; "The spirit of the times may alter, will alter . . . from the conclusion of this war we shall be going down hill." On the other hand, however, Jefferson did not shiver about losing the sense of his own station. He never asked himself the question "Who am I?"[150]

Members of the American elite who were not blessed with Jefferson's high birth were often beset with personal insecurities. At the same time, they could become easy prey to allegations of a lack of character. Jefferson knew his character and birth at once, and he transferred upon some of his foes, especially upon Alexander Hamilton, the troubling accusation that *they* lacked birth and character.

In 1792, Jefferson wrote to George Washington about this peculiar man, "whose history, from the moment at which history can stoop to notice him, is a tissue of machinations against the liberty of the country which has not only recieved and given him bread, but heaped it's honors on his head." In Jefferson's view, birth abetted the acquisition of character. Being identified as a "tissue of machinations" was the opposite of being publicly acclaimed as a man of character. Gilbert Chinard has commented on this passage in such a brilliant way that no paraphrase would be appropriate: "In one sentence," Chinard wrote, Jefferson "had expressed not only condemnation of Hamilton's policies but all the scorn of a Virginian, of the old stock, for the immigrant of doubtful birth, who was almost an alien. He knew full well the weight that such a consideration might have on the mind of Washington; it was a subtle but potent appeal to the solidarity of the old Americans against the newcomer." Jefferson drew a clear line between men of character and those who, for a series of reasons, could hardly attain one.[151]

My Age Requires That I Should Place My Affairs in a Clear State

Thomas Jefferson was all his life singularly able to master his corporeality, to remain at the helm, to change established patterns, and to convey many messages. Even though bodies, in general, retain a rather high level of autonomy over the mind (we are a *body*-mind system, after all), Jefferson did many exemplary things with his body. He mastered his body without shivering. He inhabited his body comfortably and efficiently. His sheer presence was often the outcome of a well-planned strategy—actually, as we have seen, more than one.

Nonetheless, at a certain point the body reclaimed control. As happens to many old persons, and despite staying limber in his mind, Jefferson started experiencing his own body as no longer entirely his own: "oneself as another," to use the title of a book by a famous philosopher. Obviously, as he was well aware, under certain conditions our being may always twist into a burden. What he called "idleness" or "indolence" makes the body system a burden. He had given advice to his daughter Martha in this sense, and had urged her to always stay vigilant: "Body and mind both unemployed, our being becomes a burthen, and every object about us loathsome, even the dearest."[152]

Jefferson was not immune from a peril worse than just lurking idleness or indolence. I am making an allusion to the "malady" called senescence. Old age and eventually death are more than an external, relatively probable threat. Irremediably, age turns one's body into a foreign "other," making it a significant "burthen." Old age disrupts the whole system made of our mind interacting with our body in turn interacting with many things that form our world. Jefferson's masterwork, a harmonious, flexible, modern, refined, even "feminine" body, at a certain point broke asunder. As a consequence, our discourse must turn medical. While we avoided this dimension so far, we cannot any longer ignore that medical performances defined Jefferson's corporeality. At a certain point, he did things medical, and increasingly so.

Interestingly enough, the aging body, a body that failed, did not disrupt Jefferson's sense of self. This body system now utterly defective did not alter the kernel of Jefferson's optimistic philosophy, while turning him into a cynical, unresponsive, and cranky character. He kept up with his sanguine expectations and constantly fostered his ambitious programs. He kept his plans going despite the fact that his body, eventually, foiled him—as we will see, even in the most basic ways. He suffered, both morally and physically, from a body that was increasingly beyond his control, of course. But old age seems not to have affected the fundamental categories upon which, and expedients through which, he built his self. For better and for worse (for worse, as we will see in part 2), he was still the same Thomas Jefferson up to the very moment he died.

Actually, over the years he had prepared himself for the inevitable physical decay, whether by reading Seneca and other classical authors or by launching warnings, to himself and others, to get ready for the "more certain event which is death," as he wrote to his daughter Martha. Jefferson had always been heedful of senescence and death, and this awareness of human finitude explains why, perhaps as a talismanic gesture, he had also played the old man since his prime—or right after his prime. He had claimed he was ready to retire, longing for retirement, and all this took place at the very beginning of his career as a national politician. As a young secretary of state, he felt (or just pretended) his fibers and nerves were already worn out: he was "worn down with labours from morning to night, and day to day." Seeking respite and "happiness" in the "lap and love" of his family, as he claimed, was the only sensible response to the fact that "the motion of my blood no longer keeps time with the tumult of the world." Young Jefferson is renowned for playing the old man: "The little spice of ambition, which I had in my younger days, has long since evaporated," he wrote. "My health is entirely broken down within the last eight months; my age requires that I should place my affairs in a clear state."[153]

Talismanic gestures asides, Jefferson seemed aware that his genetic predisposition, as we would call it today, was far from promising. His father, Peter, had died young, and Jefferson "knew" he could hardly outlast him. In 1784, he said to Abigail Adams that he did not expect to "live above a Dozen years." He must have soon realized that the best strategy he could adopt to slow the pace of such a "genetically unhappy" patrimony and prolong his life was a steady reliance on proper diet, temperance, and constant exercise.[154]

Possibly as a consequence of a good regimen, as well as a more propitious genetic predisposition than the one he dreaded, Jefferson enjoyed a life that was at once long and considerably healthy, especially for those years. He suffered from short- and long-term ailments, but none was impairing: headaches, usually of the duration of several weeks; rheumatism; a few episodes of teeth abscesses; and common colds. As to life-threatening illnesses, as much as we know he was only affected by dysentery while a young member of the Virginia House of Burgesses. Scholars have also claimed he may have been struck by tuberculosis from late 1783 to 1786.[155]

We will never know if what he said to Abigail Adams was just a joke, a posture, or another typical Jeffersonian hyperbole. However, he spent almost his entire life firmly settled on a healthy regimen, a proactive behavior indicating not pessimism or fatalism, but rather confidence and high expectations. Jefferson's healthy regimen was based, as we have seen, on walking, horse riding, moderate diet with little meat, and a few glasses of wine. He abstained from consuming tobacco and "ardent" liqueurs, albeit wine was entirely another matter. Wine was healthy. "Wine," Jefferson wrote to a Portuguese wine maker and physician, "from long habit has become an indispensable for my health." Dr. Rush had advised one-and-a-half glasses of wine per day; but "I double" the dose, he confessed to Dr. Vine Utley, and "even treble it with a friend."[156]

Besides wine, Jefferson settled on much more debatable and unpalatable habits and regimens. Since his youth, for example, he took up the practice of bathing his feet in cold water: "I have for 50. years," he wrote to James Maury, native of Albemarle County and consul in Liverpool, "bathed my feet in cold water every morning . . . and having been remarkably exempted from colds (not having had one in every 7. years of my life on an average) I have supposed it might be ascribed to that practice." For fifty, maybe sixty years, as he said to Utley, Jefferson had been faithful to this practice. He was sure his "exemption" from important maladies was due "partly to the habit of bathing my feet in cold water every morning."[157]

This Will Give Time to the Vis Medicatrix Naturae

Jefferson was an eighteenth-century man, a particular we can infer even from this perhaps little weird habit of bathing his feet in cold water. Furthermore, this eighteenth-century natural philosopher believed the doctrine that, in most cases, nature takes care of itself—*vis medicatrix naturae,* as Hippocrates, Paracelsus, Thomas Sydenham, and many others had called this mysterious, self-healing power hidden in every organism. When maladies hit, Jefferson-the-nature's-man assumed that the best thing to do was to bear the lot with confidence and endurance: "At your time of life," he encouraged his son-in-law Thomas Mann Randolph, momentarily sick, "the resources of nature are so powerful that, in a case which gives her time, they are infallible." Except in cases of consumption, "which is not yours," "I cannot recollect one instance of a chronic complaint in any person of your age not being surmounted." Waiting patiently, the "wisest physicians agree," paid better than relying on "medecine": "Keep up your strength then, by such exercise as you find does not fatigue you, and by eating such things and in such quantities as you find you can digest. This will give time to the vis medicatrix naturae, which, if it be not thwarted in it's efforts by medecine, is infallible in it's resources at your time of life."[158]

Franklin's *Poor Richard* had famously quipped: "He's the best physician that knows the worthlessness of most medicines." Voltaire had said the same, in turn spoofing the medical art: "The art of medicine consists of amusing the patient while nature cures the disease." The tenet of taking "no mede-cine" resonated with Jefferson's concept of a caring nature. In 1807, he wrote to Caspar Wistar, professor of anatomy and midwifery at the University of Pennsylvania and the author of the first American book on anatomy, that the *vis medicatrix naturae* should be the golden rule for every physician to follow. Nature "brings on a crisis, by stools, vomiting, sweat, urine, expectoration, bleeding, &c., which, for the most part, ends in the restoration of healthy action." Pharmaceutical remedies, he trusted, may at best speed up the pro-cess a little, but usually they are a hindrance.[159]

As a matter of fact, however, Jefferson took and dealt with medicines regu-larly, despite the ideological aversion we have just encountered. A strong supporter of inoculation against smallpox, a very risky procedure, Jefferson undertook a journey to Philadelphia in 1766 to be vaccinated. Over the years, he advised friends and relatives to undergo the procedure. Especially after he became president, he intensified his commitment to the vaccination. Between August and September 1801, for example, he donned the garb of the doctor himself and inoculated many of his slaves. We have lists of vac-cinations, in Jefferson's hand, dated 1802, 1816, and 1826. Jefferson experi-mented with medicines all his life. In 1792, he devised a "Recipe for the head-ach called the Sun-pain" based on "Calomel taken at night." Calomel, a very popular preparation at the time, was nothing less than mercurous chloride, an antibacteria with purgative effects, and yet highly poisonous.[160]

In a context of wild self-medication and still more crazy practices, we must reckon that Jefferson pursued mildness and sensibleness. The ordeal that George Washington underwent before he died is legendary. The practice of bloodletting was widely accepted, and Washington's doctors, during those ominous final days, extracted from him about four pints of blood, without doubt speeding his demise. But Jefferson followed another route: "In his theory of bleeding, and mercury, I was ever opposed to my friend [Benjamin] Rush," he declared to Thomas Cooper, at the time chair of chemistry at Dickinson College in Carlisle, Pennsylvania. Like many other advocates of problematic medical measures, Rush "has done much harm, in the sincerest persuasion that he was preserving life and happiness to all around him." Jefferson came to the conclusion that "cautious practice" should be the first virtue of a physician.[161]

We may well say that Jefferson lacked appropriate medical competences. And nonetheless, he was commendable in his willingness to access information. His great library, under the heading "natural history," contained over 150 writings on medical subjects, from dentistry to inoculation, from venereal diseases to various psychiatric conditions, from "onania" to the bite of mad dogs, from ophthalmic problems to "longevity." Also, it contained several medical guides and dictionaries.[162]

Bread Pills, Drops of Colored Water, and Powders of Hickory Ashes

Jefferson did not despise the medical art or doctors in general. He always regarded with interest the medical practice of the day and those physicians who refrained from bold speculative adventures in the realm of the unknown. Jefferson was particularly kind toward his personal doctors, the especially cautious Thomas Watkins and, starting from the spring of 1825, Robley Dunglison. He corresponded with many doctors, including Benjamin Rush, of course, and George Gilmer, Gustavus Horner, and Samuel Brown.[163]

A superficial reading of the letter Jefferson wrote to Caspar Wistar in 1807 may beget the mistaken impression that, all in all, he was hostile to the medicine of his day. From the assertion that "we observe nature providing for the re-establishment of order" by itself, that too many operations of nature escape "our imperfect senses and researches," it seems we have to conclude that Jefferson despised doctors. Jefferson actually lent a hand to a similar conclusion. "One of the most successful physicians I have ever known," he wrote to Wistar, "has assured me, that he used more bread pills, drops of colored water, & powders of hickory ashes, than of all other medicines put together." A statement such as this may well put the reader on the wrong track. In reality, Jefferson was simply criticizing the "adventurous physician," the one who "substitutes presumption for knolege." He was simply disparaging "fanciful theory." Jefferson knew, as he wrote in another letter a few years later, that the theories of that art "change in their fashion with the ladies caps & gowns."[164]

Jefferson himself made clear the real intention of the letter to Wistar: not mocking medicine, but rather specifying to a friend the "real limits" of both the medical art as such and his personal comfort zone. "The only sure foundations of medicine are, an intimate knolege of the human body, and observation on the effects of medicinal substances on that. The anatomical & clinical schools, therefore, are those in which the young physician should be formed. If he enters with innocence that of the theory of medicine, it is scarcely possible he should come out untainted with error." Jefferson read the "ingenious theories" of medicine, his qualifications notwithstanding. But instead of tricking him adrift, the bounty of information he could get from his personal library had the effect of restraining him, of teaching him a moral.[165]

His readings gave him a lesson in the proper corporeal style, including the virtues of moderation, sobriety, and thoughtfulness. The "adventurous physician," from whom Jefferson took distance, embodied precise visual characteristics. Reflecting on the character, the *persona* of such a physician, was the same as mulling over precise images and a precise repertoire of outdated behaviors. This doctor, and only this doctor, was entirely clownish in his manners, and Jefferson could not stand the type. This doctor made a fool of himself by speculating on secret virtues, qualities, spirits, and other metaphysical conundrums. Medical science "was demolished here by the blows of Moliere," Jefferson had written as a young man in Paris, "and in a nation so addicted to ridicule, I question if ever it rises under the weight while his comedies continue to be acted. It furnishes the most striking proof I have ever seen in my life of the injury which ridicule is capable of doing." The blows of Molière (and of Voltaire and Franklin as well) may have been excessive as they targeted the entire profession indiscriminately. But would it be possible not to spoof the *persona* of a Renaissance-like magus and a latter-day alchemist?[166]

A Wrist and Fingers Almost without Joints

At a certain point Jefferson actually became old and his body changed into a blunt instrument, an uncompromising hindrance, or maybe even a real enemy. Jefferson's corporeality, so to speak, became tyrannical, whimsical, and upsetting, and thwarted his sense of agency—albeit not his general optimistic worldview. After he retired from the presidency, his "periodical head ache" subsided—which gives us an indication that stress may have elicited these excruciating and debilitating fits. That these cyclical episodes may have had a psychosomatic base is probable, also because resting in dark rooms was more effective than the calomel and Peruvian bark (quinine) Jefferson occasionally took. But despite the abated headache, other conditions intensified. Rheumatic joints at his hips progressively debilitated him, making walking painful and eventually impossible. By 1812, while testimonies could still see him as enviably limber and in command of his postmilitary body, he acknowledged that time "presses on me with a heavy hand." One year later, secluded in his private space at Poplar Forest, he realized he was "weakening very sensibly. I can walk no further than my garden." All this was no longer just a pose.[167]

Jefferson was ready to die, like a real Epicurean philosopher. At the same time, he did not lose his knack for literary expedients and hyperboles as rhetorical means to ward off the approaching end. He kept challenging the tyrannical power of his body by joking about the whole corporeal system and the unwelcome level of rigidity he hit. On occasion, he could become a branchless tree, a trunk, a monument of a bygone era, a worn-out mechanism, or a "carcase." He played with many self-representations, all of them emphasizing the "otherness" of his own aging body. In 1813: "an old crazy carcase like mine." In 1814: "I stand like a solitary tree in a field, it's trunk indeed erect, but it's limbs fallen off, and it's neighboring plants eradicated from around it." The same year: "our machines have now been running for 70. or 80. years, and we must expect that, worn as they are, here a pivot, there a wheel, now a pinion, next a spring, will be giving way." In 1819: "First one faculty is withdrawn and then another, sight, hearing, memory, affections, and friends, filched one by one, till we are left among strangers, the mere monument of times, facts, and specimens of antiquity for the observation of the curious." In 1820: "why wish to linger in mere vegetation? as a solitary trunk in a desolate field, from which all it's former companions have disappeared?"[168]

He eventually became corporeally rigid, and not only literarily and meta-

phorically. Scarcely able to walk, as said, the right wrist he dislocated probably around 18 September 1786, while attempting to jump a fence in the
Cours-la-Reine in Paris, tormented him for the rest of his life. Near the end,
he managed somehow to write letters, but the functionality of the right hand
was gone. "My dislocated wrist is now become so stiff that I write slow and
with pain," he wrote to Adams. "Weighed down with years, I am still more
disabled from writing by a wrist & fingers almost without joints," he wrote
to Lafayette.[169]

A Spasmodic Stricture of the Ileum

While he could somehow put up with the trouble the wrist and other stiff
joints gave him, diarrhea was a different affair. Diarrhea affected Jefferson
especially in the last twenty-five years of his life. Here lies the most dramatic
measure of the alienation of his body. Bouts of diarrhea deprived him of a
big part of his autonomy. He was anxious, even scared, about what he knew
could happen. Described to Rush with some reticence as an episode occurring in 1801 "after having dined moderately on fish which had never affected
me before," diarrhea became chronic over the years. Not surprisingly, for a
long time he tried to hide his "secret" from family and friends. He wanted
to be seen as limber, straight, astride his horse, crouched at the desk like a
philosopher, or taken by many other noble activities; he was not even particularly wary of revealing that his body was becoming progressively stiffer and
burdened with age; but he could not tolerate the idea that the public could
know of his weak bowels.[170]

A few friends got notice of Jefferson's embarrassing ordeal. But this information reached them only filtered through the objectifying, de-personalized
language of medical science: "My late illness," Jefferson-turned-doctor
explained to William Short, "was produced by a spasmodic stricture of the
ileum." *Spasmodic* movements, the very opposite of those harmonic, civilized gestures Jefferson had sought to perform throughout his life, had to
be stopped. Unfortunately, the medicine of the day wreaked havoc as a rule.
The late Benjamin Rush, since the time of the Lewis and Clark expedition,
used to recommend so-called Rush's pills, otherwise known as "Thunder-
clappers," a mixture of calomel and jalap (jalap is the tuberous root of the
plant *Ipomoea Purga*), which is to say a purgative to treat diarrhea. Furthermore, jalap and calomel, as poor Jefferson was bound to experience, "brought
on a salivation."[171]

In 1825, a more sensitive Dr. Dunglison started to give Jefferson laudanum, a tincture of opium, to slow the peristaltic bouts and allow Jefferson some residual control of his body: "I certainly cannot say that I am well," Jefferson wrote to Dunglison, but "My intervals have averaged thro' this month an hour in the day and ¾ in the night with particular instances of 1 ¾. The day before yesterday I rode about my garden in a walk half an hour without any inconvenience at that time or since, and found it more reviving than in a carriage." Jefferson's major ambition became retaining some measure of control and aiming at a sort of truce in a time of war. Having a residual life during the intervals between the crises was soothing, the body again gliding away toward a compliant unnoticeability.[172]

During the previous stages of his diarrhea, Jefferson had believed he could reeducate his body by counterbalancing its ungracious excesses, bouts, spasms, paroxysms, crises, and fits with the proper rhythm and the proper activity. At the beginning of the episodes, in 1801, the president had requested for dinner Dr. William Eustis's company. Eustis was a graduate of Harvard College and a promoter of English physician Thomas Sydenham's method against diarrhea, riding "a trotting horse." The trotting horse, consequently, became the receptacle of Jefferson's hopes. In 1806, he was still expectant about this "natural," almost musical method. As he wrote to William Short, "the only remedy I believe which can be relied on for relieving an obstinate diarrhea, or weak bowels, is long journies on a hard trotting horse." He had "great reason to approve Sydenham's advice."[173]

When Dunglison began treating Jefferson, Sydenham's method had proved largely ineffectual. Furthermore, diarrhea was accompanied by frequent urination. Jefferson's prostate, apparently, was not in order. Magnesia, rhubarb, and laudanum were not enough to control urination. At this point, too many signs showed that his soft, postmilitary, postaristocratic, and modern body was no longer "his own." The body became foreign both because it maintained control over the frequency and intensity of the release of material, whether urine, excrements, or salivation, but also because it was violated. Jefferson's body was violated by a "bougie" inserted through the penis to reach into the urethra. This slender pipe made of elastic gum had to dilate the constriction of the urethra, allowing, at least in theory, the complete emptying of the bladder. Moreover, Jefferson's body was violated by huge quantities of bacteria introduced via the nonsterile bougie. Most likely, pyelitis occurred, permanently damaging the kidneys. Death, the Supreme Other, had irremediably entered Jefferson's body.[174]

The evening of 3 July 1826, Jefferson drifted in and out of consciousness, occasionally lifting his right hand and elbow as if to write. More than once he asked whether it was yet midnight. Around 4:00 A.M., the story goes, Jefferson's voice became suddenly strong and clear, and he called to his servants. He stated his last words, which were never recorded.[175]

When Jefferson died, Martha Jefferson Randolph asked Nicholas Trist, Jefferson's private secretary and the husband of Virginia Jefferson Randolph, to snip off a lock of hair—or perhaps she performed this operation herself. Understandably, Jefferson's family members wanted to preserve a corporeal trace of the man, the father, their ancestor. At 5 P.M., on 4 July 1826, Alexander Garrett, to whom Jefferson had requested to safeguard a copy of his will, sent his wife, Evelina Bolling Garrett, a letter. Garrett bid adieu to his friend by lovingly covering his body and consigning it to eternity: "Mr Jefferson is no more, he breathed his last 10 minutes before 1 Oclock today almost without a struggle. no one here but Col. Carr & myself, both of us ignorant of shrouding, neither ever having done it, ourselves or seen it done, we have done the best we could, and I hope all is right. his remains will be buried tomorrow at 5 oclock, PM no invitations will be given, all comeing will be welcome at the grave."[176]

Passage

That Jefferson was substantially able to embody naturalness, simplicity, softness, "femininity," postmartiality, and all those other relatively modern features we have met does not mean that for him the dialectic with the human
"other" had become superfluous. The "other," especially when like-minded
and like-bodied, as we have just seen apropos his chosen models (William
Small, George Wythe, or Peyton Randolph), was essential to morality, education, and the construction of character. This kind of other was included in
Jefferson's world as an example to follow in order to develop the right habits:
Jefferson's self, like any other self, was built relationally.

Tensions emerge, however, and things become more problematic when
other bodies, marred by "peculiar" behaviors and "strange" and "less-than-
normal" characteristics, are taken into account. Another "other" existed outside the borders of Jefferson's world that served as a counterexample.

Over the last generation, many Jefferson scholars have proclaimed that
this idol should be removed from its pedestal. They have emphasized what
previous generations of historians could not see, or perhaps did not want to
see. Jefferson's cunning expedients toward Native Americans, his racism,
the intrinsic brutality of slavery (no matter how "feminine" his corporeality
and "soft" his mastery), his misogyny and lack of any serious plan for female
education—the many dimensions of his opportunism are undoubtedly there,
parts of an encumbering legacy. We know all too well Jefferson's lack of fairness especially in relation to the three big categories of the excluded and
oppressed: Native Americans, African Americans, and women.

And yet what follows is more than just a reiteration of disconcerting
themes that are now broadly accepted. It is not a survey of Jefferson's *ideas*
and what he *wrote* about American Indians, blacks, and women. The focus

is narrower, and materiality, which means corporeality, drives the research: How did Jefferson react to the physical presence of these excluded "others"? How did he conduct himself when he met an individual of this group? How did his body system, not only his mind, readjust? How did he *interact* with them?

As an old man, he became eventually "other" to himself. But when he was in control, the simplicity, gentility, "femininity," and postmartiality that he attained for his corporeal self was repeatedly tested against dispossessed and disenfranchised "others" whom he had the capacity to oppress or diminish. Historians and readers who think that Jefferson simply mistreated members of these three groups (which he certainly did), and that this must be the end of the story, miss an essential thrust of Jefferson's progressive and liberating message. Jefferson is misread each time his Enlightenment sensibility, particularly a progressive view of human history, is overlooked. His philosophy was certainly progressive and liberating; his body, as we have seen, was trying to overcome many traditional repertoires, from clothing to manners, including more rigid practices of masculinity. We should not ignore the significance of these efforts—and the energy coming to him from the Enlightenment—in exploring the ways he physically interacted with the "other."

At stake here is the narrative of Jefferson's *gradual* and thus only half-successful efforts at liberation. The world Jefferson inherited was hierarchical and deeply antiegalitarian. Nonetheless, the Enlightenment devotee, the humanist, and the egalitarian philosopher sought to liberate himself from the strictures of history and circumstances. Jefferson's corporeality sought, as well, to embrace modernity. An honest effort at liberation was acted out both mentally and corporeally. Even so, Jefferson believed it was better not to hasten and act before the time was ripe.

More than another recapitulation of Jefferson's well-known shortcomings and peculiar ideas, the aim of part 2 is to draw the precise line between what Jefferson deemed proper, timely, and effective, and what he considered untimely, if not simply wrong. Only when this line is drawn can we hope to capture Jefferson's unique effort and concrete existential situation. As a philosophical statesman, he tried to do what he thought would *gradually* bring about universal self-determination—but without risking his own progress, modernity, and civilization in this endeavor.

Jefferson was inspired by what scholars have dubbed a stadial theory of the progress of civilization. This means that Jefferson preferred to envision and implement only those ideas, measures, and policies that he believed were appropriate to the historical moment. His belief was that individuals, especially leaders and policy makers, should always prefer what is feasible to what is perfect. Though contemporary intellectuals may disagree, this gradualism, or simply meliorism, was for him the most pragmatic and expeditious way to ensure that the message and the content of the Declaration of Independence would eventually become the actual law of the country, and perhaps of the entire world. Without hastening the time, he was sanguine, the Declaration will eventually encompass all people: "may [the choice made in 1776] be to the world, what I believe it will be, (to some parts sooner, to others later, but finally to all,) the signal of arousing men to burst the chains under which monkish ignorance and superstition had persuaded them to bind themselves, and to assume the blessings and security of self-government."[1]

That he refused to endorse more ambitious plans (women in politics, immediate abolition of slavery, universal equality *de facto*), or that he clung to pseudo-anthropology, including racist and misogynist ideas and habits, means that he conceived of himself as a man whose effectiveness was limited and whose powers would soon be wasted. He kept dreaming of a better future to the very end of his life, and he prayed for it. But he knew that the more ambitious enterprise "is for the young," as he wrote to Edward Coles apropos an immediate abolition of slavery. The ambitious enterprise is "for those who can follow it up, and bear it through to it's consummation. it shall have all my prayers, and these are the only weapons of an old man."[2]

He would have happily jettisoned, perhaps, the racist and misogynist ideas and attitudes that have been discredited by the advances of modern science and philosophy, including anthropology. That Jefferson would have loved to be disproved is simply due to the fact that he endeavored to usher in a better, more humane, more just, and *wiser* world: "When I contemplate the immense advance in science and discoveries in the arts which have been made within the period of my life," the Sage of Monticello declared to Benjamin Waterhouse, professor at Harvard Medical School, "I look forward with confidence to equal advances by the present generation, and have no doubt that they will consequently be as much wiser than we have been as we than our fathers were, and they than the burners of witches."[3]

Whatever Jefferson's limits, his personal demerits, even his "notorious" hypocrisy, he sought to improve the lives of many individuals, *but starting with those "normal" white male persons whom he believed he could more easily include in his world without risking social order and, as a consequence, "progress" itself.*

On Jefferson's score there are major democratic undertakings—public acts, performances, and attempted policies, not only ideas. He wrote the Declaration of Independence; he outlined a constitution for Virginia (in 1776, in which he proposed to grant every unpropertied man "of full age and sane mind" fifty acres of land to make him propertied and hence free); he tried to abolish entail and primogeniture; he drafted another constitution for Virginia (in 1783, in which he proposed to extend the suffrage to those who had enrolled in the militia, propertied or not); he founded a public university for the new (white) leading classes; and, more in general, he worked hard to cast the legal basis of a modern nation as an effective bulwark against aristocracy and obscurantist forces.[4]

Jefferson's temporizing and closed-mindedness on many other pivotal issues do not automatically translate into duplicitousness. There is nothing paradoxical in this situation. When we go back in time, starting from our privileged station, we grasp this man trapped by all the things he did not achieve, both mentally and corporeally. Why did he not do more? Why did he not hug in public his black progeny?

True: but in this case, we hurl our disappointment at this late eighteenth-century figure that we have chosen as a more-than-historical hero. Nevertheless, when we put ourselves in the shoes of the real man, and look ahead the way he did, we cannot overlook his many achievements and real efforts. Measured against more traditional values and still more rigid hierarchies performed by his society, Jefferson emerges as an innovator, a postmartial, flexible, and "feminine" body and, at the same time, a quite radical and visionary Enlightenment devotee.

Jefferson-the-gradualist (which also means Jefferson-the-racist and Jefferson-the-misogynist) tried to facilitate democratic processes leading to the improvement of the human condition—but not everyone in his world qualified as fully human.

PART 2

Others

His Eye, the Eye of an Eagle

In late August 1822, Reverend S. A. Bumstead, from Maryland, undertook a journey to visit Charlottesville and other parts of Virginia. He spent time on the not-yet-finished campus, had breakfast somewhere nearby, but unfortunately did not succeed in meeting the famous Thomas Jefferson. On the road to Richmond, about three miles from Monticello, the reverend crossed paths with a man riding a horse. The man sported a "singular" costume: a coat with checkered gingham, probably manufactured in Virginia, and pantaloons made of the same fabric; he had no hat but held in his hand a lady's parasol. Bumstead suddenly realized who that man was. He was elated and duly recorded in his notes what for him was the most striking feature of the personage: "his eye, the eye of an eagle. . . . He cast his very penetrating eye at me."[1]

Jefferson's eyes remained lively and sharp to the end of his life. Jefferson wore spectacles occasionally, especially for reading, and he placed orders with Philadelphia optician John McAllister for eyeglasses as early as 1806—a pair of bifocals and a pair of very small reading spectacles. Despite physiological decline, Jefferson's eyes stood the test of time. "My own health is quite broken down," he wrote to Robert Mills, the architect who designed the obelisk for the Bunker Hill monument. Mostly confined in the house, "my faculties, sight excepted are very much impaired."[2]

Jefferson's eyes were noteworthy on so many levels, and not only when medical considerations are at stake. His eyes were indeed singular, rather smallish and light, an ambiguous, shifting hue difficult to categorize. Testi-

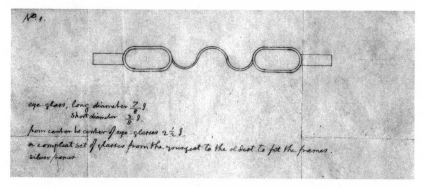

Fig. 16. Detail from Jefferson's letter to John McAllister, 12 November 1806, showing a sketch of design for spectacles. (©Thomas Jefferson Foundation at Monticello)

monies disagree as to their specific color. Francis Calley Gray from Massachusetts, for example, was sure Jefferson had "light gray eyes." Edmund Bacon, on the other hand, wrote that "he had blue eyes." Thomas Jefferson Randolph says that his eyes were hazel, while Henry Randall, once again, goes back to a somehow shifting tint: "His full, deep set eyes, the prevailing color of which was light hazel (or flecks of hazel on a groundwork of grey)."[3]

The exact color will perhaps remain a mystery, but Jefferson's eyes, "the eye of an eagle," were especially interesting and noteworthy in what they performed. Human beings, more than other species do, experience their world through their eyes. The sense of sight or vision, a "faculty" as Jefferson and his contemporaries named it, remains one of the most important among the evolutionary tools we have successfully developed throughout our history. What makes vision still more interesting, furthermore, is that such a sense is never universal and neutral, free from theory and complex social and material dynamics. This "faculty" cannot be a biological process without history, or a mere function carried on by the whole humanity in precisely the same way. Human eyes are trained to look and overlook, to spot objects that they set at the foreground as if they were actually separate and independent from a certain background. Eyes learn to draw differences, to look and overlook, thus making vision an art involving a mixture of seeing and blindness.

The brain tells the eyes what they should be watching and what they should be ignoring. Eyesight also relies on memory to make sense of what the organ sees. Cultural biases and intellectual expectations reach the eyes, and through such a complex interchange of physiology and culture humans execute distinctions and hierarchies. Consequently, whatever the color and whether or not they were actually so distinctively piercing, Jefferson's eyes brought about far deeper challenges.

Jefferson's eyes saw many things, including other body systems. He performed an interesting interplay between looking and overlooking, between drawing distinctions and making analogies, between putting on the foreground and leaving in the background. So, what did Jefferson really see when he looked at a human body, especially at human bodies as "others"?

No easy answer can be given, but each time Jefferson "saw" a human body, whether "similar" or "different," he brought to bear complex and problematic dynamics. To begin with, he saw, as did many white people of his age and peerage, that white male bodies appeared to embody a simple, natural, and timeless humanity. White bodies were not full of peculiar characteristics, but represented a "neutral" model. Like his peers, Jefferson did not unmask "whiteness." He did not reveal that this word is only a tool that Virginia society (or, rather, many societies) devised in order to reinforce hierarchies and arbitrary structures of power.

In this framework, American Indian, black, and female bodies were "seen" as being fraught with distinctive and unique characteristics, often "peculiar" details. Implicitly, certain ways of interaction were thus suggested over many others. Jefferson and his peers "described" these characteristics and behaved toward these people in ways that only reinforced white men's universality and "natural" privilege. Jefferson's eyes "saw" differences among American Indian, black, and female bodies. But a still more striking difference these eighteenth-century eyes "saw" was between these "others" and the universally human white male body. Jefferson relied upon this dichotomy even without recognizing it, without recognizing its historically conditioned genesis, much like his white male contemporaries.

Had Jefferson seen whiteness as a historically produced set of attributes—problematic because of its historical implication in slaveholding, in the dispossession of Native Americans, and in the subjugation of women—he might have been more critical of these distinctions between "self" and "other." But he did not, maybe he could not, and therefore he kept interacting with the "other" as some kind of exception to the norm. He succeeded in fashioning himself as a flexible, approachable, simple, natural, and even "feminine" modern man. But, at the same time, he failed because the other, for him, remained a rigid, nature-given "other."

This is the theme I follow through this second part. There was a struggle going on within Jefferson. Instances of betterment, progress, civilization, and his desire for more humane and fairer standards had to win over ignorance, inherited prejudices, and entrenched biases prevalent in late eighteenth-century Virginia. It was a battle between old and new paradigms that took place around as well as within Jefferson. He did not emerge from this battle as an absolute winner. He freed himself, but only partially. Correspondingly, he freed (or tried to) some persons he could reach, albeit not all of them. But he did not free himself from false natural hierarchies. What is worse, he did not free those "others" on whom his own liberated identity depended for its whiteness, its maleness, and its centrality to the notion of progress.

White Seems to Be the Primal Color of Nature

Vision is in itself dichotomic as it draws on differences between many fore-grounds and backgrounds. But the vision of a human body as a significant "other" brings such a dichotomy to an extreme. Are humans different? Of course they are. But why should such visible differences—some, not all of them—mean so much? Comparison to a constructed other provides contrast and depth to one's self. The imagined other creates the very limits of the self. This dialectic is rather simple: in order to see and know who we are, we need to focus upon what we deem we are not. The act of seeing, as well as many other intellectual performances, cannot easily take exception to this binary outlook. The most disquieting aspect, the one that usually goes unnoticed, is that through such a dichotomic, adversarial, oppositional outlook the result-ing self emerges as transparent, normal, simple, and unconstructed. As his-tory teaches, the white self of a white body took advantage of such a dialectic. The white body disappears, and historically had indeed disappeared, through the very process of its largely arbitrary differentiation from a set of chosen bodily others.[4]

Whiteness has been customarily associated with ideality and simplicity. Whites have consistently believed they were *perfectly* white. White Euro-Americans, Jefferson included, have deployed ad hoc strategies to disas-semble the other's body into features, components, and behavioral character-istics. Disassembling and decontextualizing the other's body was provisional on "seeing" that the other was composite, thus diverging from ideality, sim-plicity, and beauty.

Jefferson, obviously, did not invent the strategy of presenting the other as a variation from the norm. Buffon, for one, did it persuasively. The French naturalist voiced the widespread misconception that "white" was the primal color of nature, the model and the simple unit of measurement allowing comparisons. What Buffon "saw" was that human beings were naturally positioned along a gradation of skin colors corresponding to the gradients of latitude and longitude. Not surprisingly, as he claimed, "the most temperate climate is between the 40th and 50th degree; it is also in this zone that the most beautiful and soundly built men are to be found, it is in this climate that we can find the idea of the true natural color of man." The supposition of existing shades of whiteness, and hence of whiteness as an ensemble of particularities, was promptly rejected as nonsense. European white bodies stuck out because they suffered no gradations. They bore no multiplicity. In a patent reversal of Newton's discovery that white light *resulted* from a composition of primary colors, Buffon claimed that white skin was the original, natural color from which all other colors degenerated.[5]

It is apparent that to single out whiteness as the most noteworthy standard, one needs to approach it with strong preexisting biases, if not explicit theories. The claim that white men were the bearer of reason, and that whiteness had some kind of bearing on the fact that this group of men were reasonable, has a very ancient history. Whiteness could not suffer gradations, philosophers and naturalists argued; it could not be construed as a more or less random selection of ethnic attributes because it was seen as interchangeable with reason. Since there is only one form of reason, they claimed, there must be only one form of whiteness.[6]

Furthermore, *expecting* that whiteness could exist as a standard would not be enough if such a standard were not constantly, endemically, and successfully applied by the very white people who benefited from the notion of privileged whiteness. Standards, in general, need to be applied. And what made whiteness into a working operative standard, more than expectations, biases, and theories alone, were actual practices of white beneficiaries who availed themselves of expedients, technological apparatuses, and organized violence. History teaches that each and every interaction with a real other has been more than just an opportunity for European philosophers and naturalists to engage in wild speculations about the "natural color of man." Encountering the other has rather been an opportunity to put the theory to test. Were it not for the practices of people who identified themselves as white, availing themselves of sophisticated instruments and sly expedients, whiteness would have never become a standard. Fanciful theories of white superiority, simplicity, and reasonableness had to be put to test: European armies, militias, and bands have conquered, subjugated, or abducted Africans, Native Americans, and many other peoples. Doing so has been the most expedient way to erase from whiteness the memory of its arbitrary and troublesome history.

But many other subtler devices had been deployed to make whiteness into a standard. A clever device that helped Europeans to believe the dream of a perfect whiteness was the linen shirt. Europeans had come to actually and literally perform whiteness, thus enhancing the illusion that they were de facto white. Europeans ended up refusing the nude, maybe because of their tattered skin, maybe because of the cold weather, maybe because of biblical prejudices, or maybe because they had been nurturing strong reservations about public bathing for centuries (public bathhouses were tarnished with the suspicion of illicit sexuality). Over the centuries, Europeans had become oblivious of the difference between nude and naked—this last, nakedness, and only this last, indicating a state of deprivation. People in the nude had been wrongly seen as belonging to some form of savagery, a lower stage in the Great Chain of Being. For whatever reason this had happened, dressing had become for Europeans the most civilized gesture concerning body care.[7]

People of darker skins have retained for much longer the sense that this organ had an intrinsic value and an inherent beauty. On the American continent, people of darker complexions kept refusing the equation between garment, especially the white linen shirt, and civilization. "While Europeans developed a more self-conscious concern with whiteness and the meaning of clothing," Kathleen Brown has written, "Native Americans worried that adopting European-style clothing might compromise their beauty and comfort." West Africans as well "continued to view the skin as the body's most significant canvas." Whereas Europeans became, de facto, white and accepted the assumption that civilization entailed covering their skins with white linen shirts, people of non-European origins, to show their beauty and to make their degree of civilization visible, preferred bathing, applying ointment, or, when needed, wearing animal skins.[8]

Garments in general, and white linen shirts in particular, succeeded in turning whiteness into a marketable commodity: the internal had thus become external. On the other hand, people of non-European origins, by and large, kept displaying their "whiteness" (cleanliness, candor, and moral purity) by doing what they had done for centuries—bathing in rivers, applying ointments, or abstaining from committing depravity. The fact is that around 1700 the European paradigm to appropriately perform whiteness had been clearly defined and made dependent on specific pieces of outfit *that had to be donned.* The morality of an individual could be promptly recognized and, if needed, supplied through complex commercial networks. As Brown writes, "the gentleman's kit of a white linen shirt, breeches, stockings and shoes, a coat, waistcoat, and cravat became basic elements of male costume in the West and spread rapidly in colonized regions." Europeans won by all accounts, and turned whiteness (a moral, internal quality) into something that could be externally discerned—a given set of clothes and, by extension, a certain type of pale, tattered skin usually associated with those individuals wearing those clothes.[9]

At the beginning of the eighteenth century, Euro-Americans had become used to having their shirts snow white. When circumstances permitted, men of means put on a clean shirt nearly every day. This rather peculiar way of performing whiteness enhanced in-group cohesion and justified out-group exclusion.[10]

Degenerated Altogether

Perceived differences, like the contrast between lighter and darker skins, or clothed bodies and bodies in the nude, may be uncomfortable or strangely affirming. But are people bothered simply by what they see? Anthropologists argue that when people are worried by someone else's difference they are not so much worried by physical differences per se—skin color, traits, hair forms, bodily shapes, the amount of nudeness, and so on. They are rather bothered by behavioral differences. In other terms, people are disturbed by what they *believe* these features mean about the people who embody them. Moral expectations projected upon certain physical features turn these visual elements into signs with a seemingly "obvious" significance. Lips thick and fleshy, for example, came to signify to thin-lipped white people lazy behavior and unchecked sexuality, the antithesis of reason and virtue. During the eighteenth century, educated and scholarly white people believed they could decipher a more or less arbitrary set of verifiable physical characteristics as signs indicating, in turn, laziness, lack of self-control, childishness, or artfulness and knavishness.[11]

Dark skin had become especially troublesome after a long history of dispossession and subjugation. Europeans and Euro-Americans had turned Africans into a deprived "race"; subsequently, they could not bear the thought that all these differences between the two "races" amounted to just the plain historical fact of subjugation. They deluded themselves with the notion of something more *essential*, more natural and inborn, that could explain these *perceived* differences. The point is that people are often bothered by their "other" of choice because this "other" is not really another.

Anthropologists, sociologists, ethnographers, and psychologists make clear that people are generally eager to take up the other's behavior—"imitativeness" was the eighteenth-century word. Seeing the other as *essentially* different and inferior may be a means to downplay and justify the brutal fact of subjugation, and, furthermore, it may be a way to ward off the propensity humans have to sympathize and actually identify with one another. For whatever reason this happens, differences are often amplified. "There is a tendency to view another society's behaviours," John Szwed has written, "as the polar opposites of one's own, even if they are in reality only small variations on a common human theme." The history of human civilizations shows that differences are often amplified and, as often, that these differences are in many ways lessened. When people connect in the process of everyday interaction, they not only end up discarding many of their former beliefs but also they start learning from each other and adopting crucial aspects of the other group's behavior. More specifically, and perhaps more disquieting for some, the dominant group would most likely end up borrowing from the lower group, regardless of the theoretical and practical barriers it saw as dividing them.[12]

Institutions, social classes, and many other contrivances, both ideal and material, have been created precisely to prevent such anarchical intermixing. By and large, any dominant group fears the perspective of degenerating into an abated condition. But for very long, this group—any group—has also craved its inferior "other": people sympathize and mix together no matter the premises and consequences. Especially on the new continent, where social stratification and hierarchies were not so consistently tested, as they were in Europe, dominant groups feared that their members could absorb undesirable features and traits. This is true on many levels, from linguistic habits to moral habits. There is "One Thing" the American planters "are very faulty in, with regard to their Children," a British traveler lamented in *the London Magazine* in 1746. These southern children are allowed too much time "to prowl amongst the young Negroes, which insensibly causes them to imbibe their Manners and broken Speech." We are already familiar with the basic psychological mechanism, imitativeness, that is at work here.[13]

The poet Hector St. John Crèvecoeur raised his voice to warn his fellow white settlers about what he thought was a major danger. Moving westward and living on the very threshold of wild nature entailed being beyond the power of example and the rules of civilized society. Crèvecoeur shivered at the thought that a number of frontiersmen had already "degenerated altogether into the hunting state," becoming like American Indians or, worse, like carnivorous animals. "Eating of wild meat," he surmised, "tends to alter their temper." Whether or not this was based on a real experience, it was not infrequent to behold upper classes emulating the lowly, linguistically or otherwise, unintentionally or purposely. While American settlers were "going Indian," as Crèvecoeur feared, and planters were "going Negro," many English were "going Celtic." And this list can easily be expanded.[14]

The fear that Euro-American whites might lose their station was real. For centuries, settlers and colonists had tried to abstain from consuming American Indian foods, including maize—until and unless they were especially hungry. Travel writers had shivered at the effects the "New World," its climate and natural resources, might have on Europeans. Europeans have repeatedly feared that North America could contaminate them. Many philosophers and naturalists, including Buffon, Cornelius De Pauw, and Baron de Montesquieu, expanded on these very fears. They wrote frequently about how humans could easily go up and down the natural ladder. As Montesquieu maintained, for example, too hot or too cold climates could alter the prospect of optimal bodily and mental development offered by the temperate climate of France. Anyone could either read or discuss geographical determinism, or environmental determinism, as these theories against the fixity of human nature are sometimes called.[15]

It was likewise mind-boggling and almost unacceptable, at least to many elite Euro-Americans, to see that nature allowed the lowly to scramble up the ladder. Eighteenth-century geographical determinism spelled out the "servile demeanor" of people of African descent, including their "ugly" corporeal features and attributes, as environmental effects. Samuel Stanhope Smith's *An Essay on the Causes of the Variety of Complexion and Figure in the Human Species* (1787) argued that the physical characteristics of African Americans were a toll these people had to pay for their equatorial origin. But, as he claimed, their features would change over time, and in the long run they would become more similar to Europeans.[16]

While eighteenth-century whites could see that some of their peers were degrading into more or less ominous "others," they could also observe that some among these "others" were actually turning white. Not only was the increasing number of "mulattoes" whitening the African "race"; it was not so infrequent to behold white African Americans, either albinos or individuals suffering from vitiligo—needless to say, physiology, endocrinology, genetics, and neurology were not mature disciplines in the period. In the mid-1790s, for example, public interest was shaken by the case of Henry Moss, an African American whose skin turned white as he entered middle age. Did a case like this mean that the white-group/black-group divide was a hoax? Was the entire system of hierarchical differences fabricated? Rather than a natural quality, was "whiteness" only a word loaded with prejudices, expedients (like the white shirt), and concealed violent strategies?[17]

A Short Account of an Anomaly of Nature

During the eighteenth century, issues and problems raised by practices of whiteness, with their load of intergroup tensions, were not acknowledged as such. In the period, the notion of "whiteness" itself was, and for a very long time remained, rather opaque, multifaceted, and epistemologically ambiguous. A "quality" at once natural and moral rather than a series of *strategies* to gain preeminence over the "other," the privileges believed to be inherent in whiteness maimed the intellectual potentialities of many brilliant minds—including their ability to envisage more humanitarian options. There was a battle going on within Jefferson: his ideas of betterment, progress, and civilization and his attempts at reaching humane and fair standards had to win over ignorance, inherited prejudices, and entrenched biases. Even in his case, "whiteness" loomed very large.

Let us stay with the case study just examined. Commenting on Henry Moss, Benjamin Rush maintained that being black summed up to a hereditary and curable skin disease, which he called "negroidism." Weird though such a hypothesis may at first appear, Rush was among the few to advance a nonevaluative and nonnormative explanation: the physiological basis of blacks being black, he was convinced, had been discovered. Not only could blacks become whites, but also the whole race question, and related behaviors and modes of interactions, would eventually melt away. He wrote that whites should not "tyrannise over them [blacks]." Their disease "should entitle them to a double portion of our humanity, for disease all over the world has always be the signal for immediate and universal compassion." For Jefferson, on the contrary, African American bodies turning white did not offer a compelling argument leading to a more radical questioning of Euro-American alleged moral, social, and intellectual supremacy.[18]

In Query 6, to account for both albinos and individuals suffering from vitiligo, Jefferson embraced a less daring view. Albino bodies were an anomaly of nature, not an occurrence of larger import. He believed that white African Americans were not really white even though they were seen as white. These bodies were a mistake, a dead end, Jefferson alleged, and the whiteness of skin was deceptive. This "anomaly of nature, taking place sometimes in the race of negroes brought from Africa, who, though black themselves, have, in rare instances, white children," did not call for a revision of his ways to interact with African Americans. "They are of a pallid cadaverous white, untinged with red, without any colored spots or seams; their hair of the same kind of white, short, coarse, and curled as is that of the negro; all of them well formed, strong, healthy, perfect in their senses, except that of sight, and born of parents who had no mixture of white blood."[19]

The seven instances Jefferson recounted in *Notes* represented an anomaly, even though as individuals they were "uncommonly shrewd" and substantially healthy. Although not morally corrupt individuals or personally responsible for their color, white African Americans did not lead Jefferson to rethink race and to figure out new ways of mutual interaction, as they did for Rush. Rush, in a way, was more wrong than Jefferson: albinism and vitiligo were a congenital disorder and a chronic skin disease (albeit not "anomalies"). But more important here are the different consequences the two men drew from a certain explanation of facts. The whiteness that "white Negros" carried upon their skin was not for Jefferson real and worthy whiteness. "Real" whiteness, he claimed, must be the signal of something more essential and substantial than an observable color.

Both albinos and individuals affected by vitiligo kept being distant "others," albeit this time not because of their perceived blackness. Their hair "short, coarse, and curled," their lips, the shape of the nose, and other "essential" differences told Jefferson that these bodies were no proof that species and "races" were evolving and that Europeans should rearrange their hierarchies accordingly: "To these [albinos] I may add the mention of a negro man within my own knowledge, born black, of black parents; on whose chin, when a boy, a white spot appeared. This continued to increase till he became a man, by which time it had extended over his chin, lips, one cheek, the under jaw, and neck on that side. It is of the Albino white, without any mixture of red, and has for several years been stationary." Easily mistaken for what is whiteness, African Americans' "odd" mutating color kept representing otherness. Not only "negroid" traits but also their "pallid cadaverous white, untinged with red" was the problem. Far from being or becoming whites, these individuals made Jefferson aware of the only whiteness that counted. A tattered, reddish complexion, as he knew personally, may be deemed a shortcoming. But only such a whiteness (often hidden under the white linen shirt) was the index of real whiteness. If the eye could be deceived, the intellect should not.

A Suspicion Only

What we think, what we believe, and what we write have an impact on our conducts of interaction. By and large, Jefferson's ideas about the "other" prompted defensive reactions. Seeing is power, and Jefferson exerted his vision reactively, as power over the other's body. Seeing is power, first of all, because it happens as science and knowledge. Vision brings order into the world, from a theoretical standpoint. But seeing is power from a practical standpoint as well. When a thin-lipped, white-shirted male in a position of command saw things a certain way, it also meant that he had a nonnegligible normative impact. It was not indifferent, as social structures and hierarchies are concerned, that Jefferson kept viewing the "whiteness" of certain African American bodies as a mockery of real whiteness. It would have been different had he seen blackness at least as a temporary condition due to geographical variables (like Smith) or to a curable disorder (like Rush), and albinism and vitiligo as clear signals that the so-called natural order was changing—and that behaviors were about to change accordingly. Had he seen things this way, he would have settled on more inclusive, less defensive behaviors. But he embraced a more rigid framework.

Even if we leave out the notion of race, we can infer that there was something meaningful in the way Jefferson separated "real" whiteness from anomalous, deadlike whiteness. Such a biased vision belonged to its time, to rely on an abused phrase. It was an expression of a racialized, genderized, hierarchical, and traditional society—from which Jefferson's humanism and Enlightenment sought to emerge. But society was changing. From an intellectual standpoint, Jefferson was caught in between two extremes. This was his unique, evolving situation: he did not believe in rigid hierarchies while worshipping human differences as such; but he was not for a total dissolution of hierarchies and "natural" differences either.

Jefferson refused to look at his fellow creatures, including the nonwhite "others," the way other men from the period did. Advocating "polygenesis," for example, did not appeal to Jefferson's Enlightenment. Voltaire, Hume, Lord Kames, Captain Bernard Romans in *Concise Natural History of East and West Florida* (1775), and Benjamin Smith Barton in *New Views of the Origin of the Tribes and Nations of America* (1797) defended the belief that distinct groups were the product of separate creations. Jefferson disagreed. At the end of Query 6, he admitted of "varieties in the race of man." Natural varieties, for him, existed, "as I see to be the case in the races of other animals." In an infamous statement in Query 14 he advanced, "as a suspicion only, that the blacks, whether originally a distinct race, or made distinct by time and circumstances, are inferior to the whites in the endowments both of body and mind." Racially charged statements like these, however, were not tantamount to admitting a separate creation. As to the metaphysical origin of human differences, Jefferson's attitude bordered on caution. "The question of Indian origin," he wrote to John Adams many years later, "like many others pushed to a certain height, must recieve the same answer, 'Ignoro.'" After all, the proof that humans were a common family was given by the ability to intermarry and reproduce—and Jefferson must have known more than something about this issue.[20]

As to the second point, Jefferson was not so advanced to do away with human "natural" differences tout court. He did not act to de-mythologize whiteness and instate an equal society of individuals existing beyond given hierarchies (natural and social). His gradualism, meliorism, and the stadial theory of the progress of civilization curbed a similar wild dream. One of his most famous statement ever, "All men are created equal," should not be taken as a claim that every individual, for him, should be actually protected in her or his right to develop into a fully grown person. Similarly, Jefferson was no human rights activist demanding that every person be treated with respect by governments. Jefferson never brought equality to its logical consequences. Being *created* equal did not mean, for him, being *de facto* equal.[21]

I Had Rather Be Shut Up in a Very Modest Cottage

Intellectual tensions between old and new patterns did not occur in a void, as if they were battles of ideas, struggles of different visions, fights of disembodied minds. These tensions did not even happen in society and community abstractly considered. Especially in the context of Jefferson's Virginia, these tensions and battles took place within a very concrete structure, the family. Family was the primary stage where Jefferson's at once old-fashioned (for us) and modern visions (for him) occurred. Vision is power, from a practical point of view, because it liberates assets and possibilities for some. But vision is power also in the less enticing sense that eighteenth-century vision was not immaterial, universal, and neutral. It fell as the decree of destiny upon hapless women and men who lived very close but who were excluded from progressive dynamics.

We have to insist on the family if we want to understand where Jefferson's corporeal dialectic with the "other" started. His flexible, harmonious, post-martial, and approachable self was in turn built within the family. Dubbed by sociology a primary agent of socialization, family is the most immediate and most concrete setting. Children learn to interact with others and absorb norms and values through their families. Before churches, schools, guilds, clubs, or parties start exerting their influence, families open up the repertoire of dos and don'ts. They enhance one's sense of power and possibility while drawing precise limits to one's agency.

Of course, especially by the mid-eighteenth-century Virginia, "family" elicited much more than just mother and father, love and mutual understanding, closeness and confidence. Not a mononuclear family, the structure into which Jefferson was reared was not a simple unit, but rather a complex container of processes, hierarchies, tensions, and conflict-ridden relations of race and gender. Jefferson's family, together with other Virginia families, did not represent an intimate, informal, private space where body could freely touch body. An old tradition has it that Jefferson's earliest memory was of riding on horseback, from Shadwell to Tuckahoe, comfortably carried on a pillow and protected by the arms of a trusted slave, a "member" of his family. And yet by the time this baby comfortably carried by strong black arms grew into manhood, he had to learn to contextualize, which means downplay, the importance of "the warm intimacies of the African American nurturing he had received," to borrow Rhys Isaac's words. Furthermore, family in the period retained the economic function typical of the traditional Greek *oikos*. It is no surprise that Jefferson could often refer to those residing and working at Monticello, up to 200 individuals, as his "family."[22]

Famous quotations exist that are usually interpreted as signs of Jefferson's reserved character, making him almost a provincial: "I had rather be shut up in a very modest cottage, with my books, my family and a few old friends, dining on simple bacon, and letting the world roll on as it liked, than to occupy the most splendid post which any human power can give." "I look with infinite joy," to take another famous example, "to the moment when I shall be ultimately moored in the midst of my affections." But excerpts like these should rather be taken as disclosures of the most concrete and basic platform from which Jefferson's visions-prompting-behaviors emanated. The cottage, which means Monticello, intimacies both remembered and forgotten, and books, things, children and grandchildren, relatives, free and bond laborers, nonhuman animals, and a growing network of friends and neighbors formed a specific ensemble that simultaneously rooted, defined, boosted, and limited Jefferson. The eyes of such an eagle were the eyes of a Virginia family man.[23]

Trying to understand Jefferson's challenges of old paradigms without referring to the most immediate and concrete context, fueling him with energy while, at the same time, bogging him down, would be just nonsense. But such an ensemble was evolving. The family Jefferson inherited was becoming modern, as we will see in a moment, but not so radically modern as postcolonial, postmodern eyes may want it to be.

I Have My Flocks and My Herds

Traditional Virginia family was not an end in itself. It was a means to an end. It intensified the master's self-assertion, his public honor, and the traditional modes of whiteness and maleness. In 1726, William Byrd II had written: "Like one of the patriarchs, I have my flocks and my herds, my bondmen, and bond-women, and every soart of trade amongst my own servants, so that I live in a kind of independance on every one, but Providence." The "independance," honor, and public success of the master was provisional on his ability to shut himself up within a fully functional structure from which he could safely carry out "every soart of trade." The master's goal within the traditional family was not to find a retreat from the outer world, even if he could claim the contrary. He sectioned off the world principally to carry out complex social functions. Family, furthermore, gave the master the impression that those relations between the center and peripheries were natural and simple, not based on power. As Kathleen Brown writes, the traditional household "served the very purpose of affirming male authority and social position through sociability."[24]

Economically, the traditional Virginia family was profitable. Culturally, intellectually, and psychologically, this family was the best opportunity for self-assertion and for realizing the master's identity. The planter retired periodically to the bosom of his family not to escape the world and become private, but to make the most of a consolidated hegemonic system of authority and hierarchy over compliant wives, children, slaves, and less privileged men. Paradoxical though it may appear, such men ensconced themselves inside to gain visibility and find the strength to be acknowledged outside.

Nevertheless, the family-*oikos*, once the stable center of communal activity, slowly became the locus of the private sphere, a shelter against an outer world oftentimes held to be immoral and corrupt. House and family were indeed progressively losing their function of helping the master and, going down the hierarchy, the few privileged individuals. In Virginia as well, the modern world was eroding the network of familial functions and communal connections. Whether based on something real or just founded in imagination, whether backed up by observation or just arising from fears, an "increasing consciousness of individual separateness," as Rhys Isaac writes, "was slowly becoming more general."[25]

Separateness and the growing awareness of an intrinsic value associated to every human person went hand in hand. Intellectual and social historians, and historians of manners, have made it clear that a "middle-class character" of American society predated the second quarter of the nineteenth century. We do not have to wait until the outburst of the Market Revolution, in other words, to behold epochal transformations. Expectations for a moderately comfortable lifestyle, literacy, the worship of self-respect, the myth of "hard work" as a tool to effectively climb the social ladder, and higher rates of inclusion of the "other" were gaining momentum among many late eighteenth-century Americans.[26]

Especially in the North, young men broke free from plans and patterns that families devised on their behalf and increasingly sought personal fulfillment. Romantic love based on personal choice, for example, replaced interests based elsewhere. These young men married no longer to perpetuate or enlarge family assets, but because they fell in love. Lorry Glover has demonstrated that romantic love and personal choice became "the primary basis for marriage among the increasingly influential middle class." Although comparably slower than the North, the South as well "embraced the ideals of individualism and affection."[27]

Early eighteenth-century northern and southern scions used to be poles apart. They had customarily differed, among other things, on the way they conceived of higher education. Young male southerners attended college like European aristocrats have done for centuries, to complete their *persona* and enhance their public status. They knew, and their families knew as well, that acquiring knowledge and entering a profession were secondary to being successful in securing one's honor and character. Southerners had traditionally seen college education as part of a larger process leading to a fixed ideal of manhood. Going to college was tantamount to gaining gentility, attaining refined manners, and strengthening preexisting contacts. Moreover, since attending college was not a requirement for being acknowledged as a member of the gentry, education in the South had traditionally been "less practical than ornamental." At the end of the century, however, this situation had already changed, and the North-South divide had considerably shrunk. Both in the North and in the South, status and honor, as Glover has phrased it, were becoming "more something derived from personal success than something leading to it."[28]

Southern gentlemen had long criticized the alleged commercial-mindedness and the acquisitiveness of the northerners. Northerners, for their part, had for very long portrayed their antagonists as idle and disdainful of work. Jefferson himself believed such ingrained stereotypes. He was sure northerners were constitutionally independent, industrious, but also "chicaning" and "hypocritical." Southerners, he admitted, were fiery, generous, candid, but also indolent. Whether or not these stereotypes ever exposed real traits, the fact is that the difference was disappearing. At the dawn of the new century, all northern and southern sons were asked to go past their family assets, if any, and to demonstrate their individual talents as professionals. "Because simply inheriting wealth no longer guaranteed manly status," Glover concludes, "in the minds of many Americans, southerners included, boys needed to prove themselves, through individual success, worthy of assuming power over society."[29]

Their Power to Resort to Professions

Could "independant" masters and planters, and traditional families as their "natural" places, still hope to remain the "chosen people of God"? Things had changed dramatically since Jefferson wrote his celebrated paean for the "simple and natural" way of life: "Let our work-shops remain in Europe." Jefferson was ready to put up with this new world, especially when newer generations were at stake. "With respect to the boys," he wrote to his son-in-law Thomas Mann Randolph, "I never till lately doubted but that I should be able to give them a competence as comfortable farmers, and no station is more honorable or happy than that." His "debts" and dreadful situation, however, made him aware of the fact that "we shall place it in their power to resort to professions, if that should be their choice. to that choice they have a natural title, and it seems a natural duty on us to qualify them for it."[30]

Middle-class values were on the rise, and there was nothing Jefferson could and would do to stop them. He did not plan to turn back the hands of time. But the world of professions he hailed also prompted broader cultural transformations. People who entered professions were the same "boys" who increasingly embraced the world of romantic love. Furthermore, these individuals belonged to a world where status was being reset as a consequence, no longer the necessary foundation, of shrewd individual choices.

Transformations such as these ended up privileging individuals over their traditional communities, choices over status, and success over birth, thus putting hierarchies seriously under attack. Once again, Jefferson was caught in between: he no longer belonged to William Byrd II's world of never-questioned hierarchies; but he was not a romantic either, a nineteenth-century "boy" simply longing for personal success. Jefferson kept defining himself as a family man, a paterfamilias, like Byrd did; but he did so in the precise moment when family was becoming modern. Having entered the "profession of the law," he knew something about aspirations toward fulfillment outside the household.[31]

Challenged by emerging values, the Virginia network of households waned, slowly but steadily. The traditional authority and control wielded by patresfamilias could no longer be an accomplished fact. Late eighteenth- and early nineteenth-century paternalism replaced older patriarchy, as historians usually describe the transformation, or rather they coexisted along a continuum. On many levels, paternalism represented an actual improvement in human material interactions over patriarchy. The control exerted by the master over children, wives, slaves, and small white property owners became less and less centered on physical coercion. It was more domesticated, more clearly based on new ideals of "flexible" and "feminine" manliness as equal to approachability. Paternalism was adjusted to a culture of sensibility and to an American society, both northern and southern, on its way to increased mobility and interchangeability of roles—at least to some extent. Obviously enough, the emergence of a new ethos did not signify the end of coercive power or male bodies imitating warriors. Many planters were at once patresfamilias and abusive patriarchs. All in all, slaves continued to be whipped and women sexually assaulted.[32]

In order to keep their authority alive, enlightened patresfamilias like Jefferson had to strike a balance between accommodation and intimidation, between performances in "femininity" or "simplicity" and force. They had to evolve, somehow. Many white upper-class men belonging to Jefferson's generation realized they had to do two things. They had to incessantly stage their authority: no Virginia leader at this later period could afford being negligent and oblivious of himself and to simply rest on old ingrained customs of deference. Kenneth Lockridge, in this respect, has aptly described Virginia gentry as "the most staged and theatrical of gentries." But they also had to learn to be limber, supple, more "feminine" and modern. This means that enlightened patresfamilias could no longer only repress and subjugate via direct violence over the other's body. The "other" had to be held in place, obviously, but better if intimidation took place by means of genteel approachability or by other, more "feminine" expedients, including an overwhelmingly exquisite and refined home, like Monticello. Some among these "others" had to be accommodated within the nation.[33]

An Elevated Situation, from Which He Might Contemplate the Universe

In a society becoming more individualistic and flexible, the activity of *looking* at the "others" and *seeing* them a certain way— above all women and nonwhite, nonshirted men—replaced in many cases actual coercion. New forms of interaction with the other's body, and reaction to it, were experimented with; the eye was given new powers. Being controlled or observed, even through a "scientific" and inquisitive eye taking advantage of new technological tools, was in many ways better than being beaten.

I have said that Jefferson, like other eighteenth-century men and women of higher rank, watched himself regularly, and in particular through the eyes of imagined others—nothing less than the character was at stake. "Whenever," Jefferson had written to Peter Carr, "you are to do a thing tho' it can never be known but to yourself, ask yourself how you would act were all the world looking at you, and act accordingly."[34]

But the power of the eye could operate as effectively when directed to the external other—and for this reason this powerful medicine should always be given in a proper dose. The nightmare of an excessive public exposure with no possible hideouts, laying passively, almost like an object, becoming *entirely visible* and without having the chance to "gaze back," could turn into a punishment worse than death: "Exhibited as a public spectacle," Jefferson wrote in his so-called autobiography, "with shaved heads and mean clothing, working on the high roads produced in the criminals such a prostration of character, such an abandonment of self-respect, as, instead of reforming, plunged them into the most desperate & hardened depravity of morals and character."

Many years earlier, in a "confidential" letter to John Peter Gabriel Muhlen-berg, Lutheran minister and brigadier general of the Virginia Line, Jefferson had made the case for having Benedict Arnold kidnapped and "exhibited as a public spectacle of infamy, and of vengeance." He soon recanted, however, and deleted the passage: he must have realized that the dose was improper, the measure inhumane, even for a traitor like Arnold.[35]

Civilization meant, for Jefferson, the refusal of violence as both the main source of authority and a basic male signifier. But relinquishing physical vio-lence, unavoidably, brought with itself the fear of losing power. Consequently, strategies of observation, acting in both directions (introspectively but prin-cipally toward the other), had to be sharpened and enacted constantly—what Jefferson did throughout his life. Effective power exerted through observa-tion had an evolutionary advantage over violence: observation made mascu-linity more pliable, harmonious, and modern. A masculinity relying more and more on intellectualized performances elicited the belief that the domi-nant male was the smartest exemplar. The dominant male was the one who saw almost everything (through science, knowledge, and many technolog-ical apparatuses) while he was seen only occasionally and through studied and selected performances. The dominant male's seductive power no longer came from the strength he possessed, but through the control he was able to master.

Marquis de Chastellux, in a passage I presented at the beginning of the book, told us something very important about Jefferson's self and masculin-ity, and his way of deploying power over others: "he had placed his mind . . . on an elevated situation, from which he might contemplate the universe." Contemplation, in Jefferson's case, had very proactive implications. This paterfamilias succeeded where others had failed. He built sophisticated strategies of observation, while at once retaining control over others and his own image without resorting to brutality.[36]

Historians and biographers have repeatedly emphasized Jefferson's reserved character, but this is only part of the whole story. He was generous with his body and his limber, postmartial, and modern corporeality—when he wanted to be. As often, however, he was parsimonious and made several decisions to hide himself. The "other," we should never forget, prompted Jef-ferson's defensive reactions. He was indeed reserved; but his being reserved was functional to the strategy of staging power and excluding many types of women and men. In other terms, staying hidden did not necessarily mean that Jefferson only worshipped privacy. Our twenty-first-century understanding of the "obvious" threshold between public and private might be here highly deceptive.

There is hidden and hidden. Each time Jefferson pursued authentic privacy he obtained it. He destroyed the letters to and from his wife, Martha; he burned the correspondence with his mother, Jane Randolph Jefferson; his so-called autobiography says virtually nothing about the life of the man who wrote it (it says selectively something about the officeholder); his sexual habits have stirred the wildest speculations over more than two centuries, but Jefferson never leaked details; Sally Hemings and her family were "discretely hidden" within Jefferson's trove of documents—and we needed Annette Gordon-Reed's talent to join scattered pieces. On the other hand, when in his letters he "confessed" private, sensitive matters to "trusted" correspondents (the "My Head and My Heart" letter is perhaps the most famous case), he was fully aware that these issues would become public, either in the short or the long run. By the same token, Jefferson's lamentations about travelers, intruders, and enthusiasts showing up unannounced at Monticello seem disingenuous at best. Monticello was the theater and the public shrine this man had uninterruptedly reworked, from 1769 up to his death. When he wanted *privacy* he escaped at Poplar Forest. Similarly, a definitely younger and more energetic man, he had disappeared in the streets of Paris. On occasion, he had successfully been a private man, and we know almost nothing about this dimension of his personality, let alone corporeality. Jefferson could master all his resources in order to actually disappear from sight.[37]

Most of the time, Jefferson's choices of being hidden were public performances that had relevant social meaning. He wanted privacy, for sure, and yet he did more than just hiding himself. His cult of "privacy"—we should better say "decorum," or postviolent "self-possession"—was a strategy of public revelation. He wanted to be seen as a very discreet, maybe too discreet, and "feminine" observer. His private quarters at Monticello, his "sanctum sanctorum," have risen to the level of a legend. He retired in his studio regularly, leading a hidden life, and leaving others the burden to take educated guesses about what he was doing: Was he asleep? Was he studying? Was he secretly planning someone else's life?

From beneath the blinds of Monticello, he saw without being seen. To check the amount of sunlight entering the house, to regulate temperature and air flow, but also to guarantee privacy, Jefferson used louvered shutters—or

Fig. 17. "Porticles" or Venetian porches at Monticello, the two matching louvered structures enclosing the small terraces at the south and east corners of the house and flanking the southeast piazza (greenhouse). (©Thomas Jefferson Foundation at Monticello, photograph by William L. Beiswanger)

Venetian blinds as they were called in the period. Jefferson's interest in these louvered shutters went as far back as the early 1770s, when he ordered six pairs for the first version of the Big House. Ground floor windows at Monticello had inside shutters and Venetian blinds on the exterior. At a certain point, Jefferson also planned to put louvered blinds between the columns of the porticoes. He also built, on either side of the greenhouse, small seven-foot-square louvered verandas, or "porticles." He must have had compelling pragmatic reasons if he chose to ruin the Palladian style of Monticello. People looking through his cabinet door into his bedchamber bothered him. Blinds and shutters were thus to some extent utilitarian devices. At the same time, however, they were a message he wanted to launch to visitors, slaves, all the occasional intruders, and many "others." Since Venetian blinds allowed inside-out observation, he let excluded people know that he was watching. The message was that this postmilitary, "feminine," approachable, simple, generous, and modern master was heedful. As Jack McLaughlin writes, Jefferson "was a man who revealed to others only what he chose to; he remained fixedly concealed behind what we would call his defenses—*observing all but seldom revealing.*"[38]

A New Mode of Obtaining Power of Mind Over Mind

The English philosopher Jeremy Bentham, at the end of the eighteenth century, devised a new model of prison, the "Panopticon" (literally "to observe all"), able to minimize personnel while maximizing control over inmates. (In Greek mythology, Argus Panoptes was a giant with a hundred eyes.) Even though it was impossible for a single custodian to simultaneously observe all inmates, the effectiveness of the institution, according to Bentham, depended on the fact that inmates could not know if and when they were being watched. The Panopticon's power depended directly from the dissociation of the dyad see/being-seen—plus the relevant fact that inmates had internalized the more-than-just brutal power of the overseer. By this singular mixture of knowing and not-knowing, being seen without seeing, the Panopticon, as Bentham wrote, was "a new mode of obtaining power of mind over mind, in a quantity hitherto without example." Under the power of unseen eyes, inmates were expected to behave as though they were watched at all times. Although the prison was never built, Bentham believed he could apply this model to hospitals, schools, "houses of industry," and many other institutions.[39]

The symbolic power of the eye, especially when hidden from sight, is very effective. More than by its feasibility, late eighteenth- and early nineteenth-century enlightened and genteel leaders were captivated by the symbol of modernity Bentham was able to conjure. With a genial stroke, Bentham translated God's metaphysical eye into a mundane reality. Like God's eye, Bentham's was a powerful eye, all knowing, effective, and, above all, hidden. During "barbarian" times, rulers had enforced the drive for discipline through actual force. But the enlightened age discovered that a monitored social space, whether real or imagined, especially when the observer was hidden, was just as effective. When people think they are observed, they regulate themselves accordingly. How would you act, Jefferson asked Peter Carr, if all the world was looking at you?

Jefferson himself observed and exerted power through his eyes. That he observed the others means more than one thing. He studied exotic American Indian populations; he scrutinized slaves' behavior; he supervised younger whites, male and female, imposing strict schedules for their education and expecting regular updates. We will return expressly to the topic of these particular bodies as an *observed* other. For the moment, suffice it to say that Jefferson's observing the others also meant, in a very practical way, monitoring their social space.

His "academic village," first of all, was built upon the idea of eye spying on eye—Bentham would have approved. Preferring a village to a large house had certainly to do with both aesthetic and practical reasons. "Large houses are always ugly, inconvenient, exposed to the accident of fire, and bad in cases of infection," Jefferson wrote to Littleton Waller Tazewell, former member of the Virginia House of Delegates and, later, governor of Virginia. The village, consisting of small houses for professors presiding over students' lodgings, enhanced new forms of authority and control. Students' rooms should open on a central lawn, purposefully diminishing their privacy and pushing them to internalize the overseer. In the Report of the Commissioners for the University of Virginia, known as the Rockfish Gap Report, Jefferson was vociferous about "order." The university "should consist of distinct houses or pavilions, arranged at proper distances on each side of a lawn . . . these pavilions should be united by a range of dormitories, sufficient each for the accommodation of two students only, this provision being deemed advantageous to morals, to order, and to uninterrupted study."[40]

Overlooking All the Details of Their Business Myself

While this academic village was only "the Hobby of my old age," not a real Panopticon, a younger Jefferson had other chances to actually exert power through the eye. A true Jeffersonian Panopticon was his nail-making shop. "Jefferson's methods," Lucia Stanton writes, "of managing his nail makers were certainly influenced by the ideas that sustained penal reform at this time." More rational and humane modes of managing institutions, by forestalling brutal force and using incentives and well-designed monitored social spaces as proxies, were becoming popular. Philadelphia Quaker merchant Caleb Lownes, whom Jefferson met at the end of 1793, and with whom he started right away to place orders for nail rod, had worked vigorously to modernize the prison system. His *Account of the Gaol and Penitentiary House of Philadelphia* (1793) provided the model of "humanitarian" prisons in America.[41]

Jefferson's naileries operated continuously from 1794 to 1812 and more sporadically from 1815 to 1823. During the first decade, nail shops raised a handsome profit, but they turned out to be less and less profitable when difficulty in obtaining payment from purchasers and failures in the supply of nail rod became more frequent. A school, a manufacture, and a "humanitarian" prison, the nailery, as Stanton describes it, "was an experimental laboratory for working out new ideas about exercising power, a place to try to manage enslaved labor in harmony with current ideas of humanitarian reform." In his naileries, as Jefferson wrote at the end of April 1795, were employed "a dozen little boys from 10. to 16. years of age, overlooking all the details of their business myself." Jefferson tallied it as a success: "A nailery which I have established with my own negro boys now provides completely for the maintenance of my family, as we make from 8. to 10,000 nails a day and it is on the increase." Success was due to the power of his personal control and constant monitoring. By 1800, Jefferson was still rejoicing about this experiment: "my nailery flourished, and still flourishes greatly, employing 16. boys at a clear profit of about 4. to 500£ annually." When Jefferson entered office in 1801, however, he could no longer exert the power of his eyes.[42]

Overseers deployed violence, although Jefferson preferred other means. Incentives had a role, but vision and supervision did most of the job. In 1807, overseer Edmund Bacon caught a nailer, possibly James (Jim) Hubbard, who stole and hid hundreds of pounds of nails. He was eventually brought before Jefferson's eyes, not under his whip: "I never saw any person, white or black, feel as badly as he did when he saw his master. He was mortified and distressed beyond measure. He had been brought up in the shop, and we all had confidence in him. Now his character was gone. The tears streamed down his face, and he begged pardon over and over again." Actually, things were slightly more complicated than that. Hubbard did not just "see" his master. He saw the master *seeing* him and *judging* him while an entire oppressive institution supported the exclusionary practices of this same master. The slave saw himself after having internalized the master's power as if this power were legitimate and morally compelling. Jefferson paid daily visits to the nail shops, even twice-daily visits, weighing the rod constantly to make sure waste (or theft) did not exceed a "reasonable" percentage. "Considered in the context of surveillance," Stanton concludes, "his small Virginia mountain begins to take on the shape of a panopticon, with Jefferson, elevated above the surrounding landscape and its inhabitants, inspecting the workings of his world."[43]

One scholar has argued that "the principal of panopticism" is essential for an adequate reading of the entire Monticello, its gardens, and associated landscapes. It is undeniable that Monticello ended up being an observation post, a very modern and "scientific" one at that. It could not be spotted from downhill, while everyone in Charlottesville knew that the Sage of Monticello was looking through his telescopes—whether inspecting slaves, British soldiers coming to seize him, or workers toiling over the buildings and serpentine walls of the new university campus. "Power was embodied in, and expressed by, the ability to see rather than to be seen." The unidirectional unimpeded view this postmilitary, postbrutal master, thanks to his technological apparatuses, could enjoy from the mountaintop over the fields and farms below was designed to maximize the visual screening effect: modernity and science were undoubtedly on the rise.[44]

The Valuable Part of Society Condemn in Their Hearts That Knight-Errantry

"Others" were watched, observed, scrutinized, studied, described, categorized, controlled, and kept at a suitable distance, and their shortcomings or anomalies were pointed out and classified. Not surprisingly, as we will see better in the sections to come, American Indian, African American, and female bodies, because full of "anomalies," were, for Jefferson, anthropologically and epistemologically more interesting subjects to be seen through his lenses and telescopes. He was nonetheless aware that any "normal" white body could be born with "deformities" or be taken at any moment by innumerable accidents, maladies, psychiatric conditions, or psychological or moral imbalances—"passions," in the language of the period. Whether permanent conditions or episodes, these factors could change any white male body into an object of "scientific" scrutiny.[45]

Each time they fell into a more or less permanent and more or less severe condition of "otherness," both working-class and higher-class white males, like himself, invited Jefferson to acknowledge what we may call the *variation within the norm*. Many white men existed who for many reasons were "inhabitants of diseased bodies" and who happened to lose the firm, self-confident, and yet welcoming bearing that Jefferson thought should characterize "normal" male corporeality. All of a sudden, we deal with white bodies shaking, trembling, losing character out of fear or some other passion, and prey to "terrible convulsions." According to Jefferson, this was not the way the white male body should present itself to the world. The message, he believed, should be different: "I steer my bark with Hope in the head, leaving Fear astern." "Sensations of Grief" can maim even the "happiest life," and white folks out of control should thus be cured by a pathologist: "I wish the pathologists then would tell us what is the use of grief in the economy, and of what good it is the cause, proximate or remote."[46]

Pathologies, both moral and physical, could certainly seize any white male body and turn a potentially reliable individual, for example, into a drunkard, a beggar, a Tory, a Marshall, a Hamilton, an Arnold, or worse. The Tory was, for Jefferson, the prototype of the wimpy male, pathologically beset by passions, a slave to his qualms, and unable to trust his fellows. Like other "gloomy and hypochondriac minds, inhabitants of diseased bodies, disgusted with the present, and despairing of the future," Tories should be sent to the pathologist.[47]

Something can and often goes wrong among "normal" white males, Jefferson conceded. Convulsions, spasms, paroxysms, commotions, tremors, bouts, fits, and similar episodes signal a problem. Whites sometimes engage in crazy behavior, thus offering themselves as a sheer appalling spectacle—a cautionary tale for everyone. Sensational, for example, was the brutal murder of a young slave, George, committed in Livingston County, Kentucky, on 15 December 1811, by Lilburn and Isham Lewis. The Lewis brothers were the sons of Jefferson's sister, Lucy, married to Colonel Charles Lewis, and were cousins of Meriwether Lewis. But although the story of the Lewis brothers was common knowledge at the time, Jefferson never acknowledged his nephews' pathological behavior either publicly or privately. What he did acknowledge, especially after famous Meriwether Lewis committed suicide, or so it was believed at the time, was a tendency toward depression and mental disturbance within the whole Lewis family.[48]

Even when physical or psychiatric pathologies are averted, moral maladies can occur among whites. An American youth who goes to Europe "learns drinking, horse-racing and boxing. . . . He acquires a fondness for European luxury and dissipation and a contempt for the simplicity of his own country; . . . he is led by the strongest of all the human passions into a spirit for female intrigue destructive of his own and others happiness." Unruled, unbalanced white male bodies were actually everywhere to be seen, even within the circle of Jefferson's family. Charles Bankhead, husband of Anne Randolph Bankhead, Jefferson's eldest grandchild, for example, was one among the many trustworthy whites who all of a sudden lost his character and went crazy. He became a violent drunkard. In 1819, he stabbed Anne's brother, Thomas Jefferson Randolph, in his side, on the steps of the courthouse of Charlottesville. Thomas Jefferson Randolph himself was not always able to keep his temper at bay. When he was in Philadelphia, as said, studying medicine to gain a profession, Jefferson had advised him to "be very select in the society you attach yourself to, avoid taverns, drinkers, smokers, idlers, & dissipated persons generally." The grandfather, evidently, knew his grandchild's shortcomings well.[49]

In 1806, Thomas Mann Randolph, Thomas Jefferson Randolph's father, was himself challenged to a duel by John Randolph of Roanoke following an altercation over a debate about a salt tax in the House of Representatives. Jefferson gave him advice not to take up the garb of the gladiator, or the medieval knight—it would be a disgrace to be publicly seen that way. Should he present himself to the world dressed up in these long-gone costumes, Thomas Mann Randolph would just appear unfit to the progress of civilization: "The valuable part of society condemn in their hearts that knight-errantry, which following the ignis fatuus of an imaginary honour, bursts asunder all the ligaments of duty & affection, & consigns to misery & ruin innocent & helpless families."[50]

The reader can visualize, on the one side, these white men pathologically embracing old-fashioned "knight-errantry" as opposed to the better and healthier "part of society" whom every white should try to imitate—the former ruffled and agitated; the latter calm and rational. Civilization had fortunately decreed savage bodies as obsolete and undignified. Also, we find here again the motive of an "approval" sought from the best part of humankind: act as if the entire world were watching you.[51]

After the "Revolution of 1800" was won and he entered office, Jefferson made a case for replacing specimens from the Federalist era with harmonious, more modern and healthier whites. "Let us restore to social intercourse that harmony and affection without which liberty, and even life itself, are but dreary things." In older times, when brutal force reigned, it may have been normal to witness lack of harmony: "During the throes and convulsions of the ancient world, during the agonizing spasms of infuriated man, seeking through blood and slaughter his long-lost liberty, it was not wonderful that the agitation of the billows should reach even this distant and peaceful shore." History had done away with white bodies seized by "agonizing spasms," and only pathological characters still endure in this habit. Irregular passions, he contended, make an individual both unhealthy and hateful.[52]

Despite pathologies and excesses, Jefferson was not defensive against white male bodies in the way he was against the bodies of the "others." Many whites, eventually, will reenter the narrow circle. The "ligaments of duty & affection" will be reestablished. Whites can and will be friends to each other. Regardless of many *episodes* and *excesses*, the "normal" white male body remained the best example chosen by nature, and helped by the progress of history and civilization, to rise to some kind of model for humankind. True as it was that Jefferson never spoke very highly of many whites—from Alexander Hamilton to John Marshall, from Patrick Henry to Andrew Jackson—was there any other human type that should be picked for a model?

We Should Have to Strip Off the Artificial Vestments

The topic "Jefferson and religion" has been analyzed from every possible angle. Raised an Anglican, interested in English Deism, and enthralled by Unitarianism, Jefferson arrived at his mature view of religion as early as he wrote Bill No. 82, A Bill For Establishing Religious Freedom, in 1776, finally adopted in 1785 and known as the *Virginia Statute for Religious Freedom*. A freethinker and an advocate of the separation between church and state, Jefferson's views of religion were nonetheless far from a simplistic and ideological refusal of the matter. God and religion were, for him, important issues, both as social phenomena and from a personal, spiritual point of view. Federalists' allegations that he was an "atheist," of course, must be interpreted under the label of political campaigning: they belong to the violent political discourse typical of the 1790s.[53]

Jesus fascinated Jefferson. Teaching a system of morality superior to any other, Jesus made us aware of "our duties to others." "Of all the systems of morality antient or modern, which have come under my observation," Jefferson wrote in 1813, "none appear to me so pure as that of Jesus." Jesus was a prophet and a moral teacher, not the Son of God, and yet he performed wonders, albeit not miracles in some conventional sense. In 1804, Jefferson came up with a compilation of excerpts from the Gospels, which he literally sliced out with a razor from the Bible. Known as The Philosophy of Jesus of Nazareth, this first edited version of Jesus's teachings, and an attempt to make the worthy parts as distinguishable from the less worthy "as diamonds in a dunghill," left Jefferson not fully satisfied. In 1820, he assembled what for him was a better version, known as The Life and Morals of Jesus of Nazareth.[54]

Instead of reviewing all the shades and different components characterizing Jefferson's religiousness, what we can do, and I will do, is to see the issue of Jefferson's fascination with Jesus from the point of view of his invention of whiteness. By means of his versions of the Gospels, Jefferson tried to strip from Jesus the clothes of priesthood, superstition, and falsity. He tried to dress this figure up with the garb of simplicity and, of course, to provide him with a functional whiteness. He wanted to normalize Jesus's *persona*, to peel off of layers of tradition and peculiar characteristics. He wanted to divest him of particularities and attributes, thus making him into a paradigmatic, natural, normal, passion-free, healthy, and perfectly white body that could help Jefferson to define the "other."

Jesus, for Jefferson, represented life in its simplest, at once most rational and natural forms. Jesus's bodily simplicity was what he was looking for. "It is the speculations of crazy theologists," Jefferson wrote a few months before setting himself to work on the new version of his edited Gospels, "which have made a Babel of a religion the most moral and sublime ever preached to man, and calculated to heal, and not to create differences." Jesus did not try to bring about disharmonies; he did not want to "create differences." According to Jefferson, Jesus's teaching was all about performances in simplicity, not limited to what he said and preached. It was his *example* and not only his doctrines, according to Jefferson, that needed to be rescued from the deception of priesthood. How did Jesus move? How did he behave? What was his style? Clothing? Manners? "Restoring" Jesus's elegant simplicity is an underlying theme we cannot help noticing each time Jefferson addressed Christianity. "I trust with you," he wrote to François Adriaan Van der Kemp, "that the genuine and simple religion of Jesus will one day be restored: such as it was preached and *practised* by himself."[55]

Jesus practiced simplicity, according to Jefferson, and set his (white) corporeality as an example and a universal standard. This is what made his figure so valuable to counteract monarchical sophistication, aristocracy, priesthood, Federalists, and any "long train of et caeteras" Jefferson sensed he had to offset. In 1787, he had advised Peter Carr to look after the style of this personage, a character, and a *persona:* "You will next read the new testament. It is the history of a personage called Jesus." Stripping off his artificial vestments was a metaphor Jefferson relied on—but there was more to it than just a metaphor. Jefferson believed Jesus was actually waiting to be liberated, in a very corporeal sense, from hefty apparatuses and the cumbersome, aristocratic-like apparel: "In extracting the pure principles which he taught," Jefferson wrote to his friend John Adams, "we should have to strip off the artificial vestments in which they have been muffled by priests, who have travestied them into various forms, as instruments of riches and power to them. We must dismiss the Platonists and Plotinists, the Stagyrites and Gamalielites, the Eclectics the Gnostics and Scholastics, their essences and emanations, their Logos and Demi-urgos, Aeons and Daemons male and female, with a long train of Etc. Etc. Etc. or, shall I say at once, of Nonsense." One can easily picture these Gothic and misty figures, with their weighty load of evil seductiveness, standing in stark opposition to a white-dressed and white-skinned Jesus.[56]

Jefferson set out to counterpoise Gothicism. More than a metaphor, it was for him a real danger. "I am laboring," he wrote to DeWitt Clinton in 1822, "to save my fellow-citizens from the Gothic barbarism into which they are sinking for want of the means of education." Jesus's white "normality," which means an intrinsic educational power emanating from his simplicity, is the kernel one starts to behold once Jesus is cleared of all the priestly, Gothic regalia hampering his freedom of movement. Priesthood and aristocracy, or whatever the name Jefferson happened to choose to indicate artificiality, crafty sophistication, and the gruesome layers of traditions, were at once Jesus's enemies and the enemies of sound republicanism. Even before doctrines were discussed, Jefferson's praises of Jesus's simplicity were an invitation for his correspondents to imagine a striking visual alternative: Jesus's corporeality, on the one hand, and, on the other, "the artificial structures they have erected to make him the instrument of wealth, power, and preeminence to themselves," as Jefferson wrote in 1815. These two extremes "are as distinct things in my view as light and darkness: and, while I have classed them with soothsayers and necromancers, I place him among the greatest of the reformers of morals, and scourges of priest-craft, that have ever existed."[57]

White male bodies, as models, were beyond particularities as well as beyond tradition and its pollutants, including the "artificial vestments" in which they have been "muffled by priests." White bodies should aspire to such a condition, and Jefferson observed and classified Jesus in terms of the achievement of civilization and whiteness. When true to themselves, like Jesus was, white bodies had no attributes, no characteristics, no traits, except their "natural" simplicity.

Filled Me with Awe and Veneration

Not all white males of course could aspire to become perfect like Jesus. But those who failed, failed occasionally—as said, their variation was within the norm. When whites fell under surveillance, it was their failed character, their passions, or a pathological condition, and not anthropological characteristics, to strike Jefferson's imagination. When whites were at stake, Jefferson's discourse was clearly moralized; if not moralized, it was medicalized. All of Jefferson's white enemies, or those like-minded and like-bodied white men he disliked and those with whom he fell out, failed either on a moral level or on a pathological level.

Other "others" existed, however, whose minds and bodies—especially bodies—had become naturalized by law, custom, and science. American Indians, blacks, and women were the three principal "others" functional to Jefferson's definition of white normality and simplicity. He did not simply despise these three "others." What we find is rather a mixture of attraction and repulsion, of praise and blame, of awareness—awareness of the underlying social dynamics—and a total lack of insight. But the three groups, for him, bore an inbuilt, natural inferiority, a diminished corporeal constitution that only the eyes of a natural historian or an anthropologist would assess in the proper way. Scrutinizing and classifying eyes, like Jefferson's, made many differences "natural," which means ultimately nonnegotiable. Jefferson's *naturalizations* explain his questionable ways of interacting with these excluded "others."[58]

Jefferson wrongly believed that Native Americans were already nearly dead. The "melancholy sequel of their history," as he labeled it in Query 11, elicited the consoling impression that the modes of interaction between white and "red" communities, however brutal, had been long decided, decided in the past. It was not clear to Jefferson whether the cause of the "disappearance" of Native Americans must be attributed to natural and inborn factors, like an insane lust for spirituous liquor, smallpox, and an inexplicable stubbornness in resisting agriculture, or whether it was the consequence of some kind of illegal "abridgment" of their land perpetrated by whites. Jefferson thought this last option unlikely: "I find in our historians and records, repeated proofs of purchase."[59]

To a certain extent, Jefferson-the-natural-historian acknowledged Native Americans' dignity and nobility, of both character and deportment. Jefferson approached at least some Native Americans and listened to them. The eloquence of John Logan, the Great Mingo, as famously referred to in Query 6, helped to rescue American animals, including humans, from Buffon's "imputation of impotence." By taking his start from Logan's eloquence, Jefferson concluded that Buffon was wrong and that the American Indian's "vivacity and activity of mind is equal to ours in the same situation."[60]

Fascination with the American Indian character, their mind and eloquence, is also testified to by Jefferson's vivid recollection of Outacite's speech. Jefferson was at the College of William and Mary in the spring of 1762 when a Cherokee chief he knew from earlier visits at Shadwell delivered a farewell oration to his people at Williamsburg before departing for England to meet the king. In his remembrance, Jefferson suffused the entire episode with vivid romantic colors: "The moon was in full splendor, and to her he seemed to address himself in his prayers. . . . His sounding voice, distinct articulation, animated action, . . . filled me with awe and veneration, altho' I did not understand a word he uttered."[61]

Neither More Defective in Ardor, Nor More Impotent with His Female

Since his boyhood in Virginia, and especially during the years of his governorship, and later his presidency, Jefferson encountered many real, corporeal American Indians, whether delegations or single individuals. When he retired, he often conjured the memory of past encounters. Jefferson stayed consistently curious about Native American corporeality, their manners and customs, not only about their character and eloquence. But he remained substantially distant and detached, and developed only an intellectual interest. (Political motives and opportunism, obviously, loomed very large.) Maybe he could not, maybe the occasion did not present itself, but as a matter of fact he never tried to draw examples of Native American bodies into the circle of his friends and intimates. Acting on occasion as a political theorist, or a policy maker, or a scientist, Jefferson kept Native Americans at a distance. He always treated them "objectively."

In both Query 6 and Query 11, Jefferson's longest essays on the natural history of Native Americans, he praised many corporeal attributes. To counteract Buffon's representation, in Query 6 Jefferson claimed that the American Indian male "is neither more defective in ardor, nor more impotent with his female, than the white reduced to the same diet and exercise." The American Indian may be sly and eager to play tricks on enemies, but he is brave and dignified, "he is brave, when an enterprise depends on bravery." The male American Indian body was not postmilitary and rather complied with an obsolete code of honor: "he will defend himself against an host of enemies, always choosing to be killed, rather than to surrender, . . . he meets death with more deliberation, and endures tortures with a firmness unknown almost to religious enthusiasm with us." Somehow left behind by the progress of civilization, the American Indian was, however, "affectionate to his children, careful of them, and indulgent in the extreme," progressively less so when we "recede from the centre." "His friendships are strong and faithful to the uttermost extremity," but the Indian shows less attachment to abstract society or to the modern idea of nation. Nothing surprising, given Jefferson's postulate of the Indian being outdated, and belonging to a previous stage in the Great Chain of Being.[62]

The American Indian male, especially, was for Jefferson a Stoic figure, endeavoring "to appear superior to human events." But he was peculiar in his overall carriage. "His eagerness for hunting, and for games of chance" made him an ideal warrior-type, but for this same reason, he was out of step with civilization. Had civilization not excluded them, they would have made excellent citizens. Had they entered progress, "we shall probably find that they are formed in mind as well as in body, on the same module with the 'Homo sapiens Europaeus.'" But they have been defeated by "history," and "eloquence in council, bravery and address in war" have become the sole "talents" they have remained capable of displaying. "Of their bravery and address in war we have multiplied proofs, because we have been the subjects on which they were exercised."[63]

All in all, Jefferson treated the generic American Indian kindly and, as said, "objectively." He took extreme care, for example, to name Native American communities, or nations, especially in Query 11: the Powhatans, Mannahoacs, and Monacans, this last "the most powerful." And then the Nottoways, Meherrins, Tuteloes, Massawomecs, and Chickahominies. In the tables he appended, Jefferson added many more "tribes." Nonetheless, the impression a modern reader gets when going through these pages is that Jefferson did not address these societies like a social historian or an ethnologist would do. Unquestionably, no empathy, no sense of compassion, no closeness, no sense of responsibility, let alone guilt, emerges. He wanted to comprehend these communities to some extent; but he was especially concerned about classifying them along a precise "natural" hierarchy setting whites and American Indian "brethren" far apart. These peoples seem not to have a real past and a history of their own. What is worse, they seem to be irremediably "gone." Native Americans' habits, behaviors, and traditions seem not to have coevolved along with their environments. Habits, behaviors, and traditions seem not to be fully consistent and coherent. American Indian societies seem unaffected by either development or progress or cultural stratifications. These people were, for Jefferson, no longer alive and did not belong to world history, but rather acted like living fossils.

Magi, Archimagi, Cunning Men, Seers, Rainmakers

This is what "naturalization" elicits: when, many years after *Notes*, John Adams asked his friend to provide further information about Native Americans, Jefferson wrote what should probably be considered his third longest treatise on the subject, discussing a huge array of literature and theories. In this famous letter, Jefferson was still more explicit than he had been in *Notes* about American Indian "strangeness" and intrinsic "peculiarities": "You ask further, if the Indians have any order of priesthood among them, like the Druids, Bards or Minstrels of the Celtic nations?" They, all of them, according to Jefferson, belonged to a stage anterior even to Christian or Jewish history—living fossils, indeed. They never knew priesthood or proper social hierarchies. Their sorcerers should be rather called "by their proper names, Jongleurs, Devins, Sortileges," or "praestigiatores" and "Magi, Archimagi, cunning men, Seers, rainmakers." They are "persons pretending to have communications with the devil and other evil spirits, to foretel future events, bring down rain, find stolen goods, raise the dead, destroy some, and heal others by enchantment, lay spells etc." American Indian spirituality was tantamount to a reenactment of those despicable figures that Jews, for example, used to call "Soothsayers, sorcerers and wizards." They were the equivalent of those obscure characters that both Jews and Christians called "Jannes and Jambres, their Simon Magus, witch of Endor, and the young damsel whose sorceries disturbed Paul so much; instead of placing them in a line with their High-priest, their Chief priests, and their magnificent hierarchy generally."[64]

By means of all these details, Jefferson wanted Adams to picture American Indians as sharing space and time with these prehistoric figures. Indian conjurers must not be "ennobled," Jefferson was convinced. The fact is that the "present state of the several Indian tribes, without any public order of priests, is proof sufficient that they never had such an order." According to Jefferson, Native Americans were defeated by history in many ways: "Their steady habits permit no innovations, not even those which the progress of science offers to increase the comforts, enlarge the understanding, and improve the morality of mankind. Indeed so little idea have they of a regular order of priests, that they mistake ours for their Conjurers and call them by that name." At this later stage of his life, Jefferson never wavered on the notion that Native Americans were condemned to remain outsiders. The time to boast of their qualities in order to disprove European notions of an American inferiority was gone.[65]

For Jefferson, Native Americans simply were, and ultimately always would be, outside of history: their traditions opaque and primitive, their corporeality nothing more than peculiar. In Query 11, he had praised them for their strong corporate identity, but this is problematic too. When younger, Jefferson had admired American Indian "lawlessness," the fact that those people had "never submitted themselves to any laws, any coercive power, any shadow of government." Jefferson had been sensitive to the fact that Native Americans were bound together not by contracts and calculi, not even by constraint, violence, and a despotic power: "Their only controls are their manners, and that moral sense of right and wrong, which, like the sense of tasting and feeling, in every man, makes a part of his nature." Problematic is the fact that they were nature, for Jefferson, and had never known institutions, administrations, procedures, internal tensions, debates, class and gender conflicts, and, in a word, the *transformations* wrought by history.[66]

When the urgency to refute Buffon decreased, Native Americans' "otherness" increased accordingly. Furthermore, Jefferson always remained faithful to his postulate to interpret Native Americans' identity from the perspective of natural history. When he studied American Indians, Jefferson could not empathize, but he could not even become a historian; he remained a *natural* historian or a taxonomist. He could not notice the ferocity of his acts of naturalization of American Indians and that such a naturalization was a cultural artifact. It was cruel to construe these peoples as evicted from historical processes and to picture their intellect and their forms of social organization as primitive, prehistorical examples of living fossils. But Jefferson did not see his allegation of "lawlessness" and naturalness as intrinsically derogatory. At least at the time of *Notes,* he was convinced he was praising and not objectifying them.[67]

Inveloped in the Clouds of Their Antiquities

There is an evolution in Jefferson's way of approaching Native Americans: over the years, they became increasingly peculiar, stubbornly nostalgic and visionary, to be more precise, more like their prophets. Jefferson downgraded Tenskwatawa ("the Open Door"), the Shawnee prophet, to a fool or worse. "More rogue than fool," he wanted to "reform" his "red brethren" by a "return to their pristine manner of living." He was a fool both in his pretense "to be in constant communication with the great spirit" and in his metaphysical fantasy that Native Americans would have been created "distinct from the

Whites, of different natures, for different purposes." As to the origins of American Indians, Tenskwatawa did not come up with a more cautious and enlightened opinion, like Jefferson did: "Ignoro." A worse form of peculiarity was Tenskwatawa's commitment to look back, including his clumsy attempts at convincing his "red brethren" to "return from all the ways of the Whites to the habits and opinions of their forefathers." Jefferson had repeatedly denied that looking backward instead of forward was a good strategy. But Tenskwatawa was precisely "inveloped in the clouds of their antiquities, and vainly endeavoring to lead back his brethren to the fancied beatitudes of their golden age." "It is that bigotry," Jefferson had already realized in 1810, "which keeps the Indians in a state of barbarism in the midst of the arts."[68]

When Jefferson said that Tenskwatawa was "inveloped" in antiquity, such an accusation should be taken literally and materially, as a denotation of precise corporeal characteristics. American Indians dressed "peculiarly" and had "peculiar" manners and tastes. The "habits of their bodies" ran counter to any sincere progressive drive. As he wrote to Adams, American Indians were convinced that "they must not wear linen nor woollen, but dress like their fathers in the skins and furs of wild animals." Linen made whites literally white, as we have seen, while the obduracy to don skins and furs made American Indians "natural," but only in a bestial, primitive way.[69]

In 1807, Jefferson had offered precise instructions to General Henry Dearborn. The secretary of war was then involved in a campaign to remove Native Americans beyond the Mississippi River, and Jefferson told him that the best way to pacifically "gratify" Indians was to capitalize on their peculiar, childlike, flashy styles. "Explorers" should just provide them with those "articles" that are "in highest value with them." Give them "*blue* beads. this is a coarse cheap bead imported from China . . . it is far more valued by the Indians than the *white* beads of the same manufacture, & answers all the purposes of money, being counted by the fathom." Give them, he advised, "common brass buttons, more valued than any thing except beads." Give them "knives. with fixed wooden handles stained red, usually called red handle knives, & such as are employed by the N.W. Co. in their indian trade." Give them "battleaxes & tomahawks"; "sadler's seat awls, which answer for mockasin awls"; "some glover's needles"; "some iron combs"; "some nests of camp kettles. brass is much preferred to iron, tho both are very useful to the indians, *size, from one to 4 gallons.*" He had naturalized them in the first place, and the only conclusion Jefferson could draw was that bestiality, foolishness, and puerility went hand in hand.[70]

The Same World Will Scarcely Do for Them and Us

If distancing Native Americans, however this took place, helped Jefferson to better inhabit his "modern," "normal," and "simple" body, it also made it impossible to draw real individuals into the circle of friends. He "knew" American Indians were essentially childlike, primitive, bestial, naive. And although history had already defeated them, as Jefferson claimed, they were dangerous and violent as well.

Intellectual expedients and biased representations, which means narratives, were not enough to distance and objectify fit and healthy Native Americans. If Jefferson hoped to live comfortably within his "normal" white body, he had to take into account harsher solutions. And to accomplish this, he was ready to put his hard-gained postmartiality and "femininity" at risk. Through the summer of 1776, the Cherokees launched guerrilla raids against isolated Virginia settlements, killing several people. No easy appeasement was in sight. "The situation in Kentucky," as Anthony Wallace writes, "had become desperate; the population had been reduced to about one hundred armed men." In the 1780s, skirmishes and battles still went on. White bodies faced off against people who had begun to think of themselves as red, and drastic measures were sometimes necessary. "Frequent murders," Jefferson wrote in 1780, "having been committed by the Cherokee Indians of the Chickamogga towns . . . , we directed Colo. Campbell in the month of June to raise 500 men from our counties of Washington and Montgomery in order to destroy those towns." In Jefferson's mind, "distinguishing the friendly from the hostile part of the nation" was both humane and strategic. While foes should be chastised, he intended "to spare no assurance of friendship and protection to the former." In 1786, violent episodes were still rather frequent: "The Creeks have made a formidable invasion of Georgia. Some scattered Indians have done mischeif at Kentucke; they are however disavowed by their tribes."[71]

Updates about skirmishes, mutual killings, and official expeditions against American Indians appear frequently in Jefferson's correspondence. To keep hostile Indians at bay, he often relied on extreme measures. Ideals of justice should not hamper urgent policies: "The two principles," Jefferson wrote to an Indian agent in 1786, "on which our conduct towards the Indians should be founded are justice and fear. After the injuries we have done them, they cannot love us, which leaves us no alternative but that of fear to keep them from attacking us. But justice is what we should never lose sight of, and in time it may recover their esteem." Ideals were important, but obviously they should never thwart policies. In the mid-1770s, after many guerrilla raids, Jefferson had already realized that Native Americans "will now be driven beyond the Missisipi and that this in future will be declared to the Indians the invariable consequence of their beginning a war." To his friend John Page he declared: "I would never cease pursuing them [the Cherokees] while one of them remained on this side of the Misisippi." A few years later, Governor Jefferson gave the frontier leader George Rogers Clark a similar message about the appropriate way to deal with American Indians north of the Ohio River. If a campaign was to be waged "against these Indians [the Shawnees, principally], the end proposed should be their extermination, or their removal beyond the lakes or Illinois river. The same world will scarcely do for them and us."[72]

On the eve of retirement, Jefferson admonished Kitchao Geboway, an Indian leader, to just abstain from any design of attacking whites: "You see that we are as numerous as the leaves of the trees, strong enough to fight our own battles, and too strong to fear any enemy." "The tribe which shall begin an unprovoked war against us," Jefferson equally warned the Wyandots, Ottawas, Chippewas, Potawatomis, and Shawnees, "we will extirpate from the earth, or drive to such a distance as that they shall never again be able to strike us."[73]

Jefferson did not step back from using either force or trickeries. To promote Indians' "disposition," as the president wrote to the governor of Indiana Territory, "to exchange lands which they have to spare & we want, for necessaries, which we have to spare & they want, we shall push our trading houses, and be glad to see the good & influential individuals among them run in debt, because we observe that when these debts get beyond what the individuals can pay, they become willing to lop th[em off] by a cession of lands."[74]

Amalgamated and Identified with Us

As to race relations, Jefferson partook in a preexistent system of subjugation and dispossession, and he is definitely accountable for that—historically and not personally. Two further things, however, must be pointed out. The first relates to his policies and sweeping solutions. Aware that either massacres for years on end, leading to extermination, or removal would be the only two options available, he set the second alternative as a "humanitarian" solution. On many occasions, Jefferson advocated removal. But he did not perceive, as we do, an ultimate contradiction between removal and humanitarianism. Christian Keller has written a very interesting essay on the way Jefferson sought to harmonize removal, assimilation, and humanitarianism. Keller contends that distancing Native Americans from settlers and squatters, and in general from the onslaught going on along frontiers, became the kernel of a philanthropic, melioristic program. Jefferson believed that any prospect of amalgamation and acculturation would be hampered by contact. Physical contact should be prevented because of numberless prejudices about American Indians in the settler's mind. Reports of massacres, scalping, and ritual torture, whether fabricated or real, dated back to the early stages of colonization of the American continent. Moreover, ethnocentric government agents and missionaries, Indian resistance to land cession, growing intrusions of settlers on Indian land, and the government's increasing inability to isolate Indians all called for urgent implementation of Jefferson's plan of humanitarian removal.[75]

The second thing that must be pointed out has much to do with Jefferson's commitment to distinguish between friends and foes. We may question the very supposition of assimilating peaceful and already subdued Native Americans, or *acculturating* them, but Jefferson considered it the best thing to do. Cultural relativism, or simply fairness in acknowledging cultural and intellectual independence, was beyond Jefferson's visual field. "You know," he wrote to geographer and explorer Alexander von Humboldt, "the benevolent plan we were pursuing here for the happiness of the Aboriginal inhabitants in our vicinities. we spared nothing to keep them at peace with one another, to teach them agriculture and the rudiments of the most necessary arts, and to encourage industry by establishing among them separate property. . . . they would have mixed their blood with ours and been amalgamated and identified with us within no distant period of time."[76]

In theory, at least, "different" bodies could have "amalgamated," while striving to assume whiteness as the only standard. This was, for Jefferson, civilization. In the long run, American bodies would all look alike within the nation, at least exteriorly, as to their manners and styles. President Jefferson lectured his "brothers," the Senecas, via an address to the chief and prophet Handsome Lake, who accompanied a delegation in Washington in 1802. He lectured them on "the ruinous effects which the abuse of spirituous liquors" produce. Alcohol, he said, has already "weakened [Indian] bodies, enervated their minds, exposed them to hunger, cold, nakedness, & poverty." The reference to "nakedness" is especially interesting—as if being nude and refusing to wear white linen had nothing to do with intentional choices, or history, and was simply related to a vice. Jefferson's equation was that to look like "us," "they" should wear our clothes. Jefferson called for a radical revision of Native Americans' corporeality: "I once had hopes that the Southern tribes were nearly ripe for incorporation with us. the facility with which the cotton plant enables them to clothe themselves renders their civilization easier than that of the Northern tribes, who are obliged to resort to the beasts of the forest for covering." Jefferson's hopes were "damped" by continuous wars producing an "implacable a hatred of us" and the deepest skepticism as to "all counsels coming from us."[77]

But Native Americans chose not to cover their bodies, and no clear signal of "civilization" was ever offered. Just like unruly children, Native Americans refused these "wise" counsels. "Children" and Indian corporeality as "childish" were qualifiers that Jefferson frequently deployed—once again a consequence of having formerly distanced these people via his many acts of naturalization.

On the eve of retirement, for example, President Jefferson addressed Indian nations by emphasizing his personal role as a father and touching on other "fathers" to come: "My children, this is the last time I shall speak to you as your father, it is the last counsel I shall give." American citizens will soon "choose another chief and another father for you. . . . Be assured, my children that he will have the same friendly disposition towards you which I have had, and that you will find in him a true and affectionate father." Our people, Jefferson continued, "look upon you as brethren, born in the Same land, and having the same interests." At least before the War of 1812, Jefferson trusted these "children" could ascend to the status of "brethren": "You propose, my children," he wrote in another Indian address, to "become citizens thereof, and be ruled by our laws; in fine, to be our brothers instead of our children. . . . But are you prepared for this? Have you the resolution to leave off hunting for your living, to lay off a farm for each family to itself, to live by industry?"[78]

Remounting Thro' the Gloom of Ages towards Their Origin

This was Jefferson's real situation: quite often, Native Americans, at least many of them, made him furious, perhaps even triggering in him "martial" reactions; most of them, their minds and bodies alike, were for him "inveloped" in antiquity. Furthermore, as time went by, Jefferson experienced increased difficulty in making sense of their identities. Also, he came

Fig. 18. Entrance Hall or Indian Hall at Monticello, displaying artifacts and items shipped by Meriwether Lewis and William Clark from their expedition to the West. (©Thomas Jefferson Foundation at Monticello)

to despair about the practicality of assimilation. On the whole, the author of *Notes* was more expectant than the older philosopher, natural historian, and policy maker. What did not change was the way he saw Native Americans: Jefferson had all his life debased and objectified them, thus making them into a specimen of natural history. But "debasing" and "objectifying" or despairing and becoming increasingly unable to acknowledge the historical role these people still played in the colonization of North America cannot support the allegation that Jefferson simply "hated" or "despised" Native Americans. Notwithstanding all these difficulties, both practical and theoretical, he kept being attracted by Native Americans. The Indian Hall he put up at Monticello is the most evident response to a genuine, long-lasting *intellectual* appeal.[79]

Rather than "hate" or similar irrational feelings, the limit of Jefferson's modes of interaction and defensive reactions vis-à-vis this dimension of "otherness" is that he remained a rather traditional distant "father." He patronized. He thought his decisions were for the best. As to Indian "affairs," he never tried to don the costume of a caring, approachable, touchable mother. Maybe his roles as a public official prevented him from doing that. But as a matter of fact Jefferson never empathized. At most, he acknowledged the "injuries" a generic white "we" had "done them." Personally, he kept interacting with Native Americans objectively and intellectually, even when, *especially* when, he manifested high curiosity. Intellectual curiosity, in this sense, was a substitute for compassion and responsiveness. By looking at Native Americans through the lens of nature, and all the while remaining substantially unable to classify these people once and for all, Jefferson was mostly preoccupied with finding reliable examples, illustrations, and precedents for the American *white* nation. Through the Indian Hall he mainly represented *himself*.[80]

American Indians, for Jefferson, were left behind; but, at the same time, he hoped they could eventually be proved to be linked to European populations that had migrated into the Americas. Maybe, he hoped, they were not so aboriginal, primitive, and prehistorical to be totally irrelevant to the new nation. As we have seen, Jefferson denied the hypothesis of a separate creation. Assorted hypotheses about Indians' origins abounded in the late eighteenth century, making any sensible conclusion particularly difficult.

The analysis of Native American languages, by the same token, did not allow any clear-cut assumption. Jefferson had long been interested in collecting and preserving Indian vocabularies—another argument that counts for the intellectual appeal these original inhabitants had for him. Gathering information on Indian languages appeared to Jefferson a good method to verify if their origins could be traced back to some European or Middle Eastern population. It mattered a lot to establish whether American Indians were in the last analysis Europeans, or nearly Europeans. "I have long imagined," Jefferson, for example, wrote in 1799, "that if there exists at this day, any evidence of their descent from any nation of the old world, it will be found in their languages." Regrettably, as to the Indian origins and a common identity, "many hypotheses have been hazarded but none of them satisfactory."[81]

Although Jefferson was seriously on the lookout for hard evidence attesting to some degree of continuity between whites and native populations, he eventually despaired of finding reliable data about either a common identity between Native Americans and Europeans or for Native Americans among themselves. It was clear to Jefferson that collecting more and more vocabularies of Indian languages might increase the probability of establishing the degree of continuity. "I have several vocabularies," Jefferson wrote in 1798, "and have many out in the hands of my friends who are in situations to fill them up with the languages of different tribes." Unfortunately, once again, "the opinion I hazarded on the multiplicity of Indian languages radically different, was not on such foundations as to give me entire reliance on it." Much has been collected in order "to obtain a clue to their origin," but "my object being the true fact, I do not permit myself to form as yet a decisive opinion." Jefferson could not arrive at a definitive opinion on either of the two problems.[82]

These two problems, however, kept him busy. "The question," Jefferson wrote in 1805, "whether the Indians of America have emigrated from another continent, is still undecided. Their vague and imperfect traditions can satisfy no mind on that subject. I have long considered their languages as the only remaining monument of a connection with other nations or of the want of it, to which we can now have access." As to the second problem, collecting vocabularies would likewise show Indians' "connections with one another." Jefferson did not entirely discard the Middle Eastern hypothesis. As to the "red nations of Asia" (nations that, however, "I have never seen"), "a comparison of our collection with that will probably decide the question of the sameness or difference of origin."[83]

In the 1810s and 1820s, Jefferson kept amusing himself with hypotheses while perusing the wildest literature on the topic; but he had lost hope to arrive at certitude. Linking the origins of "our Indians" to the fugitive Trojans was really "amusing," as he acknowledged. Similarly, connecting them to the Jews, to the Tartars, and to the Persians was definitely entertaining. But the more this mature philosopher mulled over the issue, the more he despaired of "remounting thro' the gloom of ages towards their origin." By the 1820s, he could not help putting emphasis on the fact that "the analyses of their languages unfold to us structures of speech so radically different from those of the whole European families." Linguistically, culturally, and corporeally, Indians could after all represent only a radical "other," a conclusion Jefferson did not favor but had to accept. Not only their linguistic identities but as well their "peculiar" traditions and still more peculiar "naked" bodies could signal a type of "otherness" that Jefferson and his age were not equipped to welcome.[84]

Real Distinctions Which Nature Has Made

When Jefferson looked at African American bodies, he created another set of counterexamples to white "normality." In many ways, this is a simpler topic to analyze. While he tolerated, even commended, elements of Indianness, he frowned upon blackness. In this case, Jefferson's *racism* is the necessary point of departure. He may have lacked sincere empathy and commiseration when he interacted with Native Americans, but racism was absent. Even if American Indians were naturalized and objectified, these "nearly-dead" people seemed defeated more by history, circumstances, or bad choices, including their childish stubbornness not to embrace white style. They were not outranked by nature. While many circumstances certainly divided blacks and whites into parties, according to Jefferson the "real distinctions which nature has made" loomed much larger.[85]

The difference between his attitudes toward Native Americans and African Americans is striking. Instead of evoking at least the hypothesis of assimilation, acculturation, or incorporation, instead of trying to find in blacks' experience on the American continent coordinates and precedents functional to the (white) nation, Jefferson only cast eloquent warnings. In Query 14, Jefferson-the-physical-anthropologist expressed his famous, never recanted speculations. Let us start with ideas and opinions, first, and then move to Jefferson's modes of interaction:

> The first difference which strikes us is that of colour. Whether the black of the negro resides in the reticular membrane between the skin and scarfskin, or in the scarfskin itself; whether it proceeds from the colour of the blood, the colour of the bile, or from that of some other secretion, the difference is fixed in nature, and is as real as if its seat and cause were better known to us. And is this difference of no importance? Is it not the foundation of a greater or less share of beauty in the two races? Are not the fine mixtures of red and white, the expressions of every passion by greater or less suffusions of colour in the one, preferable to that eternal monotony, which reigns in the countenances, that immoveable veil of black which covers all the emotions of the other race?[86]

Differences, Jefferson claimed, were "fixed in nature." More than that, those differences were the "foundation" of precise moral and aesthetic qualities that Jefferson habitually censored. In dealing with the "negro" body, he thus jumped from a natural, physical, descriptive mode to a mode in which he expressed norms and values—what is usually termed a naturalistic fallacy. Black color was ugly, he claimed, monotonous, less preferable than white. It was for Jefferson a deficit to lack, for example, a "fine mixtures of red and white." We have already encountered Jefferson pronouncing the lack of such a red and white (a quality, by the way, of which Jefferson himself abounded) as a deficit. African American albinos were "of a pallid cadaverous white, untinged with red." Albinos were ugly, but "regular" blacks were no less unpleasant. The color black itself was at once ugly and morally questionable, even intrinsically deceitful, as it hid "emotions." Surprisingly, blacks had for Jefferson almost no eyes, no expression, no face, no hands, no gestures and elaborate manners, no verbal and nonverbal codes through which they could convey thoughts and meanings.[87]

His method of jumping from facts to qualities and values (or, better, disvalues) was problematic; but his "scientific" discourse, meant to better observe and categorize blacks, rested on decontextualization. Jefferson's naturalizations targeting blacks made them, at the same time, highly decontextualized—their expressive and culture-ridden bodies almost dismembered and anatomically isolated. Jefferson's membranes, scarf-skins, bile and blood, glands and pulmonary apparatuses, fluids and perspirations, were not neutral, "objective" characteristics of these bodies. As we may say, Jefferson *framed* black bodies.

Several times in Query 14 Jefferson deployed a language centered on physiological elements arbitrarily selected: "They secrete less by the kidnies, and more by the glands of the skin, which gives them a very strong and disagreeable odour. . . . Perhaps too a difference of structure in the pulmonary apparatus . . . may have disabled them from extricating, in the act of inspiration, so much of that fluid from the outer air, or obliged them in expiration, to part with more of it." Behavioral elements were also arbitrarily selected: "They seem to require less sleep. A black, after hard labour through the day, will be induced by the slightest amusements to sit up till midnight or later, though knowing he must be out with the first dawn of the morning." "Science" allowed Jefferson to see certain things, to construe certain corporeal differences as natural, while completely ignoring the larger context of social and cultural conditions.[88]

In this precise case, anatomical decontextualization made Jefferson's eyes extremely weak. Had he not subjected "negritude" to such a high level of anatomical "objectivity," Jefferson might have more easily seen that this "race" of people, *his* blacks, was in no way different; he might have seen that his blacks were simply wounded by exploitation, suffering, and cultural deprivation. Jefferson did not understand, for example, that certain behaviors, like sitting up until midnight seeking for "amusement," were due to the slave's effort to feel social connection and regain the warmth lost during the alienating toil of fieldwork in his master's fields. Slaves made the deliberate decision to sacrifice sleep because they pined for either family or community. After the scientist and natural historian had abstracted single elements from the large context of slavery, thus framing these bodies, the Enlightenment humanitarian could more easily avoid engagement. He could hardly afford to empathize with these fellow human beings or let alone interact with real individuals as if they were simply other men and women—not carriers of so many deficits.

In the same way that Jefferson-the-natural-historian "observed" that enslaved African Americans needed less sleep, he also "observed," to take another example, that the men of this "race," if they could, would choose, sexually or otherwise, the "more elegant symmetry of form" of white women's bodies. Blacks' "judgment in favour of the whites," Jefferson concluded, was demonstrated by the fact of their males preferring white women, "as uniformly as is the preference of the Oranootan for the black women over those of his own species."[89]

Jefferson was not original on this last topic. European explorers had repeatedly associated Africans and apes, as to their corporeal characteristics. But the fact is that after naturalizing and decontextualizing black bodies, Jefferson had liberated his racism: their "want of forethought" makes them only stupidly brave; "their griefs are transient"; their existence "appears to participate more of sensation than reflection"; albeit "in memory they are equal to the whites," their reason is "much inferior, as I think one could scarcely be found capable of tracing and comprehending the investigations of Euclid"; in imagination "they are dull, tasteless, and anomalous." Idealized Indians, on the other hand, "often carve figures on their pipes not destitute of design and merit"; they can "astonish you with strokes of the most sublime oratory," but "never yet could I find that a black had uttered a thought above the level of plain narration; never see even an elementary trait of painting or sculpture."[90]

Degrade a Whole Race of Men

An Enlightenment devotee, Jefferson was not entirely convinced of his judgments upon blackness. The reader can actually find many warnings in Query 14: "The opinion," Jefferson wrote, "that they are inferior in the faculties of reason and imagination, must be hazarded with great diffidence." Jefferson was aware that hasty conclusions would "degrade a whole race of men from the rank in the scale of beings which their Creator may perhaps have given them." Black and red races, Jefferson allowed, "have never yet been viewed by us as subjects of natural history." His hypothesis of African American corporeal and mental inferiority was, as he said, "a suspicion only." However, as he also said, any "lover of natural history" knows that "different species of the same genus, or varieties of the same species" possessing "different qualifications," exist in nature. Awareness of gradations and natural hierarchies "in all the races of animals" would easily excuse "an effort to keep those in the department of man as distinct as nature has formed them." Jefferson's scientific training as a collector of specimens, classifier, and observer of nature, in other words, allowed him to rate his suspicions as highly probable.[91]

A couple of pages before offering his "suspicions," Jefferson had already concluded that "the improvement of the blacks in body and mind, in the first instance of their mixture with the whites, has been observed by every one, and proves that their inferiority is not the effect merely of their condition of life." It was an "unfortunate difference of colour," and only disappearing into whiteness could save these people. Jefferson never doubted his own judgment about the "ugliness" of African Americans—whether or not further observation would eventually back up his "suspicions," and whether or not natural historians would ultimately establish that the faculties of blacks are equal to those of whites. Red bodies were in a sort of dialectical continuity, no matter how problematic, but black bodies from the start were, and up to the end remained, the white body's opposite other.[92]

A black body was ugly, abnormal—even when, or especially when, it was seized by the highest of human sentiments, love. Love did not ennoble blacks, Jefferson claimed in *Notes*. Black love was grotesque, a parody. "Their love is ardent, but it kindles the senses only, not the imagination"; "love seems with them to be more an eager desire, than a tender delicate mixture of sentiment and sensation." We can easily picture these hapless bodies as convulsed, tribal, revealing what was for Jefferson the ultimate obstacle to every hypothesis of emancipation, acculturation, and civilization: the color black would end up staining the white. Philanthropists and advocates of the liberty of human nature, as Jefferson wrote, were "anxious also to preserve its dignity and beauty." "Among the Romans, emancipation required but one effort. The [white] slave, when made free, might mix with, without staining the blood of his master. But with us a second [effort] is necessary, unknown to history. When freed, he is to be removed beyond the reach of mixture."[93]

Ominous ideas such as these, needless to say, belong to a precise period of Jefferson's life. With all the cautiousness and "suspicions" only, the author of *Notes* had indeed treated African Americans as if these people had no history, no families, no specificity, no individuality, and no dignity. During the same period, Indians were singled out by their proper names—Powhatans,

Mannahoacs, Monacans, Meherrins, Tuteloes. Blacks, in contrast, remained an undifferentiated racial mass of naturalized subordinated humanity.

Even the qualities and corporeal performances Jefferson praised in African Americans reflected precise biases and an ongoing, albeit largely unconscious, process of naturalization: "In music they [blacks] are more generally gifted than the whites with accurate ears for tune and time, and they have been found capable of imagining a small catch." Maybe further observation would contradict the suspicion "that nature has been less bountiful to them in the endowments of the head." In effect, Jefferson was convinced, "in those of the heart she [nature] will be found to have done them justice." When blacks pilfer from their masters it is not for a "disposition" but because of "their situation"; there is no "depravity of the moral sense." Obedient and submissive, African Americans' integrity was nonetheless reduced, at least in *Notes,* to a machinelike reflex. Blacks were "rigid," once again unimaginative and utterly predictable: "we find among them numerous instances of the most rigid integrity, and as many as among their better instructed masters, of benevolence, gratitude, and unshaken fidelity."[94]

Hic Niger Est, Hunc Tu Romane Caveto

Naturalizations, a gradualist approach, lack of time for fresh research, and of course slavery as a thriving institution combined to form a lethal amalgam. These factors, at once theoretical, biographical, and material, did not help Jefferson recognize that blacks' radical "otherness," including their "ugliness," was *only* the outcome of material, social, cultural, intellectual dynamics. In no way can human "otherness" be a natural fact and a point of departure. African Americans were obviously *kept* in a condition of difference. Many expedients were in use, none of them invented by Jefferson or exclusive to him; they ranged from direct violence to other, subtler trickeries.

We do not have to insist on the fact that African Americans' bodies were made the target of continuous, planned acts of violence, both private and institutional. Systematic institutional violence or, in other words, slavery was obviously the main culprit. But blacks were stifled in their condition of minority and otherness by several other artifices. Prejudices, mental habits, and linguistic patterns formed an invisible alliance that was detrimental to any hypothesis of African Americans' liberation. Lucia Stanton, for example, sees a revealing index in the fact that Jefferson habitually used diminutives when he referred to his slaves. It was far from neutral that Edward, for example, had become "Ned," or Frances "Fanny." "His views on racial inferiority," Stanton writes, "pushed the blacks around him down the 'scale of beings.'"[95]

Automatic, prereflexive associations between the word "black" and many forms of negativity operated as effectively. In many cultures across time and space, the color black had consistently elicited bad connotations. "The blackest traitor who has ever disgraced the American history" is but one among the many automatic associations in Jefferson's mind. Expressions like "the blackest slanders!" or the more elaborate "I would say with the poet [Horace] 'hic niger est, hunc tu Romane caveto' [That man is black of heart; of him beware, good Roman]" are revealing tropes in Jefferson's writings. Possibly worse, for several exponents of white Euro-American culture, as cultural anthropologists would agree, "black" ushered in "obvious" negative metaphysical powers—the Death, the Unknown, the Evil. On a more prosaic level, centuries-old links between dark complexions and dirt, both physical and moral, have been convincingly tracked down. As Frantz Fanon has summarized the problem, "the torturer is the black man, Satan is black, one talks of shadows, when one is dirty one is black—whether one is thinking of physical dirtiness or moral dirtiness."[96]

But material processes other than violence were at play as well. Jefferson-the-caring-grandfather who in his avowals sought "to feed & clothe them well" at the same time contributed to a very expedited way to debase his chattel slaves. It was far from neutral that chattel looked visually like chattel. It was not Jefferson's personal fault, but the clothing allotment that every master provided at his plantations trapped African Americans within precise graphic stereotypes.[97]

In December 1794, Jefferson started recording the food and clothing he gave to his slaves. This master was attentive but not strikingly generous: his slaves received a summer and winter outfit each year, a blanket every three years, and shoes for those who were more than ten years old. Jefferson's slaves wore "negro cloth," coarse "kearsies," duffels, osnaburgs, blue and checked linen, coarse "garlix" and calicoes, checked cottons, and Scotch plaids. Visually, Jefferson's slaves stayed faithful to what slaves in America were supposed to wear. It was cheaper, more functional, and more sensible to rely on these types of fabrics and coarse, practical, pregenteel cuts. But this was precisely part of the problem: by wearing their allotted clothing, African Americans in bondage were misled into believing that their diminished self-representation was "logical" and "natural." Masters, for their part, could not heed that the dirtiness of these "others," including their "brownishness," was the effect, not the rationale, of a diminished status.[98]

Give Wool to Any of My Negro Women Who Desire It

Jefferson was considerate, and no person escaped his care: "I am very glad to learn that the negroes have recieved their clothes," he wrote in 1814. "Not having enough [wool] for our people here," he wrote the same recipient in 1815, "we will try a mixture of hemp & cotton for the negro children here." To the very end, he remained solicitous toward everybody: "I hope the negro-clothing is in it's way," he wrote in 1826. Obviously, not all of Jefferson's slaves were treated equally. The memorandum Jefferson wrote for overseer Edmund Bacon in 1807 shows his *relative* generosity. It also reveals that many differences existed within the household: "Clothes for the people are to be got from mr Higginbotham of the kind heretofore got. I allow them a best striped blanket every 3. years. . . . mrs Randolph always chuses the clothing for the house servants, that is to say for Peter Hemings, Burwell, Edwin, Critta and Sally. colored plains are provided for Betty Brown, Betty Hemings, Nance, Ursula, and indeed all the others, the nailers, labourers, & Hirelings may have it if they prefer it to cotton. wool is given for stockings to those who will have it spun & knit for themselves. . . . give wool to any of my negro women who desire it, as well those with mr Craven as others, but particularly to the house women here."[99]

The point here just as elsewhere in this book is not to induce the conclusion that Jefferson was stingy, evil, a monster. He was generous, at least selectively. Notwithstanding his naturalizations, his problematic theories about inferiority, and his gradualism, he provided for the basics for all of his slaves. But he did not, and could not, radically break the established patterns of discrimination and brutality, including his double, perhaps multiple standards. The vast majority of the blacks Jefferson owned were not so lucky as to being able to choose the "wool" and other commodities they desired or simply needed. They did not have the chance to exert their choice, thus empowering themselves. Whether he liked it or not, Jefferson saw and treated these people as he was expected to see and treat them: as laboring bodies. All in all, and independently from his racial biases and other "scientific" ideas, what he did was to distance whites from blacks, the "normal" from what he thought was the "abnormal," and himself from the persons who were in his possession.[100]

The vast majority of the black bodies Jefferson owned signified labor.

Before any theory of "natural" inferiority or a gradualist approach or a thought and idea whatsoever could even *start* to produce an effect, black bodies were already kept in that "operative" condition. This type of body figures prominently, for example, in Jefferson's Farm Book and every time he made a point about agriculture, about horses, cattle, crops, and so on. This was African Americans' obvious "natural" context.

After Jefferson quit his position as secretary of state, at the end of 1793, to return to Monticello, he took a renewed interest in farming, its tools, techniques, and operations. Enthusiasm for agriculture and planning on slaves' labor were one and the same: "I am for throwing the whole force of my husbandry on the wheat-field, because it is the only one which is to go to market to produce money," he wrote to John Taylor in December 1794. "I count on potatoes, clover and sheep. The two former to feed every animal on the farm except my negroes, and the latter to feed them, diversified with rations of salted fish and molasses, both of them wholesome, agreeable and cheap articles of food." To feed them cheaply and clothe them adequately were instrumental to enhancing production.[101]

Correspondence about hiring "negroes," lending them, and conducting many forms of transactions abound. These bodies were and remained materials for trade; they represented both labor and economic assets—and all this took place before Jefferson's critical sense could even start acting. In 1798, for example, Jefferson was embittered by the fact that the "tax on lands houses & negroes goes on." Four years later, while discussing "blackseed" and "greenseed" cotton and "pine lands mixed with oak & hickory bushes" and "lands yield[ing] 4. 5. 6. barrels to the acre," Jefferson concluded that "a good negro labourer, young will sell for from 550. to 600. D. Ned Rutledge's whole stock young & old averaged lately 480. D." In many cases, it is impossible to ascertain if Jefferson's discomfort about "this kind of labour" was motivated by humanitarian or rather financial and utilitarian reasons: "I find I am not fit to be a farmer with the kind of labour we have," he wrote in 1799. Since enhancing efficiency was a goal to attain, he could not help lamenting that this kind of "labour" was especially unreliable and discontinuous.[102]

In spite of a notorious and indeed commendable aversion to sell slaves or break up families, Jefferson was impelled to look at these enslaved bodies through a utilitarian lens. There is no way to minimize that Jefferson was reared into a system that physically coerced these persons into functionalized spaces (fields, kitchens, or shops) and turned these bodies into economic devices. Blacks were less than "signs," like Native Americans were: African

Americans did not remind Euro-Americans of a "link" with the continent. They did not elicit a sense of belonging. Each time Jefferson relapsed into his actual normality, the daily life of a master, he *obviously* saw black bodies moving about the field or the house to carry out functions. In other words, to keep alive the perception that these bodies were more than assets or devices performing a function, Jefferson had to sustain a psychological effort—often, for him, an impossible one. Relapsing into normality, and not thinking hard enough, he bounced back to the obvious vocabulary of functions, markets, taxes, money, and transactions.

As to this last point, he knew that selling slaves was highly lucrative, often more than the profit brought by their labor in the fields. Jefferson had good financial reasons, for example, to complain about the high mortality rate of infant slaves at the plantation of Poplar Forest. In 1819, he wrote that "the loss of 5. little ones in a year induces me to fear that the overseers do not permit the women to devote as much time as is necessary to the care of their children." Overseers were wrong in focusing on the productivity of the fields exclusively, but Jefferson's complaint was motivated by more than humanitarian reasons. The "breeding woman," he knew, could generate a far more cost-effective staple.[103]

Jefferson could not ignore that the Louisiana territories his presidency had secured increased the market for Virginia slave breeders. In the same letter to overseer Yancey, Jefferson himself betrayed the mentality of a breeder. More than in anything else, at least on this occasion, he was interested in reproduction: "I consider the labor of a breeding woman as no object, and that a child raised every 2. years is of more profit than the crop of the best laboring man. . . . with respect therefore to our women & their children I must pray you to inculcate upon the overseers that it is not their labor, but their increase which is the first consideration with us."[104]

I Remember the Appearance of the Interior of That Cabin

A brutal system made Jefferson's eyes myopic at best. Of course, a number of other victims existed that demand incomparably higher levels of compassion. But one consequence was that Jefferson missed a lot about African American selves, bodies and minds alike. Not only did he not fully grasp, as said, the reason why his slaves sat up "till midnight." He did not see their beauty, their history, their dignity, their efforts, their ingenuity, and the many dimensions of an ongoing drama. Among other things, he overlooked entire sets of corporeal dimensions. Whether or not Jefferson was personally duplicitous and evil (for example, engaging in slave commerce and breeding despite an ideological "aversion"), the fact is that the words he uttered about African Americans elicit one visual perception over many others. Jefferson gives us the image of the black body as crouched, dirty, dressed in rough osnaburg, bearing a hideous grin, diminished, and disfigured by stupidity and hard labor.

Counterfactuals, of course, have no room in historical narratives, but had Jefferson not been Jefferson-the-gradualist-meliorist or Jefferson-the-grieving-Virginia-master, he would have beheld the effort many African Americans exerted in order to appear different from those crouched, stupid, and dirty bodies—simple means to an end. In the slave cabins on Mulberry Row, especially those occupied by the large Hemings family, we catch a glimpse of what kind of nonstereotypical self Jefferson's luckier "servants" were trying to preserve.

Jefferson's last great-grandchild, Martha J. Trist Burke, upon visiting John and Priscilla Hemings's cabin, was possibly impressed by just that kind of effort. Little Martha was less than three years old when she saw what her great-grandfather had probably never noticed, or at any rate had never talked about—that African American slaves obviously liked cleanness, tidiness, and little comforts. Amid the direness of their situation and relative material deprivation, many blacks staged corporeal performances of dignity. Each time they could, they stepped outside of functionalized spaces and moved on a "private" stage of their own choice, with character, decorum, and full-fledged humanity. "I remember the appearance of the interior of that cabin," great-grandchild Martha wrote in her journal, "the position of the bed with it's white counterpane & ruffled pillow cases & of the little table with it's clean white cloth, & a shelf over it, on which stood an old fashioned band box with wall paper covering, representing dogs running, this box excited my admiration and probably fixed the whole scene in my mind."[105]

Some black bodies, within Jefferson's own plantation as well, moved against a background made of white clean cloth and conjured *petit bourgeois* coziness, delicacy, and "femininity." Maybe, at some point in his life, Jefferson did enlarge his observations of these hapless persons, "natural specimens" though they were, discovering that more dimensions belonged to black identity, whether corporeal or spiritual. But no conclusive evidence remains. The big chapter of the "negro" fashion, their style and taste, is missing from Jefferson's narrative. Among other things, historians have reached decisive conclusions that enslaved blacks were aware of style and produced style. We cannot be certain if Jefferson ever grasped the liberating, *creative* power couched in either black fashion or in simple pillows, white counterpanes, clean white tablecloths, and boxes covered with paper representing dogs running.[106]

As White As I Am

Although African American bodies were deemed "naturally" different, theoretical and perceptive thresholds have always been rather blurred. Albinism and vitiligo, as discussed above, were only the two most manifest cases, but they were "anomalies," for Jefferson. These cases were relatively easy to rationalize: freaks, tricks, diseased bodies, peculiarities of nature, these people did not carry "real" whiteness. They seemed neither to launch a call for liberation nor for a revision of established patterns of discrimination.

The perceptive threshold was more seriously called into question each time "interbreeding" and "miscegenation" took place. Blacks "staining the blood" of whites were a source of anxiety for both medical reasons and for the fact that "apparent" perceptive patterns were being disrupted. Could "negritude" be negotiable? Was it flexible? Were black bodies becoming simple and "modern"? Comte de Volney visited Monticello in June 1796. He found Sally Hemings's nephews and nieces "as white as I am." The same year, the Duc de La Rochefoucauld-Liancourt noticed slaves who had "neither in their color nor features a single trace of their origin, but they are sons of slave mothers and consequently slaves." Biographer Henry Randall visited Monticello many years later. Thomas Jefferson Randolph told him about "children which resembled Mr. Jefferson so closely that it was plain that they had his blood in their veins." Randall refers to Thomas Jefferson Randolph saying that "in one case . . . the resemblance was so close, that at some distance or in the dusk that slave, dressed in the same way, might be taken for Mr. Jefferson." A gentleman dining with Jefferson "looked so startled as he raised his eyes from [Jefferson] to the servant behind him, that his discovery of the resemblance was perfectly obvious to all."[107]

Was black "otherness" just an enormous conceit? Was it contrived simply to maintain the slaveholding class's privileges? It was apparent that among Virginia slave owners, the self was becoming the other. Yet Jefferson's generation, and many other American generations to come, were convinced they could explain the rationale beneath these corporeal differences. For them, differences existed; they *had to* exist. Sally Hemings was "near white," percep-

tively, and yet, as to her "substance," she was a "negro." Color per se, qualities we see and touch, did not make one free or slave in eighteenth-century
Virginia. One of Sally's grandmothers was African, the other was white
European. Also, her two grandfathers were white. Her mother, Betty, was a
mulatto, and her father was, of course, white—John Wayles, Thomas Jefferson's father-in-law. Isaac Jefferson says Sally was "mighty near white," with
"long straight hair down her back." Thomas Jefferson Randolph describes
her as "light colored." But despite her appearance, she was not really white.
Under Virginia law, Africans could over several generations become whites,
but only through a single pathway that had to be measured.[108]

The letter Jefferson sent to Francis Calley Gray on 4 March 1815 is a very
interesting document, especially from an epistemological point of view. This
letter tells us something important about the way a system of knowledge can
be based on erroneous premises and about the way an entire enlightened
age and even a brilliant mind, like Jefferson's, could be trapped in erroneous
questions and wrong theoretical models. Instead of dismissing Gray's query
on "what makes a mulatto" as downright ludicrous, and instead of picking up
the occasion to openly criticize Virginia law for its, in turn, ludicrous attempt
at defining a "mulatto," Jefferson took the "mulatto question" very seriously.

"I told you 4 crossings with the whites" make a "mulatto," he wrote Gray.
But Jefferson looked even deeper: "I looked afterwards into our law, and found
it to be in these words. 'every person, other than a negro, of whose grandfathers or grandmothers any one shall have been a negro, shall be deemed a
mulatto, and so every such person who shall have one fourth part or more of
negro blood; shall in like manner be deemed a mulatto.'" More interestingly,
Jefferson believed that the issue of the blood mixture was "a Mathematical
problem of the same class with those on the mixtures of different liquors or
different metals." If mathematics was "ever my favorite" study, in which "all
is demonstration & satisfaction," as he wrote in 1811, the account of these
"fractional mixtures" was for Jefferson no less than fascinating, worthy of a
sophisticated analysis. The problem raised by white and black blood mixing
was worthy of an "Algebraical notation."[109]

Most likely, Gray's query struck a chord with Jefferson. The ensuing intricate calculi tell us something about Jefferson's character and personality as
well as about the "truth" he thought he could discover: challenge Jefferson on
the terrain of a question involving the possibility of measurements and calculi and what you will get is a diagram, a graph, or an intricate table.

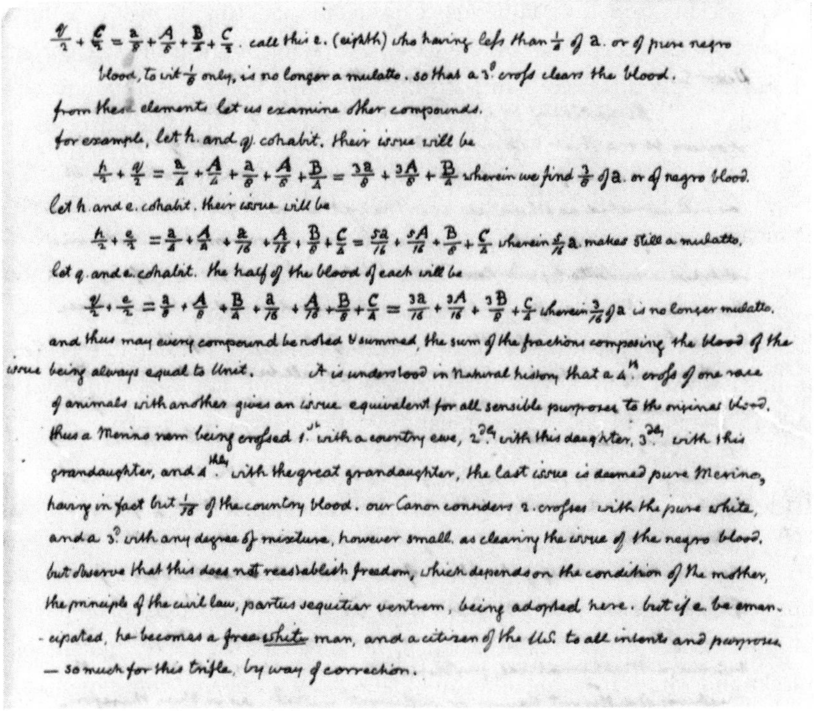

Fig. 19: Detail of Jefferson's letter to Francis Calley Gray, 4 March 1815.

But at least in this case there was more: Jefferson was an enlightened thinker embracing science while rejecting occult qualities and metaphysical substances. Like other minds of the time, he was nonetheless wary of approving of just-what-he-saw—at least in many fields of human experience. In this case as well, he had a feeling he needed rationalizations and calculi to keep track of the gradations, breaks, and leaps within the given fixed natural hierarchy, leading from the black body to the white. These calculi were obviously complicated. The reason for such a complication was that the model to account for human "races" and their intermixing was problematic from the outset, no less wrong than the Ptolemaic model in respect to the Copernican—hence the complicated calculi and conceptual conundrums (like epicycles and other complications) geocentrists needed to make sense of the things they observed.

Jefferson could master corporeal "gradations" rationally and mathematically. This kind of "scientific" method warded off the anxiety of confusion and especially empathy. Mathematics, rationality, and the rhetoric of natural history assessed corporeal "differences" in what for him was the sole correct approach: "it is understood in Natural history that a 4th cross of one race of animals with another gives an issue equivalent for all sensible purposes to the original blood. thus a Merino ram being crossed 1st with a country ewe, 2dly with this daughter, 3dly with this grandaughter, and 4^{thly} with the great grandaughter, the last issue is deemed pure Merino, having in fact but 1/16 of the country blood." Human bodies must be treated the same way: "our Canon considers 2. crosses with the pure white, and a 3^{d} with any degree of mixture, however small, as clearing the issue of the negro blood." Human differences, in other words, were neither a moral nor a social nor an intellectual nor a cultural issue. They were given in nature, not made by a group of white men.

Indelible Lines of Distinction Between Them

In many ways the line of separation between white and black bodies could not be clearly drawn. Not only were "quadroons" and mulattoes perceptively "almost white," but the business of daily life called for several renegotiations. Blacks and whites lived together, and this very fact triggered consequences.

Many black bodies were an enduring intimate presence in Jefferson's real, material life—beyond the life he led, alone, in his mind. He interacted with Jupiter, Burwell Colbert, Joseph Fossett, George Granger Sr. and Jr., the Hemingses, and many other black persons, both male and female. They had access to Jefferson's corporeality. He kept endorsing his racism and his "natural" hierarchies up to the end, but without doubt these body systems were more than characters in a literary narrative or a chapter in Jefferson's problematic arithmetic of race.

He may have not relied expectantly upon their mental faculties or their political autonomy, but in fact he took interest in the life of many of his enslaved African Americans. He freed at least some of them. Jefferson trained many slaves and made them into carpenters, joiners, valets, stone-cutters, hostlers, coachmen, shoemakers, weavers, spinners, blacksmiths, tinsmiths, nail-makers, gardeners, stablemen, and domestic servants. Unfortunately, this is no clear indication that the humanity of these persons ever emerged full-fledged from below a more or less dark pigmentation and hit Jefferson's eyes. The embodied Jefferson situated himself in the world of his enslaved people, but we are not aware of the precise degree of sharing and emotional proximity that Jefferson experienced. Was his interest motivated by pragmatic reasons? Did he want to enhance the "competitiveness" of his plantation? Did he feel affection? Compassion? Love? Were blacks means to an end or simply ends?[110]

Many eighteenth-century Virginia masters felt not only affection and compassion but love as well. As Joshua Rothman writes, they "embraced their interracial families in their homes and raised their multiracial children as they would have any white child." This did not happen sporadically. In a context in which liaisons between whites and blacks were tolerated when carried out discretely, but were publicly condemned each time they trespassed the household, many masters became nonetheless overtly attached to their mistresses. Heartless domination and rape may seem the sole, obvious pattern to describe white men's and black women's interactions, but *emotional* boundaries cannot be clearly fixed. Whites may have despised blacks, but as often whites and nonwhites, or "almost whites," lived intense emotional lives. Racial distinctions and "gradations" were the cornerstones of Virginia society, but "both forced and consensual sexual connections between blacks and whites were constituent of familial and communal life in that society." Not sporadically, daily life disproved widespread theories and mathematical demonstrations about a "natural" separation. Many masters succumbed to the power of limber and beautiful African American body systems.[111]

There is an obvious emotional and physical chemistry that takes place each time two persons, a woman and a man, or any other possible combination, live together. Esteem, either intellectual or moral, compassion, affection, not necessarily love, may and do in fact occur. While we cannot rule out the hypothesis that Jefferson felt a degree of emotional attachment, at least toward *some* African Americans (Sally Hemings will return at the end of this book), what looks more plausible is that he always worked very hard to defend the problematic, artificial differences he had so ingeniously devised and in the end called "natural." The undifferentiated mass of these individuals, the "race," was and remained, for him, the problem.

Since the time of *Notes,* Jefferson had focused on keeping distance. "Distance," in all its declinations, remained the foremost descriptor of Jefferson's modes of interactions toward blacks. At least in public, he never yielded to renegotiation. In *Notes,* Jefferson had given appalling figures, and the specter of rebellion had been conjured to rhetorical effect: 270,762 Virginia inhabitants out of 567,614 were blacks. It was enough for him to feel that the republic was besieged. Rebellions in Virginia and the nightmare of the Haitian Revolution (1791–1804) had kept the white ruling class awake. Jefferson did not personally go through open violent rebellions—except in 1822, when three slaves from Poplar Forest attacked the overseer and allegedly stabbed him. Within Jefferson's plantations, relative social harmony reigned. He was a fairly mild and beloved master, possibly because he had known from the time of the Revolution that slaves could be creatively "un-loyal." Nineteen of Jefferson's slaves had sought their liberty by joining British forces, but many others had repeatedly engaged in daily acts of resistance by running away, or stealing food and goods, or working at a slow pace.[112]

To safeguard "distance," Jefferson did not rely on punishment, direct confrontation, or repression—if not sporadically and in exceptional cases, as seen. Rebellions, in turn, had to be obviously suppressed—and Jefferson's attitudes toward the Haitian Revolution, for example, left no doubts as to his resolve. Planning, prevention, calculations should do most of the job, however. Jefferson was perhaps more frightened by promiscuity, opaqueness, and "confusion" than by open hostility.[113]

Blacks and whites, in the long run, should simply stop living together. Jefferson's peculiar plan of recolonizing blacks somewhere else to prevent a catastrophic race war, as he claimed, is problematic from many points of view. But there was more here than just the anxiety to avert a declared war between two races. Deportation was perfectly coherent if foiling temptation and corporeal "confusion" was a target to be pursued. Recolonizing blacks somewhere else, better if far away, was a logical countermeasure if the "natural" difference between white and black races was given in nature. As Jefferson wrote in his so-called autobiography, "Nothing is more certainly written in the book of fate than that these people are to be free. Nor is it less certain that the two races, equally free, cannot live in the same government. Nature, habit, opinion has drawn indelible lines of distinction between them."[114]

Should this fantastic plan have been carried out, it would have counted as another brutal act of aggression waged against this already brutalized people. Jefferson had started thinking seriously about deportation at the dawn of the nineteenth century, after the slave conspiracy in Virginia known as Gabriel's Rebellion (August 1800). And he kept advocating the feasibility, convenience, and coherence of the plan to the very end. In 1802, he had fantasized about "transporting" slaves "guilty of insurgency" to Africa: "we might, for this purpose, enter into negociations with the natives, on some part of the coast, to obtain a settlement, and, by establishing an African company, combine with it commercial operations, which might not only reimburse expences but procure profit also." But maybe, since the English Sierra Leone Company had already begun "colonising civilized blacks to that country," it would be more reasonable "incorporating our emigrants with theirs, to make one strong, rather than two weak colonies."[115]

Motives to defend the plan of deportation of both insurgents and "freed negroes and persons of colour" were at once utilitarian and theoretical, or rather ideological: a seemingly good strategy to prevent "confusion" of body colors and natures. Whether Africa or the West Indies, as Jefferson seemed to prefer by the end of his life, blacks could not be kept in dangerous close proximity to white bodies. Turning emancipated slaves into "serfs," another of Jefferson's ideas, would definitely be "better than keeping them in their present condition," but still preferable would be "expatriation"—as if they had a "Fatherland" to begin with. "I consider that of expatriation to the governments of the W. I. of their own colour as entirely practicable," he wrote in 1826 to William Short, "and greatly preferable to the mixture of colour here. to this I have great aversion; but I repeat my abandonment of the subject."[116]

Let Your Clothes Be Neat, Whole, and Properly Put On

Let us now consider the third and last form of "otherness," women. (And for this third group as well the discourse remains fundamentally anthropological—it is about Jefferson interacting with undifferentiated women, with the gender, with female "nature" as a whole, some notable individual exceptions notwithstanding.) Anthropologically, a woman's body, no less than her "soul" and mind, has been deemed "different" from the male standard for centuries. Elaborate theories, or simply myths, have been devised to trap women within real or imagined cages. Biblical culture, Classical antiquity, and the Middle Ages begot countless ideas of a radical, even demonic, "otherness." Abnormality, supernaturality, and so on were qualities repeatedly attributed to the "weaker sex"—no matter the race and the social class. Everybody knows that witches were still executed in late seventeenth-century Massachusetts. Fortunately, few of these ideas survived intact into the age of the Enlightenment.[117]

Jefferson and his generation had no theory of a radical otherness. Of course, they had biases and innumerable unconscious prejudices that in many ways belittled women's value, both spiritually and corporeally. They had anxieties and put blame on this perhaps more problematic type of human "other." Women stick out as moving within a less organized epistemological space when they are compared to either Native Americans or African Americans. American Indians were "primitive" bodies, and, as Jefferson believed, they were defeated by history; blacks were an "inferior" and "ugly" race, furthermore kept within unbreakable limits by the institution of slavery. But in many ways (white) women were, on the whole, models expected to play important roles within the new nation. They were not simply the *negative* double of an ideal male normality: stupid, ugly, and construed as insignificant, either for racial or for historical reasons.

A tension is here evident: during the age of Jefferson, women could be virtuous and vicious at the same time. A woman's nature was believed to bring to bear specific virtues. She could be read as simple, modest, welcoming, a "republican mother," and therefore could contribute in a significant way to the pursuit of general happiness. At the same time, however, she was especially dangerous. Although not as dangerous as the Evil or the Devil, a woman was often perceived as voluptuous, uncontrolled, irrational, and seductive. She wielded power, sexually and beyond the sexual domain. The reaction such a female power triggered was unsurprising. This power had to be curtailed, and almost every expedient was admissible. Recurring to violence other than sexual violence was not infrequent, but jokes, innuendos, and many other strategies were endemic.

Women were definitely subject to hierarchies, but they posed a special threat to eighteenth-century male "normality." The problem was that they were not simply the distant, negative "other." Described as the "weaker sex," they were near, dwelling in intimate spaces, allowed to dispense peace. Wives, mothers, and many other types of women enjoyed significant levels of equality. Race distinctions, conversely, made relations much more rigid. Women were regarded as inferior to men but, as Dallett Hemphill writes in her study of manners in America, "gender inequality was not the most fundamental form of inequality in this culture; instead, it was the mildest form." Relative equality explains why women's behavior was rather unconstructed. Eighteenth-century conduct literature, for example, advised women to abstain from making bold statements in public or putting up antireverential and defying attitudes. They were expected to appear in public not as if they were poised to conquer their vital space, like warriors and Amazons. Yet "they were also advised that the intimacy of their relations with the opposite sex allowed some talk," Hemphill concludes. The "weaker sex" had an impact by being in the perfect position to "sollicit" many favors, to borrow from Jefferson a revealing verb.[118]

That women as a whole were no longer depicted as monsters, or devilish creatures, did not mean that they were automatically considered "normal" either. Their generous bodies, which could sooth a male, hosted a set of "peculiar" characteristics. Both in Europe and in America, men looked at women's bodies as at once attractive and repulsive objects—no matter how accomplished or refined and visibly upper class single female individuals may have been.

By the eighteenth century, the notion that the female body was intrinsically filthier than a male body was still widespread. "Only with great difficulty," Kathleen Brown has written, "could a woman conquer the natural loathsomeness of her body. This acute sensitivity to the filth of the female body reflected centuries of wisdom about its special corrupting power, only recently overlaid with a veneer of gentility." Mathew Carey's popular *Lady's Pocket Library* (1794) insisted that every woman, especially the younger ones, should work hard to contain her bodily functions, like eating and drinking, and to appear neat. A woman would easily elicit disgust. Fathers, tutors, and all the males who had promoted themselves to the role of controller repeated the advice to "guard your body" over and over again. "Above all things and at all times," Jefferson, for example, wrote to eleven-year-old Martha, "let your clothes be neat, whole, and properly put on. . . . A lady who has been seen as a sloven or slut in the morning, will never efface the impression she then made with all the dress and pageantry she can afterwards involve herself in. Nothing is so disgusting to our sex as a want of cleanliness and delicacy in yours."[119]

Women were near, virtuous, to a certain extent strong and effective, and for all these motives lovable. But male love came at a cost. By and large, love is rarely pure. It is hardly free from obscure, unconscious dynamics, and often leads to compromise, to pettiness, and sometimes to violence. Men were eager to love this loosely constructed "other," whose "weaknesses" were often tolerated. Genteel culture made considerable room for the "weaker sex," but it was understood that the woman should never launch too serious challenges to male leadership, male sense of control, and especially male "normality." When gender roles were being subverted, and both men and women presented themselves as entirely normal, disappointment or puzzlement could easily surrender to rage.[120]

I Mean the Influence of Women in the Government

The Revolution did little to change women's subordinate position within society. The men who led such epochal change seemed not disposed to "remember the ladies," as Abigail Adams had justly remarked. Especially in the 1790s, while the fear of disorder due to the social upheavals of the French Revolution censored political participation, women's political activity shrunk even more. And yet the right to vote and women's official political participation are not the sole parameters to assess women's activity or, let alone, their real political influence.[121]

No discourse on eighteenth-century American and Virginian women can ignore the fact that the "weaker sex" wielded power. Women's informal activities did not suffer from legal strictures. Historians have convincingly shown that informal political opportunities for women continued well into the era of the Federalists and Jeffersonian Republicans. Before and after the Revolution, many women participated in the local political culture of Virginia. Especially upper-class women and candidates' wives kept providing freeholders with lodging, food, and drink. Similarly, they had many opportunities to perform politically, as producers of domestic manufactures, nurses and laundresses in the army, petitioners who sought redress of grievances from their government, or simply as consumers and boycotters: "consumption was powerful," it has been written. The conclusion is that although the law cordoned off women from the formal polity, many other activities existed that complicate our understanding of the relationship of women to political culture and power.[122]

Better-off widows in particular had access to the public sphere. A *feme sole* (the opposite of a married woman, or *feme covert*) was allowed to buy and sell land, negotiate contracts, and manage the household with servants and slaves. Widows usually remarried, but those who did not could exert a degree of independence. Widows and other single women counted as a considerable economic, and hence political, force: they owned nearly 20 percent of Virginia land.[123]

Those women who married, or remarried, helped enfranchise men through the land they brought as a dowry. This, in turn, gave many of them indirect power to influence their husbands. For his part, the husband or soon-to-be husband could not ignore that his woman was often essential to his personal success. Male offspring of notable Virginia families (the Byrds, the Lees, the Jeffersons) were raised in the conviction that the woman they courted, and ended up loving and choosing, was an asset. When a man "admired" his female companion, her beauty, her simplicity, her virtue, he dealt with meanings that transcended romantic or individualist love. Love, once again, was never pure. As daughters, spouses, mothers, widows, and spouses again, women had title to property and hence authority.

As a matter of fact, the woman was "his" nearly as much as a man was "hers." Consequently, influential upper-class men in particular had all the interest to overlook that a harsh struggle was going on whose outcome could determine who was in real control of the household. Almost all men grew anxious, as they had to constantly reinforce and reenact their authority. When elite men are concerned, the struggle was principally economic and political. And it was intellectual too: the Enlightenment was a good environment for many female philosophers and activists. In several other cases, within almost every family, whether legal or illegal, whether upper or lower class, battles were about hearts and sex. Many men were understandably not especially keen on focusing the attention upon this not-yet-decided battle, but by looking at any "modern" woman they could not fail to notice that she had grown powerful, despite the law and a weaker physical strength.[124]

Genteel culture conceptualized women's power and taught them to better master it. Educated American women could plunge into a growing body of conduct literature advising them on the proper canons of behavior for a post-deferential society. Especially upper-class women had become considerably more aware of their seductive power: "Rather than asking women," Hemphill writes, "to show deference in their behavior to superior men, as they had in the past, revolutionary-era authors advised them to behave in such a way as to avoid arousing men sexually."[125]

As a result of many painful renegotiations, deferential society waned, while Enlightenment ideals and goals spread on both sides of the Atlantic. The transatlantic Enlightenment made strong "philosophical" cases for the primacy of reason; the reliability of human understanding; the value of individual freedom, willfulness, and self-determination; confidence in method and education; and above all the belief in progress—the most "romantic" among the Enlightenment tenets. The Revolution did not bring immediate substantial progress for women, as said, but as decades wore on, the "weaker sex" won many battles in the name of egalitarianism and *real* Enlightenment. By the early nineteenth century, women were included in the male world to a much greater degree than ever before. Especially in New England, a new middle-class woman, pairing the new professional man dressed in black, engaged in new worlds of competition. While some men liked this transformation, others, obviously, did not.[126]

Virginians of Jefferson's generation, of course, frowned upon these novelties. They were almost shocked at the disgraceful lack of restraint women had started to show. Women, especially European ones, seemed to act more willfully and wickedly than ever, bringing about a "kind of influence" not taken into sufficient account by shortsighted Parisian reformers—while American reformers should. "In my opinion," Jefferson wrote from Paris in 1788, "a kind of influence, which none of their plans of reform take into account, will elude them all; I mean the influence of women in the government." Society was changing, and grateful though Jefferson was for its many achievements, he could not make sense of the custom that allowed women "to visit, alone, all persons in office, to sollicit the affairs of the husband, family, or friends." Women's "sollicitations" begun to outstrip the household, and such a practice was bidding "defiance to laws and regulations." The "corrupting" effect of such a peculiar, undesirable outcome of Enlightenment noble ideals was striking. Jefferson did not grasp, let alone favor, the transformations that were making women more daring, more practically relevant, and their corporeality less deferential. He rather focused his attention upon the "desperate state to which things are reduced in this country [France] from the omnipotence of an influence which, fortunately for the happiness of the sex itself, does not endeavor to extend itself in our country beyond the domestic line."[127]

Woman the Fountain of All Human Fraility

This last quotation epitomizes prejudices, misogynist utterances, slanders, and false naturalizations whose effect was to cage women into an essence not of their own choice. Similar statements were crafted to diminish the stature of this "weaker" other. They tell us that women, according to Jefferson, were not supposed to lobby, maneuver, or strike bargains to reach an aim, precisely what men, especially politicians like Jefferson, had been doing in order to increase the chances for the American nation. They tell us that women should relinquish power, at least the power that extended beyond the "domestic line."

Furthermore, a quotation such as this is more than just circumstantial or tailored to the character of the recipient of the letter, the patriarch George Washington. It is programmatic, and through the following sections we will see these precise themes (misogyny, slanders, and naturalizations) emerging time and again, standing in an unsolved tension with Jefferson's progressive sensibility.

Misogyny is a childish way to compensate the perception that power belongs to "less-than-worthy" individuals. Jefferson did not stay a misogynist for long, although in his Literary Commonplace Book he entered harsh misogynist quotations. There is a peculiar alternation of citations about arbitrary political power and about women that is certainly revealing of juvenile sentiments of rage and frustration. Misogynist quotations were entered between 1756 and 1764, but Jefferson kept these earlier angry entries when, in 1768, he edited the Literary Commonplace Book. Jefferson copied Milton's famous tirade against women (n. #241):

This Novelty on Earth, this fair Defect
Of Nature? And not to fill the World at once
With men, as Angels, without feminine?
Or find some other Way to generate
Mankind? This Mischief had not then befall['n,]
And more that shall befall: innumerable
Disturbances on Earth through female Snares,
And straight Conjunction with this Sex!

He also did not forget Thomas Otway, *The Orphan* (n. #306):

I'd leave the World for him that hates a Woman.
Woman the Fountain of all human Fraility!
What might ills have not been done by Woman?
Who was't betray'd the Capitol? A Woman.
Who lost Marc Anthony the World? A Woman.
Who was the Cause of a long ten years War,
And laid at last old Troy in ashes? Woman.
Destructive, damnable, deceitful Woman![128]

Of course, Milton's or Otway's ideas were not Jefferson's, and yet it cannot be accidental that he made the choice to enter these quotations. Furthermore, Milton and Otway appear as out of context, and this fact increases the misogynist effect. We should not take these specimens as conclusive evidence against Jefferson. Whatever the reasons that pushed this young man to select these quotations instead of many others he may have liked better, by 1770 Jefferson's misogyny disappeared. The Literary Commonplace Book veers toward different directions, political, philosophical, and existential. He was in the early 1770s a married man, and he must have realized that the "weaker sex" was more than what his decontextualized Milton or his in turn decontextualized Otway thought.[129]

The Instrument of Vengeance against an Inconstant Lover

Young Jefferson grew into a more mature and less "enraged" man, in himself more flexible, postmartial, and even "feminine." But slanders, innuendos, and prejudices crafted to remark the "natural" distance occurring between male and female corporeality, not only between male and female spirituality, did not disappear. I could easily pile dozens of quotations, from his letters and other writings, to give the reader the sense that Jefferson was part of a culture and a society that still clung to antiwomen sentiments and attitudes. Notwithstanding women's relative empowerment and his personal veneration for the Enlightenment, Jefferson did not renegotiate either the spaces of male-female spirituality or, let alone, those of male-female corporeality. I will provide a few cases just in order to veer quickly toward a more important topic—Jefferson's naturalizations of the female body.

The reason why I am exempted from providing a longer list of antiwomen quotations is that, after all, a worse form of slander and a better example of Jefferson's prereflexive denigrating attitudes is given by the style he invariably adopted when he dealt with women. Each time, invariably, he became half ironic and half overblown sentimental: "Here I am, Madam, gazing whole hours at the Maison quarrée, like a lover at his mistress. The stocking-weavers and silk spinners around it consider me as an hypochondriac Englishman, about to write with a pistol the last chapter of his history."[130]

It was not only the "silly" aristocrat Madame de Tessé who forced him to don this slightly naughty *persona*. Jefferson could not help doing precisely this each time he wrote to women, no matter how accomplished they were. In Boston first and then in Paris in 1784–85, Abigail Adams repeatedly challenged Jefferson on the issue of women's rights and capabilities. John, Abigail, and Jefferson spent time together, and, most likely, the two men had to listen to Abigail's passionate Enlightenment arguments many times over. But when John and Abigail moved to London in May 1785 (John was appointed ambassador to Great Britain) and the Jefferson–Abigail Adams correspondence began, we have this cheeky *persona* constantly on the stage. Besides one hasty, tongue-in-cheek reference to a gender-neutral language ("I pray you to observe that I have used the term *people* and that this is a noun of the masculine as well as feminine gender"), Abigail's compelling arguments about gender equality did not trigger any momentous transformation. Not only did Jefferson not amend his *notions* about women's natural inferiority. Probably worse, he did not renounce his customary half-ironic attitudes.

On too many occasions, Abigail deserved better than being rewarded with gossiping about princesses, chevaliers, and old countesses, or entertained, for example, with jokes about "an Ordonance" for Parisian drivers to "wear breeches." Most of the time, Jefferson and Abigail Adams gossiped and, occasionally, flirted.[131]

Truth be told, Jefferson admired Abigail Adams; he praised her *womanly* thoughtfulness, sensitivity, and intuition; he asked her little favors (as she did to him); he trusted her with his younger daughter Maria (Polly) when in 1787 she arrived in London from Virginia (accompanied by Sally Hemings), and the two friends grazed together merrily upon many intellectual fields. Jefferson took this particular woman, Abigail Adams, *as seriously as he could*— definitely more seriously than he ever took Maria Cosway. But, almost invariably, the reader can immediately realize from the sheer epistolary style that Jefferson is addressing a woman.

While Jefferson could not take women's minds more seriously than he did, with men he felt he could freely crack dubious jokes about women's deeds and behaviors: "The principle of retaliation," as, for example, he wrote from Paris to his friend James Madison, "is much criticised here, particularly in the case of Rape." Obviously, a reader of Cesare Beccaria's *On Crimes and Punishments* (1764), Jefferson could have delved into a philosophical conversation on the merits and limits of a retributive account of punishments. He could have easily emphasized the *reasons* why retaliation is "indecent & unjustifiable." He chose instead to end his letter with a remark on the "temptation women would be under to make it the instrument of vengeance against an inconstant lover, & of disappointment to a rival." Why would he assume that women, all women, would have acted that way?[132]

It was just an innocent witticism, but Jefferson was exposed to conditioning forces, even before he could exert his critical sense. In 1814, to take an analogous example, he congratulated John Mason on his wife's determination and success in producing homespun. "Mrs. Mason is really a more dangerous adversary to our British foes, than all our Generals. these attack the hostile armies only, she the source of their subsistence. . . . I hope too she will have more followers than our Generals, but few rivals I fear." We cannot tell for sure whether this letter conveys a sincere celebration of women's informal political activity and his appreciation for women being relevant. Most likely, Jefferson could not resist being funny at the same time he drew precise lines of distinction between serious and less serious political behaviors and performances, respectively the male and the female worlds. The point is that Jefferson's prereflexive attitudes and automatic responses—I mean the joke as a psycho-physical response and an act of readjustment, independent of its content—are revealing. He may have not been aware, but through his "innocent" jokes he sustained women's "otherness."[133]

There is not much to argue about the fact that Jefferson saw women a certain way. In his visual, pictorial representations, female figures impersonated roles sometimes worth a witches' party or Euripides's *Bacchae*. An old man, for example, Jefferson looked expectantly at the imminent opening of his university. Especially the University of Virginia, he believed, would halt the diffusion of religious fanaticism. For the time being, he beheld a heavy "threatening cloud of fanaticism" polluting the "atmosphere of our country." As he told the philosopher Thomas Cooper, appointed as first professor of natural science and law at the University of Virginia, Unitarianism would eventually "humble this haughtiest of all religious sects." Meanwhile, he was scared by what he "saw" taking place. Jefferson identified one of the main springs of fanaticism: "In our Richmond there is much fanaticism, but chiefly among the women: they have their night meetings and praying-parties, where, attended by their priests, and sometimes a hen-pecked husband, they pour forth the effusions of their love to Jesus, in terms as amatory and carnal, as their modesty would permit them to use to a more earthly lover."[134]

While it is implausible that Jefferson at a certain point returned to a representation of the "weaker sex" as a demonic other, it is similarly doubtful that he actually ever took part in "praying-parties" happening precisely along the "amatory and carnal" lines here described. This is rather one of his famous hyperboles: exaggerated images he often deployed to stress his point—the point being that women can be dangerous. As we know, his happy pen could convey powerful images, and the "hen-pecked husband" must have been, to him and his recipient alike, as scary as religious fanaticism itself. More than just religion is at stake here, more than just a fear of revivalism and irrationalism, more than just a reenactment of the classic topic of Enlightenment disdain for religious enthusiasm, superstition, miracles, and incomprehensible rituals. Jefferson is saying that gender roles should not be subverted, and that women should not perform in the public arena—and certainly never let their "sexually wild" corporeality go unchecked.

More Susceptible of Impressions of Mind and Body

Science gave Jefferson precise indications about what women "naturally" were. In general, they were made of a softer fabric and were basically emotional. (White men, on the other hand, were "naturally" sturdier and rational.) Women as a whole were described as "more susceptible of impressions of mind and body," as Dr. Rush wrote, "more subject to nervous diseases than men." If they were "more long-lived than men," the reason was that women's "natural softness" required "more time to become solid, and then to decay."[135]

Jefferson's views were to a certain extent more advanced than the average opinions on women's roles still prevalent in Virginia. For him, women were not a mere plaything and an ornament destined to amuse men. In particular, white women of means could excel, despite a more "fragile" constitution, but only by providing moral examples, by acquiescing to their "delicacy" and "modesty," and by circumscribing their corporeality within the household. White women could aspire to the roles of republican mothers and virtuous wives, devoted to enhancing virtue, to providing for the education of the children should the father be lost. But on a more physical level, all women were made to give birth. Andrew Burstein is right when he insists that "Jefferson's seeming inattentiveness to his wife's difficulties as a child-bearer, his impregnation of her six times in ten years, leading to her death, may be viewed in the context of his belief in woman's natural role."[136]

According to Jefferson, women should comply with their softer corporeality and find their social and physical places accordingly. They were good creatures, mothers and sometimes carriers of republican values, but only when they remained within their designated sphere. They betrayed their "nature" each time they trespassed over forbidden territories. Jefferson never wavered in the opinion that women, their bodies and minds alike, should abstain from direct competition with men. "I think it impossible to find a better woman," he wrote John Jay describing Madame la Marquise de Brehan, sister-in-law to Monsieur de Moustier, "more amiable, more modest, more simple in her manners, dress, and way of thinking." Women who entered politics, as we will see shortly, betrayed "simplicity" and "modesty." In the same way, should they do improper things with their bodies, no matter how seemingly innocent, they would betray themselves. There were many things women could do to either manifest or to increase their power, which Jefferson could not understand.[137]

Women's dresses should never make these bodies conspicuously noticeable. Jefferson, as already pointed out, objected to the practice of sending American youth to Europe. A "spirit for female intrigue" will invariably seize every young man. He will end up destroying his happiness. A "passion for whores" will destroy his health. But the problem was also that "the voluptuary dress and arts of the European women" will lure him into despising "the chaste affections and simplicity of those of his own country." In the 1780s, he had known firsthand the performances that Parisian women were able to put up each time they donned their fancy dresses. Jefferson was then undergoing a "dandy" phase himself. That European women did too much with their style is a typical paean of the period. From this point of view, as he wrote in another famous letter to Anne Willing Bingham, the Philadelphia intellectual and famous salonnière, a comparison of European and American women is like "a comparison of Amazons and Angels."[138]

Jefferson did not appreciate that fashion, and women's interest in it, was a statement, an attempt at self-fashioning and self-empowerment, and a calculated strategy to conquer space. And yet he had done it throughout his life—many people of course do it. He did not understand that by choosing "voluptuary" dresses these Parisian women were not betraying their nature. They were simply enhancing their bodies, at times playfully, maybe precisely to exert their power of seduction. They were trying to convey messages, exploring the external environment, and attempting experiments in self-liberation. They were doing what they did by relying on the sharper weapons that were available to them. For his part, Jefferson moralized. And he could only moralize because he had naturalized women in the first place: these exemplars deviated from what for him was a natural standard.[139]

Anne Willing Bingham, on the other hand, had grasped the liberating power implicit in Parisian women's voluptuary dresses. Women's attractiveness, she knew, was premeditated, a means to an end: "The Women of France interfere in the politics of the Country, and often give a decided Turn to the Fate of Empires." Since women were too often denied the opportunity to speak and to exercise "the gentle Arts of persuasion," Bingham concluded, it was "by the commanding force of superior Attractions and Address" that they could hope to obtain "Rank and Consideration in society." Fashion was nothing less that *intellect in action,* and everyone should be "bound in Gratitude to admire and revere" these Parisian champions. Far from "frivolous" or "ridiculous in their Characters," these women sought to enhance their effectiveness and visibility. Coming forth was praiseworthy: "The Arts of Elegance are there [in Paris] considered essential, and are carried to a state of Perfection; the Mind is continually gratified with the admiration of Works of Taste."[140]

"Fashion in dress," Kate Haulman has written, "was both an acknowledged form of feminine power and important to men and women alike as a site for expressing social status." But since Jefferson had already opted for naturalization, since he "saw" what a woman's nature fit her for, he could only moralize. What Jefferson did was typical—and still is. He bought fancy stuff throughout his life in order to convey his own messages and achieve goals, and he claimed that women should be restrained either in their consumption or corporeal performances. In this case, he was more than just "evil" and "duplicitous"; he was in the process of building women's "otherness."[141]

Again from Paris, Jefferson wrote to Abigail Adams about what for him was a source of national money drainage. The "luxury of our ladies in the article of dress" bothered him, but, fortunately, American women "begin to be sensible of the excess of it themselves." The reformation with which he agreed was nothing short of "the adoption of a national dress." A republican costume for women sounds to our ears authoritarian at best, an efficient way to undercut women's expression and power. But he did not see the question this way. If, on this occasion, Jefferson thought the adoption of the republican dress improbable, it was just because he feared women "have not resolution enough for this."[142]

An Innovation for Which the Public Is Not Prepared, Nor Am I

These remarks about fashion and women's "excessive" penchant for luxury are maybe trivial asides. More serious consequences of Jefferson's naturalization of women, as an intellectual expedient to curtail their increased power, emerge each time some of them sought to enter either politics or the public administration. More fragile bodies, women should stay away from what "nature" decreed were exclusive male fields. We have already seen what Jefferson wrote to Washington about "the influence of women in the government" and their daring and inappropriate "sollicitations." In 1807, he was still on the same positions: "The appointment of a woman to office is an innovation for which the public is not prepared, nor am I." These were actual behaviors, practical decisions eliciting material consequences for the life of real individuals, not only a philosopher's ideas: each time he could, Jefferson wanted to make sure women, both as a group and as single individuals, stayed away from public affairs.[143]

Principles and moral convictions frequently prompt material consequences. And Jefferson's opinions were not like the everyday person's opinions. It was consequential that this influential man, a public official, a policy maker, could not allow "hypothetical" situations in which it was appropriate or productive for women and men to mingle "promiscuously" in the public arena, their different natures and bodies merging into each other. Jefferson kept moralizing: "were our state a pure democracy," Jefferson wrote to Samuel Kercheval, women "would yet be excluded from their deliberations." They "could not mix promiscuously in the public meetings of men." They could not precisely "to prevent depravation of morals, and ambiguity of issue."[144]

In 1824, Jefferson was all the more convinced that women were by their natural constitution too unequal to be treated as peers. Several states had already amended the defects in their constitutions, he said to John Pleasants, while the Virginia constitution still remained "in opposition to the principle of equal political rights, refusing to all but freeholders any participation in the natural right of self government." Jefferson's inclusive bent was far from universalistic: while the "very great majority of the militia" could rightfully lament being "unrepresented in the legislation which imposed this burthen on them," while "the majority of our free and adult male citizens" could similarly lament either unrepresentation or exclusion, not all social categories could do the same. "Among the men who either pay or fight for their country, no line of right can be drawn." At the opposite, "by mental or physical disqualifications" nature has "marked infants and the weaker sex for the protection, rather than the direction of government." While "the exclusion of a majority of our freemen from the right of representation is merely arbitrary," the same cannot be said for women.[145]

However friendly he may have been to particular women, Jefferson maintained that while the "line of right" should not separate peer from peer, it must be clearly drawn between men and women. Women's exclusion from equality, and certainly from the "direction of government," was the consequence of the fact that nature had "marked infants and the weaker sex" a certain way. Heeding their "otherness" was for him the same as acknowledging a natural truth. Exclusion was motivated by the fact that these persons *were* different, in no way *made* different.

Jefferson rationalized women's exclusion from politics and in general from the public arena as an act of justice. In Query 6, the same query that examined trees, plants, fruits, animals, albinos, and Buffon's contentions, he alleged that American Indian women were "submitted to unjust drudgery": "This I believe is the case with every barbarous people. With such, force is law. The stronger sex therefore imposes on the weaker. It is civilization alone which replaces women in the enjoyment of their natural equality." Among barbarians, the stronger sex imposes on the weaker, while civilization and science acknowledge what women "naturally" are. We, civilized men and natural historians, Jefferson believed, "respect those rights in others which we value in ourselves. Were we in equal barbarism, our females would be equal drudges." Jefferson saw something wrong in the habit American Indians embraced of letting their women "attend[] the men in their parties of war and of hunting." There seemed to be something abnormal in the fact that "the man with them is less strong than with us, but their woman stronger than ours; and both for the same obvious reason; because our man and their woman is habituated to labor, and formed by it."[146]

It was far from an imposition, for Jefferson, to actually try to confine Euro-American women within the household. The sum of total happiness would soar if only the "weaker sex" were allowed the chance to stay inside. "Our good ladies, I trust," Jefferson wrote Anne Willing Bingham, "have been too wise to wrinkle their foreheads with politics. They are contented to soothe & calm the minds of their husbands returning ruffled from political debate. They have the good sense to value domestic happiness above all other, and the art to cultivate it beyond all others." In this letter where Jefferson compared American women to angels, and Parisian women to Amazons, he also claimed that Bingham would eventually discard her opinion that "a Parisian," either a woman or a man, "is happier than an American." Jefferson conjured an idyllic image of American domestic life, one of his most famous hyperboles: "Recollect the women of this capital, some on foot, some on horses, & some in carriages hunting pleasure in the streets, in routs & assemblies, and forgetting that they have left it behind them in their nurseries; compare them with our own countrywomen occupied in the tender and tranquil amusements of domestic life, and confess that it is a comparison of Amazons and Angels."[147]

Jefferson's hypothesis was that women would never be happy if they simply kept chasing "pleasure in the streets." Intended as assistants or supporters who would put men's minds and bodies in order, women have other occupations. "The tender breasts of ladies were not formed for political convulsions," Jefferson wrote to his friend Angelica Schuyler Church, "and the

French ladies miscalculate much their own happiness when they wander from the field of their influence into that of politics." With his daughter Martha, Jefferson was very clear about the type of happiness women in general, and his daughters in particular, were expected to "hunt"—especially as Martha got married and in her father's view fulfilled her "natural" self. Her new condition, Jefferson contended, "will call for abundance of little sacrifices. . . . The happiness of your life depends now on the continuing to please a single person. To this all other objects must be secondary; even your love to me, were it possible that that could ever be an obstacle. But this it can never be."[148]

I Have, Like You, Preserved My Old Folly

Just like men, women vary among themselves. There has never been a "women community" or a transgenerational, transsocial, transracial condition of "being woman." Furthermore, strong personalities and healthy bodies, including women, especially women, did not accept falling into socially conformed roles and conventional sets of corporealities. Many of these defiant body-minds, strong-willed subjects, talented, educated, informed (like Martha Washington, Abigail Adams, Dolly Madison, or Martha Jefferson Randolph) kept carrying out thoughts and bodily performances upon which their masters, husbands, tutors, and superiors could not but frown upon. These women had to be tamed.

Martha Jefferson Randolph, for one, eventually got trapped, as *we* would say, into her role of wife, mother of eleven children, and mistress of Monticello. Physically and materially, at a certain point in her life, when she got back to Virginia in 1789, she started moving within "appropriate" spaces, like parlors, kitchens, storerooms, and so on. Jefferson eventually succeeded in sealing her off the Parisian stimuli and "excesses"—which teaches us that the threshold between, on the one hand, Jefferson's philosophical opinions or his famous misogynist utterances and, on the other, his modes of interactions is rather porous, especially when we come to the narrow circle of his family. (His daughters, in particular, were his personal laboratory.) But it took Jefferson a while to train Martha. It took him energy. For a period, she could have become a Parisian, an "Amazon." Paris during those years was an avant-garde setting where Parisians were experimenting with new roles and styles. "Performances of domesticity," to use Cynthia Kierner's happy phrase, eventually held sway, and Martha's body veered toward more traditional harbors. Motherhood, Kierner observes, became "the defining feature of Martha Jefferson

Randolph's adult life, and family relationships dominated her comparatively insular world, as they did for most rural women of her time."[149]

But the world she left back in Paris talked about other possibilities. Martha Jefferson's friends from the Abbaye Royale de Panthémont were mostly comprised of daughters of French and English aristocrats. And yet for about five years these contacts underpinned young Martha Jefferson's supposition that alternative roles could better channel her individual, perhaps a little whimsical, aspirations. Her short-lived desire to become a nun may have just expressed her desire to keep on enjoying the independence, if not the transgressions, she had discovered at Panthémont. Catholicism was indeed seductive and aesthetically enticing, if not wholeheartedly fulfilling. Its rich rituals and ceremonies would eventually seduce more than one Protestant: the conversions of the writer and poet Friedrich Leopold zu Stolberg-Stolberg, of the famous poet Friedrich von Schlegel, and of the Swiss jurist Karl Ludwig von Haller are but a few eighteenth-century cases of conversion among many others that could be recalled. At the time, Catholicism was artistic and romantic. By 1788, young Martha had made up her mind, as she told her friend Bettie Hawkins, that her corporeality would be encircled by nuns and priests and populated by Catholic churches, by saints, fonts, and polyptychs.[150]

That convents may be liberating sounds weird to many twenty-first-century ears. But within this precise convent school, as well as in the representations she had of the life in convents, Martha had discovered playfulness, fashion, sociability, but also unprecedented levels of power and independence. Many letters written by her friends (especially after she left school to go back home) reveal that Martha was happy there. Unfortunately, the letters Martha sent to her friends and classmates have not survived. But from the many letters her friends sent to her we can conclude that, for a while, she gained unprecedented levels of self-assertion, self-determination, agency, and corporeal self-confidence: she was "herself" being on her own in the context of Catholic pageantry, and she was "herself" in a way that in Virginia she could never match again.

Upon learning that Martha would not return to Panthémont after a summer break in 1789, Marie de Botidoux cried her eyes out: "it has been decided that you will not come back here. . . . You have no idea how sad I am. I cried last night despite all my attempts to turn my mind away from such thoughts, and I am crying again at this very moment." She found the only partial solace in the "acknowledgment" that Martha's return to American simple life was "natural" for her happiness: "Farewell, dear little Jefferson. If you loved me as much as I love you, you could have an idea of the sorrow I feel seeing you go. But you cannot. Besides, you have the best father in the world, who wants and seeks nothing but your happiness. You are going to be reunited with your family who, surely, will adore you as soon as they know you and will take great care in entertaining you. I, on the other hand, stay in a convent, where I will be alone this summer."[151]

Botidoux got to know Martha Jefferson intimately and in a "different" way—far from those roles Martha would eventually embody within the Jefferson household. The two young women kept being fond of each other, and years later Botidoux could not believe Martha had become a mother, even a matron. For her, Patsy was still a sassy wild creature with spirited eyes, often disheveled in her garb, running about merrily each time she could, albeit she knew she should not. Botidoux kept treasuring all her life the memory of "our old follies." For her, those "follies" clearly bespoke of many roads not taken: "How I would like to know your children," she wrote in 1801, "and how I would like to see you one more time! I would not be out of place at all on your outings, for despite all I have suffered, prison, proscription, etc., I have, like you, preserved my old folly. . . . When I meet an American, it is an intense pleasure for me to speak of you and of our old follies."[152]

Botidoux teaches us that Martha Jefferson, this specific version of a young Patsy, was intellectual and spiritual, social, fond of conversations, curious, even popular; that her corporeality was lively, fun, keen on partying, artistic, generous; that this woman felt she belonged there; that she was exploring possibilities and roles, even contradictory ones. Martha Jefferson could have become a salonnière herself, like some of her aristocratic pals did, or a nun. She could have lived in a metropolis, or in a court, or in a convent. In a very material sense, different outfits could have covered her body. But Jefferson brought her back to the role "nature" had chosen. He had an early "perfect knowlege of the situation in which you will be placed." Her happiness was at stake, and Jefferson had no intention to allow that Martha's Parisian experience would end up mellowing the sinews of her republicanism.[153]

This Faithful Internal Monitor

While the mass of black bodies had to be distanced, excluding individual exceptions, female bodies had to be controlled—*all* female bodies. It was an act of justice and civilization, Jefferson believed, to control women, to control their expression in dress, politics, or labor. His belief was that control had to be rational, based on nature, and productive of altruistic effects. Exercising control on both women's minds and bodies, as this eighteenth-century flexible and civilized man thought, was a way to create bulwarks to women's happiness: "it is your future happiness which interests me," as he repeatedly told his daughter Martha.[154]

His letters to Mary and Martha, especially to his older daughter, are particularly revealing on the topic of control, the monitoring of women's social space. "Above all things and at all times," we have already seen, "let your clothes be neat, whole, and properly put on." Said from a man who, later in his life, often indulged in worn-out clothing, which others deemed improper, this intimation sounds problematic. In the same letter, Jefferson also advised orderliness and control, self-control to be more precise: "I hope therefore the moment you rise from bed, your first work will be to dress yourself in such a stile as that you may be seen by any gentleman without his being able to discover a pin amiss, or any other circumstance of neatness wanting." Given the importance for a young woman of having a tidy, ordered person, Jefferson was not above little blackmails and eliciting guilt: "I shall be very much mortified and disappointed if you become inattentive to my wishes and particularly to the directions of that letter which I meant for your principal guide."[155]

Little Mary also was repeatedly urged to accept her responsibilities. Jefferson was then in Paris, and Mary was staying in Virginia with her aunt, Elizabeth Wayles Eppes. Jefferson made her know that her father's love was conditional on her willingness to satisfy certain objective conditions, like studying, bearing oneself correctly, and wearing a bonnet: "I hope you are a very good girl . . . that you never suffer yourself to be angry with any body, that you give your playthings to those who want them, that you do whatever any body desires of you that is right, that you never tell stories, never beg for any thing, mind your book and your work when your aunt tells you, never play but when she permits you, nor go where she forbids you. Remember too as a constant charge not to go out without your bonnet because it will make you very ugly and then we should not love you so much."[156]

Maybe Jefferson was only being ironic. Maybe, given Mary's complexion, he was concerned that the late-September sun could make her tanned and freckled. Or maybe, most likely, through his insistence on the bonnet, he wanted to instill the sense that certain corporeal performances were preferable over many others, especially for a woman. With no doubts, he wanted to make sure his daughters grasped the importance of not losing what he thought was laudable: watching themselves regularly through the eyes of others and behaving accordingly. It was essential to the process of becoming a white woman of means, an "other" in this sense, to stir the impression of being observed and constantly judged by real others who were in a position of command. To this regard, the fiction of an "internal monitor," a proxy for the external one, worked perfectly well. Should you do something wrong, Jefferson wrote Martha, "you will feel something within you which will tell you it is wrong and ought not to be said or done: this is your conscience, and be sure to obey it. Our maker has given us all, this faithful internal Monitor."[157]

Their Short Reign of Beauty and Splendor

During these few last examples, Jefferson was addressing his beloved daughters. But it is impossible not to assume that all "good" women, for him, should accept supervision and conform to the same strict regimen. For sure, Jefferson gave plenty of advice to both young men and women alike. Perils always lurked. But women's happiness and realization were especially fragile, precarious, and in need of constant surveillance. Every detail, no matter how seemingly trivial, like freckles or a bonnet, counted.

In what can be considered his most methodical reflection on female education, the letter to Nathaniel Burwell of 1818, Jefferson still conveyed a precise representation of a role-abiding, nature-abiding, and for this reason harmonious and happy female body. His thoughts on details, the "ornaments" and the "amusements" of life, are particularly interesting: "These, for a female, are dancing, drawing, and music." Not only does dancing constitute a "healthy exercise, elegant and very attractive for young people." More than that, this civilized activity gives proof that young persons, each according to his or her sex, have succeeded in mastering their bodies according to the rules of society. "Every affectionate parent would be pleased to see his daughter qualified to participate with her companions, and without awkwardness at least, in the circles of festivity, of which *she occasionally becomes a part*. It is a necessary accomplishment, therefore, although of short use, for the French rule is wise, that no lady dances after marriage."[158]

Such a young female body dancing elegantly should, at the same time, demonstrate that roles and "natural" functions have been adequately internalized. The "internal monitor," once again, should be awake. Dancing should never become a profession or a passion for life: a woman may dance and become the main actor of a party, although only "occasionally." At a certain point, this activity must be stopped altogether: "This is founded in solid physical reasons, gestation and nursing leaving little time to a married lady when this exercise can be either safe or innocent." For females, drawing and music as well were useful ornaments. But, again, these activities were means to an end, the end of every woman being private, the wise mastering of the household economy: "I need say nothing of household economy, in which the mothers of our country are generally skilled, and generally careful to instruct their daughters." Boys and girls had different roles, and Jefferson sustained these roles fiercely: "The order and economy of a house are as honorable to the mistress as those of the farm to the master, and if either be neglected, ruin follows, and children destitute of the means of living."[159]

Bonnets, dancing, and everything a woman did, all the minutiae of her material life, according to Jefferson, should never undermine gender differences. Questioning roles would reduce women's otherness, but at the same time it would reduce "happiness" and "progress." Only by following "nature," Jefferson believed, could male and female happiness be preserved. He envisioned happiness as an aim to attain—which is commendable. He carried out improvements over more coercive, rigid, traditional patterns of gender relations. But his line of reasoning (that is, that "happiness" had to be the consequence of what "nature" dictated) shows that Jefferson did not see what we, twenty-first-century readers, should see.

Behaviors and standards that Jefferson deemed natural, objective, or founded upon sound facts were in reality effects of the prevailing strategies of social control. He had happiness in sight, but he did not see that women's penchants, desires, and roles were the outcome of the far from natural *fact* that their bodies and minds were being closely controlled and exploited for managing family estates, and producing children. Our eyes, not Jefferson's, should become and remain the eyes of an eagle. In assessing gender differences, as well as many other social and "biological" differences, we should not overlook that, as a rule, we *end* with them. Amazons, angels, warriors, leaders, philosophers, fathers, mothers, dancers, musicians, and so on, are by and large negotiable *personae,* and both male and female bodies easily adapt to these roles. Women's aspirations and dispositions, their delicacy and modesty, the "softer fabric" and an inbred welcoming disposition, are far from wired in their body systems.

As the French sociologist and feminist thinker Colette Guillaumin has made clear, males' superior sense of mastery of the world is merely the consequence of a greater *license* afforded to male children in many societies. Men have often a better control over physical space, and females are more vulnerable, and "more subject to nervous diseases," only because self-appointed rulers have made and still make them so. Girls are different from boys, a minus in some respects, only because they are given less freedom to associate with peers, fewer chances to play with their bodies, to don and doff bonnets at pleasure, because they are more closely guarded and are often constrained in nature-abiding roles. Girls have traditionally become the "other" because their activities have been more often restricted to maintaining the space of the home. Biological differences may and do actually exist; but their meanings are of our own making.[160]

But Jefferson obviously disagreed. The "license" this relatively modern and flexible Virginian was prepared to afford to women expired rather quickly. This means that a woman, for him, could briefly blossom into visible space, explore this space, invent her corporeality, improvise, but she had to vacate the public stage and retire, the sooner the better, into concealed and private areas. Women, Jefferson was positive, were physically like hyacinths, tulips, irises, belladonnas, tuberoses. "Like the belles of the day," Jefferson told Ann Cary Randolph Bankhead, his eldest grandchild, flowers "have their short reign of beauty and splendor, & retire like them to the more interesting office of reproducing their like." Instrumental to a smooth passage of the generations, and hence to the very life of the American republic, women's bodies must yield passage: "The hyacinths and tulips are off the stage, the Irises are giving place to the Belladonnas, as this will to the Tuberoses E.c. as your Mama has done to you, my dear Anne, as you will do to the sisters of little John."[161]

The Girl Who Is with Her Is Quite a Child

Control and love, needless to say, are not mutually exclusive. As a friend and companion, a sexually active man, a father, and later a grandfather, Jefferson loved many persons, female and male, and he did so this way or another: his wife, daughters, grandchildren, and friends were not all treated the same. Each time, he sprinkled these relationships with higher or lower doses of observation and control.

Love has always been a rather complex and opaque matter. It has many meanings, of course, and often self-contradictory ones. For this very reason, we will never know if Thomas Jefferson was ever purely "in love" with Sally Hemings. We need to discuss Thomas Jefferson and Sally Hemings here for reasons other than the supposition of a candid romantic love. The topics discussed so far, male control over the female body, the woman's internalization of her "natural" roles and places, and gender and race hierarchies, need to be brought to a new level—these categories need to be tested against what is perhaps one of the most interesting case studies ever. Jefferson rationalized the woman's body system as a complex other, but what about Sally Hemings, this exceptional female other, this "other's other"?

It is hard to tell whether Jefferson ever considered black enslaved women as a whole to be a rightful part of the "weaker sex." In a letter written while in Paris, the young minister and a devotee of the Enlightenment had called enslaved women "the tender part of our species," thus acknowledging their vulnerability as compared to men. But instead of providing satisfactory answers, this letter opens further questions—precisely the ones here at stake. Jefferson was on this occasion discussing agriculture and debating about the most suitable crops for women and children, a workforce too often misemployed "in labours disproportioned to their sex and age."[162]

It is one thing to accept a biological and functional weakness, or to devise strategies to soften the lot of these hapless individuals; quite another thing is allowing African American women to qualify and enter the moral category of the "weaker sex." An interesting literature exists that highlights eighteenth- and nineteenth-century American "weaker sex" (the embodiment of fragility, modesty, virtuousness, and republican exemplarity) as a privilege of whiteness, not just an attribute of femaleness. As a matter of fact, the moral individuality and complex personalities of African American enslaved women all but disappeared from Jefferson's visual field—with the exception of perhaps a few members of the Hemings family. It was the effect of the Virginia brutal system of oppression. African American women are actually there, scattered in Jefferson's Farm Book, in his Memorandum Books, in his letters to overseers, but simply as assets of his estate. The black enslaved woman was there (and not-there) as a breeding female producing a certain number of "little ones in a year," a resource whose "profitability" was for Jefferson beyond discussion; she was there (and not-there) in the pseudoscientific discourses we find in Notes, when she is depicted as the target of choice of the male orangutan; she was there (and not-there) in the callous computations of anatomical characteristics.[163]

Sally Hemings's case is different. To Jefferson's eyes, she was more than just an economic asset, a quasi-beast, or a set of anatomical characteristics. But was she a member of the "weaker sex"? A huge literature explores the liaison between Jefferson and this anomalous slave. "Revisionists" and "defenders" form two competing, albeit not equivalent, teams. From the moment James Callender fired the allegation that "by this wench Sally, our president has had several children," people have taken sides, pro or con the scandal, the wrongdoing, the unspeakable sexual act. By and large, *this act* has captured the attention. Some notable exceptions notwithstanding, not too many pages are devoted to trying to make Sally Hemings, the woman, into a real, historical, more-than-economical, nuanced personality and equally nuanced body. Within the debate over the act, especially over Jefferson's "guilt" or "innocence," this person was and largely remained the slave, the concubine, a type, an abstraction, something rigid and frozen, a representative of African Americans as a group, and once again an undifferentiated "negro" body.[164]

It is unquestionable that Sally Hemings was a special figure for reasons other than the fact that she (allegedly, some "defenders" would say) bore Jefferson his children and provided him with "safe" sexual gratification. Possibly, Jefferson-the-young-widower read certain books on *materia medica,* got anxious, and then decided to take *her* as a concubine. The Swiss medical theorist Samuel Auguste André David Tissot in his best-selling book *De la santé des gens de lettres* (1768 in French, 1766 in Latin) had denounced the risks associated to poor diet, lack of exercise, and insufficient or inappropriate sexual behaviors, like "self-pollution" (masturbation). Fearing the unhealthy effects of erudition and hours on end spent at the desk, Jefferson may have made his deliberations and chosen Sally Hemings as his therapy.[165]

It may be. Or perhaps everything just happened less cerebrally and calculatedly. While we will never know if love, and what specific kind of love, passed between the two, what we know is that the Jefferson-Hemings story can be narrated from many different angles: moralistic, medical, romantic, or with an emphasis on harassment and exploitation. Dynamics of sex and power are no doubt intertwined in their relationship. But their relationship was also one of control, on Jefferson's side, and mutual observation. Hemings spent a big portion of her life with Thomas Jefferson. In many ways, he watched her. Jefferson had to watch such an interesting figure—interesting in the sense of personality. Hemings, as Gordon-Reed writes, "combined what Jefferson regarded as the best in white people with what he regarded as the best in black people, an evidently appealing blend of the head and the heart." Moreover, she was a still more interesting exceptional female corporeality. Corporeally, Sally Hemings was the "other" of the female "other": she was black and (nearly) white at the same time—and not only white in that grotesque sense predicated of some albinos who were of "a pallid cadaverous white, untinged with red." Light-skinned Hemings was not, for Jefferson, an example of an "anomaly of nature." She was essentially African, but her hair was not coarse and curled but "long straight" going "down her back." Most likely, she could even blush.[166]

In many ways, Hemings was the "other" of the female "other," at once chattel and family, simultaneously enemy—like any other African American—and partner, at the same time far-off and near, diverse and similar. Furthermore, she was this "other other" in a very dynamic sense. Hemings not only was one of the most multidimensional body-minds Jefferson ever dealt with. She was singularly plastic as well. Under Jefferson's eyes, Hemings underwent profound transformations, inside as well as outside: a slave mulatto child, Hemings eventually took the shape of an educated and experienced woman, a mother, the mother of Jefferson's progeny. A passive, totally dependent subject, Hemings eventually embodied what for Jefferson was female accomplishment (in the sense I describe below)—perhaps the most striking example of accomplishment. Even if Sally Hemings's name appears rarely in the letters of Jefferson's entourage, she has never been a negligible quantity. For Jefferson, she was not invisible. The way Jefferson must have seen Hemings—through her corporeality and through the acts she carried out, more than her inner character—is the point of view from which I will conduct my analysis of the liaison. I concentrate not on the sexual acts and the consequences of these acts, but on the many more acts that Hemings performed and that Jefferson scrutinized. Again, it is all about Jefferson's eyes—to look, see, and be seen. But let us start from the beginning.[167]

Sally Hemings arrived in London in June 1787, met by Abigail and John Adams. She was then a fourteen-year-old accompanying nine-year-old Mary (Maria, or Polly), Jefferson's younger daughter. The two girls spent a few weeks in the bustling city of London, eventually fetched by Jefferson's butler, Adrien Petit. They arrived in Paris, another bustling city, in July. After little Lucy died of whooping cough in the autumn of 1784—Sally and Mary were left in Virginia with Uncle Francis and Aunt Elizabeth Eppes—Jefferson had started planning Mary's trans-oceanic trip. In 1784, the Eppeses had lost a daughter as well, also called Lucy, and they were extremely sympathetic toward Jefferson's anxiety. He had hoped to have Mary escorted by an older slave woman, but, her being unavailable, the Eppeses had chosen Sally. Abigail Adams wrote that "the Girl who is with her [Mary] is quite a child."

Doubting that she could be of any help, Abigail however noticed that the two girls seemed fond of each other. In addition, as she remarked, Sally "appears good naturd."[168]

Had Sally really needed "more care" than Mary, as Abigail Adams alleged in another letter, had she really been "wholy incapable of looking properly after her, without some superiour to direct her," it would have been improbable that the Eppeses would have chosen her over other slaves who were available. Most likely, under that childlike bearing and unassuming attitudes, Hemings was already dependable, visible, and noticeable in many respects. She was a child, for sure, but quite a child.[169]

Sally Vous Dit Bien des Choses

The twenty-six months Hemings spent in France, from July 1787 through September 1789, brought to a full ripeness her preexistent qualities, both moral and physical. Mary duly joined her older sister at Panthémont. Most likely, Sally stayed home, at the Hôtel de Langeac, but an exceptional experience began. Whether or not she received formal schooling, she saw an exciting city, went out on social occasions, gazed at the style of French dresses, met with the people who came to Jefferson's house to dine or pay visits, and, most important, started to picture herself *developmentally*, beyond the crushing institution of slavery, as having some kind of future. We cannot know for sure if and when she came up with the idea of remaining in Paris by herself or with her brother James. Maybe an early pregnancy (she was already pregnant when she embarked on the trip back to Virginia) nipped this plan in the bud. Many hypotheses may be advanced. What is certain is that thanks to Paris, Sally Hemings began to see herself differently—her mind enlarged and her body endowed with a new level of agency. This sheer fact, as Annette Gordon-Reed writes, "may have changed the way others, including Thomas Jefferson, saw her."[170]

Hemings was strengthening her level of visibility, and Jefferson could have not overlooked this fact. People in general noticed her, including Martha's and Mary's friends. Had she simply been perceived as "the slave," the aristocrat Marie de Botidoux, for example, one of Martha's friends, would not have urged Martha to give regards to "Mademoiselle Sally." Likewise, had she simply been an obnoxious servant, Mary would not have written her friend Kitty Church, the daughter of Angelica Church, that Sally as well sent her regards: "*Sally vous dit bien des choses.*" These clues allude to the fact that, in Paris, this person took part, that she left a mark, becoming all the more noticeable. Her presence increased, and she achieved this for reasons other than her natural beauty.[171]

Hemings was definitely beautiful: testimonies agree on this point. This "mighty near white" and "bright" woman, to borrow Isaac Jefferson's phrases, has always been seen as "very handsome." "Dashing Sally," as another famous characterization went, was unanimously considered a striking beauty. Thomas Jefferson Randolph, Jefferson's grandson, said that she was "light colored and decidedly goodlooking." Good-natured and good-looking, the years she spent in Paris added to her charisma.[172]

There is no surprise that Jefferson's enemies, including some among his twentieth-century "defenders," could easily freeze Hemings's considerable presence into an example of lascivious seductiveness and corruption. Still, something positive emerges even through harsh and derogatory descriptions: after all, this "African Venus," this "black wench" who, according to some, was not averse to the practice of "romping with half a dozen black fellows," has always been seductive and, in the eyes of some people, even exotic, verboten. Many eyes have seen Hemings as sexually arousing: such a "most abandoned prostitute of her color" was eloquently depicted as "pampered into a lascivious course of life, with the benefit of a French education." Desire is hidden beneath assessments of her as more "lecherous than the other beasts of the Monticellian Mountain." Many men, then and now, would be stimulated by a similar "healthy and obliging prostitute, who could be suitably rewarded, but would make no importunate demands."[173]

These men who depicted Sally Hemings as a lustful whore had an agenda to carry out. Also, they were often animated by racism. They wanted not only to debase Hemings morally but also to make her corporeality into something abstract, an exaggeration, a caricature, thus increasing either the abnormality or the unlikelihood of the Hemings-Jefferson sexual intercourse. In addition to hiding desire, characterizations such as these have the obvious purpose of increasing the distance between her and Jefferson, between her and us, thus lowering the level of human empathy.

It is unquestionable that an actual liaison existed, both sexual and more than sexual, and that Jefferson did not see Hemings along these hypercaricatural, hypersexualized lines. Jefferson saw her as a familiar presence, a real, corporeal person who was experiencing, moving from a minus to a plus, growing socially, enhancing her manners and style, learning to properly relate to friends and acquaintances. She was a familial, blossoming body.

He Promised Her Extraordinary Privileges

Jefferson could not overlook certain facts. I said earlier that, to Jefferson's eyes, Hemings was at once diverse and similar. An air of resemblance hovered above the Jefferson clan, which included many Hemingses. In a biological sense, Sally Hemings was beautiful, and she was family, the half-sister of Jefferson's deceased wife. Most likely, Hemings looked like her, sharing some of her mannerisms, gestures, postures, and overall corporeality. Hemings's demeanor and physical appearance must have left Jefferson with no other choice but to categorize this young woman as an obvious member of his close entourage. But Hemings resembled Jefferson too. As Winthrop Jordan wrote, "it seems probable that her language sounded to Jefferson very much like his own." Being reared inside Jefferson's residences and trained as a lady's maid, and all the more after the Parisian years, it is likely that Sally Hemings's language was very familiar. Not only could the two understand each other in French, but the material features of Hemings's language, the accent, timbre, and tone of her voice, elicited immediate closeness. "I think her diction may have been nearly as important as her color in shaping his thoughts about who she was," Jordan resolved.[174]

Gordon-Reed is right when she underscores the interconnectedness of the way we see ourselves and the way others see us. It is actually a circular, self-reinforcing process. Hemings saw herself a certain way, and consequently Jefferson saw her a certain way. And vice versa: he saw her as family and she saw herself as family—an essential imbalance remaining, of course, between Jefferson-the-master and Hemings-the-slave. Hemings remained a slave all her life, but neither her soul nor her body ever endured slavery in the most extreme forms many other African Americans experienced, toiling in the fields and suffering harrowing deprivation and extreme physical pain. Especially after she returned to her "natural" place, Monticello, thus reentering the Virginia slave system, the load of domestic work she had to do obviously increased. Similarly, her seven pregnancies were definitely a heavy burden. But she kept perceiving herself as belonging to the Jefferson clan. After all, many members of the Hemings family, Gordon-Reed argues, have over the years "responded to Jefferson in ways that suggest they thought of him as more a version of an in-law than the rapist of their family members." On his part, Jefferson never put Sally Hemings in the position to convey the representation of her body as crouched, dirty, and wholly disfigured. There is no reason to postulate that Sally Hemings or other persons from her family must have rooted their identity within the slave community. There was no "slave culture" or "African American community," to begin with, providing for preconstituted fixed identities.[175]

Hemings had all her life shared key moments with Jefferson. Probably some time in 1775 she had come with her family to Monticello and, as soon as her age allowed, had started doing errands for Martha Jefferson, her older half-sister. When Martha's end approached, she was at her deathbed. With high probability, she felt she belonged in that circle, or clan, for which Jefferson was universally reckoned as its "natural" center. This sense of belonging to a precise family, her master's family, helps in understanding why both siblings returned to Virginia. She could have stayed in France on her own, in theory, but apparently the fear of disconnection and the anxiety of losing direction weighed more than the burden of slavery from which she knew she *personally* could never escape (and she knew her progeny would).[176]

Upon her return to Monticello in 1789, she resumed her position within the family. No matter the actual role she carried out, whether Jefferson's chambermaid, Mary's and Martha's maid, house-keeper, house-servant, or seamstress, Hemings achieved her destination. She accomplished her projects. Of course, she did not accomplish herself individualistically, as *we* may prefer. When this nearly-white-woman-being-actually-black got home, she was already pregnant, and many pregnancies were yet to come. Her role as a mother and her body as a maternal body loom very large in the definition of her accomplishments. Hemings saw her own many accomplishments. And Jefferson saw her accomplishments as well.

Sally Hemings was by then an accomplished woman, not only because of her Parisian education; not only because she was "happily" back where she belonged; not only because she was visibly beautiful; not only because, as she knew, her progeny would become white, be free, and escape the oppression that blacks—enslaved and free alike—faced. She was an accomplished woman because she succeeded in becoming what Jefferson thought a woman, and a woman's body, should become.

The fact that, back at the Little Mountain, Hemings did not start staking claims for her rights, personal self-determination, or individual accomplishment is decidedly important. Madison Hemings said that Jefferson "promised her extraordinary privileges," but we have to understand what those privileges really summed up to. Sally Hemings never became the mistress of Monticello. She never tried to jump to a different role but stood within the hierarchy without questioning her position. She never sought to steal Martha Jefferson Randolph's "official" functions. By the same token, she never performed some kind of extravagant, sumptuous, or "lascivious" way of life. In 1789, she probably lived in the stone house on Mulberry Row (Weaver's Cottage), where her sister Critta was known to have lived. In 1793, she may have moved into one of the three new log cabins, 12 by 14 feet, on Mulberry Row. Sometime between 1803 and 1807, she possibly occupied one of the "servant's rooms" in the South Dependencies, between the South Pavilion and the dairy. It is also likely, as Thomas Jefferson Randolph pointed out to biographer Henry Randall, that Hemings simply contented herself with "a smoke blackened and sooty room in one of the collonades." We do not know for sure where Hemings lived. (The best-case scenario has her living in a "room to herself at Monticello.") But what we do know is that Monticello never became hers. Her "extraordinary privileges," gauged in absolute terms, had a rather short range.[177]

Whatever the precise terms of a specific deal, if a deal or pledge whatsoever was ever explicitly exchanged between Jefferson and Hemings in Paris, Hemings never gave Jefferson reasons to worry. By birth, she already belonged to the highest levels of the slave hierarchy at Monticello—and in those years and circumstances that was more than something. In Paris, Jefferson bought dresses for Sally, although the Memorandum Books show a consistent disproportion between the sums he gave her and the money given to his daughters—or even the amounts he employed for himself and extra "sundries." Jefferson was relatively generous, but we may and should discuss the precise measure of her "extraordinary privileges." Similarly, the Farm Book details that, upon her return, Sally was treated relatively better than many other slaves. House servants were generally treated better than those working in the fields. She definitely had "extraordinary privileges" in that, for example, she could count on nurses for her children, including her mother, Elizabeth Hemings. Likewise, she was the only enslaved person at Monticello who did not sell things to Jefferson—this indicates that she could just ask him for money. Maybe, after all, Heming's "extraordinary privileges" did exist.[178]

"Extraordinary privileges" notwithstanding, there is no basis for the contentions that this "lascivious" "African Venus" ever moved around the house "pampered" in expensive Parisian gear while putting on an air of distinction, and that Jefferson must have seen her that way. For Jefferson, Hemings succeeded in accomplishing what many other educated, genotypically white good-looking women could attain only after duress and painful discipline. Sally Hemings blossomed into a type of woman that Jefferson, as we know all too well, admired. Momentarily, he may also have found interesting the *persona*, both character and corporeality, that Maria Cosway, Anne Willing Bingham, or other Parisian salonnières put on stage: flirtatious, seductive, artistic, self-willed, independent, rather unpredictable, and "unnatural."

Hemings knew and publicly showed what a member of the "weaker sex" was "naturally" made for. And Hemings was, after all, a member of the "weaker sex." She gave Jefferson what he expected—more than sexually. Not even his daughters made him so relaxed about "natural" gender roles and "suitable" gender performances. Although Hemings did not easily fit into any category that Jefferson had created, she was clearly an "angel" rather than an "Amazon." Hemings never put him in a position to fret if she was performing what every woman was expected to perform. He never had to ask her, for example, "How many hours a day you sew?" His daughters, conversely, for their class identity and an ensuing sense of entitlement, could not make him so certain. American "angels" obviously they were, never sassy, or prissy. But they had to be verbally spurred: "Whether you know how to make a pudding yet, to cut out a beef stake, to sow spinach? Or to set a hen?" As far as Hemings was concerned, Jefferson's expectations were obviously lower, but his anxiety was lower as well. And he did not need to say anything.[179]

Everything about Hemings's corporeality and considerable presence communicated self-effacement. Phenotypically, she lacked those "objective" traits that Jefferson's racially charged physical anthropology analyzed so well— disagreeable odor, no blushing, no "tender delicate mixture of sentiment and sensation," and so on. What is more, Hemings's *persona* moved around with suppleness, delicateness, and discretion. Nothing spectacular went on in the Big House, no exhibitions, no scenes, no showdowns, and Jefferson had nothing to fear from this singular member of the "weaker sex." He had not to worry about Hemings's deviation from those norms he thought natural for a woman to follow. Starting from her body, Sally Hemings was already perceived as *essentially* anomalous (black and white, slave and family, and so on). She also knew this fact, her "anomaly," and consequently she was all too eager to abide by norms, not of her own choice, that could "liberate" her. At the end of the eighteenth century, women varied among themselves, unmistakably. Other women, like Martha Jefferson Randolph, we have seen, had to be gently and at times forcefully constrained into their "natural" roles. But Sally Hemings was a person whose center was from the start outside of herself. She never performed acts of defiance to the system—or if she ever did this in Paris, the phase was rather short-lived.

For her, the only sensible project of realization was to have her children, those who were already born and all those who would come, protected and eventually freed. By the same token, the only way she could sensibly think about her personal realization was by being acknowledged by the "Jeffersonian system" and keeping with her affiliation. True as it is that she never became public and "political" like other women did—a republican mother and a virtuous wife devoted to enhancing virtue—she nonetheless became, to Jefferson's eyes, a commendable example of the "weaker sex." Maria Cosway, Anne Willing Bingham, Jefferson's daughter Martha, to a greater or lesser extent, sent Jefferson disturbing messages. But attaining the constraints of "naturalness" that Jefferson expected women to attain was the only option Hemings could realistically choose. Each time Jefferson examined her, he was content that she could succeed on so many levels.

Conclusion

The discourse on the "others" developed in part 2 is not a criticism of Thomas Jefferson, an eighteenth-century philosopher of the Enlightenment, a man who accomplished a lot, who improved many things, who in many ways led his generation, inspired future generations, and whom we should praise on so many levels. More than a criticism or an exercise in moralization, I wanted to emphasize a sense of "otherness." Jefferson's and his generation's invention of the "other" has been contextualized and unmasked. The difference between Jefferson's gradualism, meliorism, including his stadial theory of the progress of civilization, and more humanitarian and radical measures has been contextualized as well.

Jefferson himself, both his mind and above all his body, has consequently become our "other." We see his *persona;* we contemplate his portraits; we read famous and less famous descriptions and characterizations; we study eighteenth-century clothing, manners, habits, and behaviors; we praise his corporeality, his relative modernity, his simplicity, his almost feminine softness, and his attempts at building a postmartial, postaristocratic masculinity. But we do not acknowledge this figure and its necessary expedients as belonging to our world.

Jefferson's mind—his thoughts, tenets, ideas—and his ambitious projects still survive, and hopefully they will survive for centuries on end. We still need Jefferson's Enlightenment. But his body, including the often-painful and all-too-often arbitrary dialectics between self and other I have examined, is dead. We keep studying Jefferson's corporeality, among other things belonging to his world, but we should bear in mind that *he* is no more. His factual, real, bodily self, his corporeal strategies and expedients, the fact that he allowed himself to become flexible and to attempt many experiments with his body, while the "other" had to stick to her or his "nature," all these ensembles of facts and values, acts and ideas, are forever gone.

Notes

Introduction

1. Wirt, "Eulogy on Jefferson," *Writings of TJ*, 13:xiii.
2. See Polhemus, "Social Bodies," 33.
3. See Gallagher, *How the Body Shapes the Mind*. William James wrote that "we feel sorry because we cry, angry because we strike, afraid because we tremble, and not that we cry, strike, or tremble, because we are sorry, angry, or fearful, as the case may be." James, "What Is an Emotion," 190. On William James, I am indebted to Dick Holway.

Part I: Self

1. Extract from the Diary of Ezra Stiles, 8 June 1784, *Papers of Thomas Jefferson* (hereafter *PTJ*) 7:303; John Adams to James Warren, 27 August 1784, *PTJ* 7:382. A handy and reliable list of comments by contemporaries on Jefferson's mind and character can be found at http://wiki.monticello.org/mediawiki/index.php/Notable _Comments_on_Jefferson_%28Contemporary%29#.
2. Marquis de Chastellux's portrayal of TJ, translation published in London in 1787, *PTJ* 7:585–86.
3. H. Adams, *History of the United States*, 363; TJ to Maria Jefferson Eppes, 3 March 1802, *PTJ* 36:676. On Jefferson's proactive temper, see, for example, Meacham, *Thomas Jefferson*, and Cogliano, *Emperor of Liberty*.
4. For a list of witnesses describing Jefferson's physical appearance, see http:// www.monticello.org/site/research-and-collections/physical-descriptions-jefferson#. The complete memoirs of both Isaac Jefferson and Edmund Bacon are collected in the volume edited by James A. Bear Jr., *Jefferson at Monticello*. The slave Isaac Jefferson was actually named Isaac Granger. A thorough collection of memoirs, recollections, and interviews on Jefferson can be found in Hayes, *Jefferson in His Own Time*.

5. S. H. Smith, *Memoir of the Life, Character, and Writings of Thomas Jefferson*, 35; Gadsden, *Essay on the Life of the Right Reverend Theodore Dehon*, 239; Frances Wright to Julia and Harriet Garnett, 12, 14 November 1824, Houghton Library, Harvard University. See also Thomas Jefferson Randolph in Hayes, *Jefferson in His Own Time*, 164. We will see later on that Jefferson, actually, did not age so well. For the comparison of today's average height and Jefferson's time height, see http://www.monticello.org/site/research-and-collections/jeffersons-height#. Tall stature is a socially desirable asset. See, for example, Judge and Cable, "Effect of Physical Height"; Roberts and Herman, "Psychology of Height"; and Hall, *Size Matters*.

6. Webster in Hayes, *Jefferson in His Own Time*, 93–94; Thomas Jefferson Randolph in ibid., 164; Thompson in ibid., 135–36. On Jefferson slightly bent with age, see Adam Hodgson, a merchant from Liverpool who met Jefferson in the early 1820s: "He is tall and very thin, a little bent with age, with an intelligent and sprightly countenance." Hodgson in ibid., 90.

7. Parton, *Life of Thomas Jefferson*, 165. An interesting example of Jefferson's praise of musical harmony as a bodily ideal can be seen in an original metaphor he deploys in a letter to Mann Page, 16 May 1796, *PTJ* 29:100: "It is unpleasant that we should have been made, like our watches, to wear out by degrees, lose our teeth, and become unfit for our functions. A musical glass would have been a better type, sound, strong, and vibrating in all it's harmony till some accident shivers it to atoms."

8. Margaret Bayard Smith in Hayes, *Jefferson in His Own Time*, 45. Thomas Jefferson Randolph agrees that Jefferson was "soft and feminine in his affections to his family, he entered into and sympathized with all their feelings, winning them to paths of virtue by the soothing gentleness of his manner." Thomas Jefferson Randolph in ibid., 159. Henry Adams as well emphasized Jefferson's consistent determination to stay away from "whatever was rough or coarse," and insisted that "his yearning for sympathy was almost feminine." H. Adams, *History of the United States*, 100. On Jefferson as feminine, see Ellis, *American Sphinx*, 305–6. On Jefferson as "engaging," see Joseph Story to Samuel P. P. May, 30 May 1807, in Hayes, *Jefferson in His Own Time*, 43: "His manners are inviting and not uncourtly; . . . His smile is very engaging. . . . If he chooses, he cannot fail to please." Most likely, when Jefferson smiled he did so in a contained and gracious way. Frances Few writes that "his teeth are good he shews but little of them when he laughs." Few, "Diary of Frances Few," 350.

9. TJ to Peter Carr, 19 August 1785, *PTJ* 8:407. For very similar ideas, that "of all the exercises walking is best" and that "not less than two hours a day should be devoted to exercise," see also TJ to Thomas Mann Randolph, 27 August 1786, *PTJ* 10:308. On Jefferson and sex as "part of a regimen of self-control, and important to understand if one was to enjoy a productive life," see Burstein, *Jefferson's Secrets*, especially 156–57, 186. Burstein claims that "Jefferson's taking of Sally Hemings as a concubine would have offered him a nearby sexual outlet. . . . His servant's exclusive

attention to him would also have protected him against venereal disease." Ibid., 157. I analyze Jefferson's relationship with Sally Hemings later on, and from a different angle. See also T. A. Foster, *Sex and the Founding Fathers*.

10. See Merleau-Ponty, *Phenomenology of Perception*, 159.

11. TJ to Thomas Mann Randolph, 27 August 1786, *PTJ* 10:308. See also TJ to Martha Jefferson, 28 March 1787, *PTJ* 11:250–52. For a fairly complete list of Jefferson's famous quotations on exercise, see http://www.monticello.org/site/research -and-collections/exercise#.

12. "Brute animals are the most healthy, and they are exposed to all weather, and of men, those are healthiest who are the most exposed." TJ to Thomas Mann Randolph, 27 August 1786, *PTJ* 10:308. Jefferson gave Thomas Mann Randolph advice that he also applied to himself: "I speak this from my own experience, having, from an attachment to study, very early in life, made this arrangement of my time." Ibid. Edmund Bacon, however, says that Jefferson had "a machine for measuring strength." While Thomas Mann Randolph, Jefferson's son-in-law, was very "strong in the arms," "Mr. Jefferson was stronger than he." Bacon in Bear, *Jefferson at Monticello*, 71.

13. Both Eastern and Western traditions acknowledged walking as the best method toward an enhanced psychophysical presence in the world. Aristotle's "peripatetic" school, Immanuel Kant, Friedrich Nietzsche, Henry David Thoreau, and so many other figures speculated extensively on the catharsis produced by walking. On walking, see Solnit, *Wanderlust*. Interesting on traditional Virginian "sports" is Breen, "Horses and Gentlemen." Isaac Jefferson confirms that "Mr. Jefferson never had nothing to do with horse racing or cockfighting." Isaac Jefferson in Bear, *Jefferson at Monticello*, 20. As to being ruffled, Edmund Bacon writes that Jefferson's "countenance was always mild and pleasant. You never saw it ruffled. No odds what happened, it always maintained the same expression." Bacon in ibid., 71. Jefferson managed to remain characteristically unruffled in many adverse situations. As he lectured his grandson Francis Wayles Eppes, "nothing gives one person so great advantage over another, as to remain always cool and unruffled under all circumstances." TJ to Francis Eppes, 21 May 1816, *Papers of Thomas Jefferson, Retirement Series* (hereafter *PTJ-RS*) 10:72–73. I will return to the topic of Jefferson being especially straight.

14. TJ to David Howell, 15 December 1810, *PTJ-RS* 3:257; TJ to Benjamin Rush, 17 August 1811, *PTJ-RS* 4:88.

15. TJ to John Adams, 21 January 1812, *PTJ-RS* 4:429.

16. TJ to Dr. Vine Utley, 21 March 1819, *Works of TJ*, 12:118; TJ to John Adams, 15 August 1820, *Adams-Jefferson Letters* (hereafter *A-JL*) 565; TJ to Charles Willson Peale, 18 July 1824, University of Texas, Hanley Collection; Randolph, *Domestic Life of Thomas Jefferson*, 421. On "Eagle," see *Jefferson's Memorandum Books* (hereafter *JMB*) 1371, and Bacon in Bear, *Jefferson at Monticello*, 62.

17. Breen, "Horses and Gentlemen," 249. On the traditional values attached to

horses, see Isaac, *Transformation of Virginia*, 99. And see Campbell, *Horse in Virginia*. See also *JMB* 1507 for a complete list of horse names. On Jefferson's positive appraisal of Ossian/Macpherson, see TJ to Charles Macpherson, 25 February 1773, *PTJ* 1:96–97. See also Hayes, *Road to Monticello*, 133–46, and McLaughlin, "Jefferson, Poe, and Ossian." He copied entries from Ossian/Macpherson when young in his *Literary Commonplace Book*, n. 141–45, 150–51.

18. TJ to Giovanni Fabbroni, 8 June 1778, *PTJ* 2:196. On French music, see TJ to Charles Bellini, 30 September 1785, *PTJ* 8:569. Jefferson's sincere sympathy for dancing is well summarized, for example, by a letter he wrote to Louis Xaupi (1 September 1825, Library of Congress, Papers of Thomas Jefferson) concerning "An application from young gentlemen of the Univ^ty for the appropriation of a room wherein they might recieve instruction in the use of the small sword." Jefferson did not like the idea of having students practicing the sword. Dancing was a different affair: "it's object, is the embellishment, and not the destruction, of the lives of our young citizens. . . . dancing is generally, and justly I think, considered among *innocent* accomplishments; while we cannot so consider the art of stabbing and pistolling our friends." See also Cripe, *Jefferson and Music*.

19. Ellen Wayles Randolph Coolidge, Notes and Copies of Letters to Henry S. Randall and Others, Ellen Wayles Randolph Coolidge Correspondence, University of Virginia, italics added; Isaac Jefferson and Bacon in Bear, *Jefferson at Monticello*, 13, 83. In her London travel diary, on 1 October 1838, Ellen writes: "My grandfather was a true lover of music—he enjoyed all that was good of it's kind—no one had a more true feeling for Italian music, but he likewise had a love of boyhood for the old Scotch songs. 'The Lass of Patie's Mill,' 'The Broom of Cowdenows,' 'Robin Adair' & 'Lochaber' were among his favorites." Ellen Wayles Randolph Coolidge Diary, Massachusetts Historical Society.

20. Fliegelman, *Declaring Independence*, 17, italics added. Performing bodies and the "culture of performance" have captured the attention of historians of the Early Republic. Fliegelman has popularized the phrase "culture of performance," but he remained principally interested in rhetorical and oratorical performances. On oratory and performance, see also Gustafson, *Eloquence Is Power*. Richard Beeman, Simon Newman, and David Waldstreicher, among other scholars, have insisted on the practices, performances, experiences, and behaviors (including fetes and public demonstrations) that shaped the political culture(s) of the nation. See, for example, Beeman, *Varieties of Political Experience*; Newman, *Parades and the Politics of the Streets*; and Waldstreicher, *In the Midst of Perpetual Fetes*. Carroll Smith-Rosenberg, in her recent *This Violent Empire*, builds upon the notion of "the performative nature of national identities" (42). Heather Miyano Kopelson, in her *Faithful Bodies*, has brought the individual body and its many dimensions to a really central stage. More than preceding scholars have done, Kopelson has taken up the challenge of multidisciplinarity, or rather transdisciplinarity.

21. TJ to Benjamin Rush, 17 August 1811, *PTJ-RS* 4:87. Jefferson's interest in

mathematics was real. I. B. Cohen has convincingly argued that Jefferson read and understood Newton's *Principia*. See Cohen, *Science and the Founding Fathers*, 97–108.

22. Hemphill, *Bowing to Necessities*, 3.

23. Bushman, *Refinement of America*, xii.

24. Hemphill, *Bowing to Necessities*, 18, 62.

25. TJ to George Gilmer, 12 August 1787, *PTJ* 12:26. On Monticello as an "asylum from grief," see TJ to Maria Cosway, 12 October 1786, *PTJ* 10:447.

26. Volney's journal quoted in Gaulmier, *Un grand témoin de la révolution et de l'empire*, 210; Brown, *Good Wives*, 321. Volney gives a perfect example of Jefferson's emptying violence of its content while retaining both its form and context. In the account of his June 1796 visit to Monticello, Volney wrote about a *"scène comique"* he beheld. Jefferson and Volney were visiting the fields, when the master took a whip (*"un fouet"*) to frighten work-shy slaves: *"il s'agitait, grondait, menaçait et se tournait de tous côtés"* (he hustled and bustled, sweated, and turned on every side). Slaves, expectedly, went back to idleness each time Jefferson turned his back. The scene was *"comique"* because Jefferson, evidently, was only playing a part: *"Ce tableau me rappela ces troupes de singes et de petits chiens habillés que nous voyons dans les rues de Paris danser au geste d'un bâton"* (This picture reminded me of those companies of dressed-up monkeys and little dogs that we see in the streets of Paris dancing at the motion of a stick). Volney in Gaulmier, *Un grand témoin de la révolution et de l'empire*, 210–11. Fawn Brodie (*Thomas Jefferson*, 288) describes the episode as "a piece of expected theater," recognized as such by the slaves. Even so, symbolic violence keeps being violence. Jefferson was a mild patriarch. He belonged to a culture of paternalism, and paternalism was less centered on physical coercion; it was more domesticated, more clearly based on self-control, self-restraint, the mastering of passions, and a new ideal of manliness as equal to gentility. On the distinction between patriarchy and paternalism, see Brown, *Good Wives*, 322, 462–63, n. 9. See also Jan Lewis, "Domestic Tranquillity."

27. On widespread consumption, see A. S. Martin, *Buying into the World of Goods*. See also Breen, *Marketplace of Revolution*. On falling into debt, see Sloan, *Principle and Interest*. On the elite's peculiar "desire to keep up appearances" that "helped fuel an infernal economic spiral," see Breen, *Tobacco Culture*, 105–6, 129–32. For some figures describing the trend, see ibid., 195. On the eve of the Revolution, as Breen maintains, "The days of recklessly conspicuous consumption were over." Ibid., 198. The war undoubtedly put this practice temporarily on hold. However, with the peace, consumption resumed. It is enough to cast a quick look at late eighteenth- and early nineteenth-century Virginia mansions, including Monticello, to behold a return of the age-old bias for opulence and fine things. After all, for years on end Virginia remained "a society in which material possessions counted for so much." Ibid., 207.

28. TJ to James Madison, 8 December 1784, *PTJ* 7:559. On Jefferson praising the manners of "our country," see TJ to James Monroe, 17 June 1785, *PTJ* 8:227–33. See also TJ to James Monroe, 18 December 1786, *PTJ* 10:611–13.

29. TJ to James Madison, 20 February 1784, *PTJ* 6:550. On Jefferson on an *exclusive* circle of friends and affections, see also, for example, TJ to Martha Jefferson, 15 January 1792, *PTJ* 23:44; TJ to Martha Jefferson, 17 May 1798, *PTJ* 30:354; TJ to Mary Jefferson, 1 January 1799, *PTJ* 30:607; TJ to James Maury, 25 April 1812, *PTJ-RS* 4:671.

30. TJ to Ralph Izard, 17 July 1788, *PTJ* 13:372; "Jefferson's Hints to Americans Travelling in Europe," *PTJ* 13:269–70. These "hints" were an epitome of Jefferson's two travel journals of 1787 and 1788. See also TJ to John Rutledge, 19 June 1788, *PTJ* 13:262–64, and TJ to Thomas Lee Shippen, 19 June 1788, *PTJ* 13:276–77.

31. TJ to Walker Maury, 19 August 1785, *PTJ* 8:409. See also Jefferson's famous letter to John Banister, 15 October 1785, *PTJ* 8:635–38. Jefferson had his imagination closed on so many circumstances. Lucia Stanton, for example, shows the extent of the "gradual closing of [Jefferson's] imagination that distanced and dehumanized the black families of Monticello." Jefferson had somehow to "protect himself," as Stanton says, from the brutal fact that he owned other human beings, while making calculations on them and deciding the course of their lives. Stanton, *"Those Who Labor for My Happiness,"* 18.

32. TJ, Draft of a Declaration on the British Treatment of Ethan Allen, 2 January 1776, to Maj. Gen. Howe, *PTJ* 1:276. A motion was made for a public protest by Congress, and Jefferson was appointed to draft this document. But action on the protest was eventually postponed and was not resumed.

33. TJ to Charles Bellini, 30 September 1785, *PTJ* 8:569. In this same letter, Jefferson also insists on the "tranquil permanent felicity with which domestic society in America blesses most of it's inhabitants."

34. TJ to Martha Jefferson Randolph, 5 February 1801, *PTJ* 32:557.

35. TJ to John Adams, 28 October 1813, *PTJ-RS* 6:563. On Jefferson "ultimately moored in the midst of my affections," see TJ to Martha Jefferson Randolph, 27 February 1809, *Family Letters*, 385.

36. On Jefferson bowing to every person he met and talking with arms folded, see Isaac Jefferson in Bear, *Jefferson at Monticello*, 23. On Chesterfield (Philip Dormer Stanhope, 4th Earl of Chesterfield), see TJ, *Catalogue of the Library of Thomas Jefferson* (hereafter Sowerby) #1115. On Jefferson's libraries, see Gilreath and Wilson, *Jefferson's Library*, and D. L. Wilson, *Jefferson's Books*. On Jefferson's readings, see Sanford, *Jefferson and His Library*; D. L. Wilson, "Jefferson's Early Notebooks"; and Reinhold, "Classical World." The best treatment to date of both Jefferson's early intellectual development and his reading habits is Hayes, *Road to Monticello*. Hayes deals extensively with Jefferson as a lover and collector of books.

37. Hemphill, *Bowing to Necessities*, 71. Moralistic religious guidebooks survived well into the eighteenth century. Perhaps the most popular was *The Whole Duty of Man*, attributed to Richard Allestree, a seventeenth-century clergyman. Concerning this book, Richard Bushman writes: "The moral guidebooks taught a different lesson than the manners books [or, as Hemphill has it, conduct literature]. *The*

Whole Duty of Man enjoined submission to God and continual acts of piety and charity and could easily have been divided into sermons. . . . People known to live in the courtesy-book world owned and read *The Whole Duty of Man*. The two ethics lived side by side." Bushman, *Refinement of America*, 59–60. For an introduction to conduct literature, courtesy books, and etiquette, see Schlesinger, *Learning How to Behave*; Bushman *Refinement of America*, 30–60; and Hemphill *Bowing to Necessities*, 17–30. See also Mason, *Gentlefolk in the Making*, and Kelso, *Doctrine of the English Gentleman*.

38. Chesterfield, *Lord Chesterfield's Letters*, 134; Castiglione quoted in Hemphill, *Bowing to Necessity*, 25. Henry Randall observed that Jefferson's "manners had the grace, finish, suavity and unpresumingness . . . of a well-bred Frenchman. . . . His physical, and in some particulars his mental constitution seems to us to have more resembled the man of Southern than the man of Northern Europe." Randall, *Life of Thomas Jefferson*, 1:421.

39. *JMB* 283, italics added. Both the reason for and the sources of these two lines are not ascertained. Jefferson must have liked them, obviously, whether or not he was the author. Maxims and excerpts were repeatedly entered in his Memorandum Books, possibly jotted down for later use or just to give voice and "color" to the feeling of the moment.

40. Locke, *Some Thoughts Concerning Education*, 107. Locke's *Some Thoughts* was obviously in Jefferson's library. He ordered it from Paris on 9 September 1789. See Sowerby #1107.

41. Chesterfield, *Lord Chesterfield's Letters*, 116; Locke, *Some Thoughts Concerning Education*, 107.

42. TJ to Anne Cary Randolph, Thomas Jefferson Randolph, and Ellen Wayles Randolph, 2 March 1802, *PTJ* 37:20.

43. TJ, *Notes*, Query 17, *Works of TJ*, 4:78; TJ to Thomas Jefferson Randolph, 24 November 1808, *Works of TJ*, 11:81; Locke, *Some Thoughts Concerning Education*, 109. Thomas Jefferson Randolph stresses Jefferson's repulsion for controversies: "He never indulged in controversial conversation, because it often excited unpleasant feeling, and illustrated its inutility by the anecdote of two men who sat down candidly to discuss a subject, and each converted the other." Thomas Jefferson Randolph in Hayes, *Jefferson in His Own Time*, 161.

44. TJ to Benjamin Rush, 23 September 1800, *PTJ* 32:167. On Jefferson's concern for fetid air and his craving for ventilation, see TJ to Joseph Priestley, 18 January 1800, *PTJ* 31:319–23. On the question of good air circulation in prisons, hospitals, and public buildings in general, see Clagett, *Scientific Jefferson*, 53–69. See also Shammas, "Space Problem." For famous attacks against cities, see TJ to John Lithgow, 4 January 1805, *Writings of TJ*, 11:55; TJ to Caspar Wistar, 21 June 1807, *Works of TJ*, 10:423–30, especially 423; and TJ to William Short, 8 September 1823, *Writings of TJ*, 15:467–70.

45. TJ to Maria Cosway, 12 October 1786, *PTJ* 10:449–50.

46. On the Original Rough Draught of the Declaration of Independence, see *PTJ* 1:423. On the reality of community and on virtue and happiness as intertwined, see Valsania, *Nature's Man.* On the American nation as "an expansive family of families," see Onuf, *Jefferson's Empire*, especially 78. On families, wards, states, and nations as ascending biological orders, see Valsania, "Beyond Particularism."

47. On the ethics of plain feeling, see Fiering, "Irresistible Compassion." A good example of Jefferson's flirtatious attitudes is the letter he wrote to Maria Cosway, 30 July 1788, *PTJ* 13:435: "Cease to chide me. . . . You esteem me as much as I deserve. If I love you more, it is because you deserve more. . . . Chide me then no more; be to me what you have been; and give me without measure the comfort of your friendship." The fullest discussion to date of Jefferson's debt to the eighteenth-century impassioned rhetoric of feeling and sympathy can be found in Burstein, *Sentimental Democracy*, and Burstein, *Jefferson's Secrets.* See also Barker-Benfield, *Culture of Sensibility*; Rousseau, "Nerves, Spirits, and Fibres"; and Mullan, *Sentiment and Sociability.*

48. On the "fondness for European luxury and dissipation" and so forth, see TJ to John Banister, 15 October 1785, *PTJ* 8:635–38. Jon Kukla writes that "the overall relationship between Jefferson and Maria Cosway was a flirtatious friendship enhanced by shared cultural interests rather than a passionately erotic affair." Kukla, *Mr. Jefferson's Women*, 103.

49. See Steele, *Thomas Jefferson and American Nationhood.*

50. TJ to Charles Thompson, 25 December 1808, *Works of TJ*, 11:84.

51. Margaret Bayard Smith tells us about Jefferson being proprietary about his "sanctum sanctorum": "Mr J. went to his apartments, the door of which is never opened but by himself and his retirement seems so sacred that I told him it was his sanctum sanctorum." Smith in Hayes, *Jefferson in His Own Time*, 53. On the presence of the Hemings family in Jefferson's life, see Gordon-Reed, *Hemingses of Monticello.*

52. Madison Hemings in Gordon-Reed, *Thomas Jefferson and Sally Hemings*, 247.

53. Ibid., italics added. On Jefferson freeing his slave children, see the discussion in ibid., 38–43, 52–53, 66.

54. On care and the dualism between male and female body, see Gilligan, *In a Different Voice.* Jefferson was most of the time wary of physical punishment, even toward his slaves. In 1792, for example, Jefferson wanted to inform his overseer, Manoah Clarkson, that "My first wish is that the labourers may be well treated." TJ to Thomas Mann Randolph, 19 April 1792, *PTJ* 23:435–36. Overseers, obviously, whipped slaves repeatedly. In 1812, Jame Hubbard was eventually apprehended. A twenty-seven-year-old slave who worked in the plantation nail factory, he had repeatedly run away since 1805. Jefferson wrote: "I had him severely flogged in the presence of his old companions." Jefferson was convinced that Hubbard "will never again serve any man as a slave. the moment he is out of jail and his irons off he will be off himself." He thus made the decision to sell him. See TJ to Reuben Perry,

16 April 1812, *PTJ-RS* 4:620. In 1799, Jefferson advised George Jefferson to take care of the apprehension of another fugitive slave: "there is a negro man named Jack whom I hired of a widow Mallory . . . who has run away, and has been seen at Richmond where he has a wife. . . . I would wish him to lie in jail a month or so as a punishment, & then let any body have him for the residue of the year at the rate I pay, £20. a year. [His] mistress might have him at any time, releasing my hire from thence." TJ to George Jefferson, 18 May 1799, *PTJ* 31:112. On Jefferson simplistically portrayed as duplicitous and evil, see Wiencek, *Master of the Mountain*. For a less judgmental account of the reality of slavery and violence at Monticello, see Stanton, *"Those Who Labor for My Happiness."* Jefferson's grandson Thomas Jefferson Randolph stated that "the only impatience of temper he ever exhibited was with his horse, which he subdued to his will by a fearless application of the whip, on the slightest manifestation of restiveness." Randolph, *Domestic Life of Thomas Jefferson*, 338. The point is that Jefferson was not a violent person and hence accountable *for that*; however, as we will see better in part 2, throughout his life he was immersed in a culture of violence, availing itself of violent institutions from which Jefferson-the-slave-master profited.

55. Virginia J. Randolph Trist to Nicholas P. Trist, 26 May 1839, in Randall, *Life of Thomas Jefferson*, 3:350; Martha J. Trist Burke to Ella Thurman Pratt, Thomas Jefferson Library, Thomas Jefferson Foundation.

56. TJ to John Wayles Eppes, 25 December 1809, *PTJ-RS* 2:92; Bacon in Bear, *Jefferson at Monticello*, 85, 86–87. Virginia Randolph Trist provides a very similar account of the "summer sports" that Jefferson played with his grandchildren on the terrace or around the lawn. See Virginia J. Randolph Trist to Nicholas P. Trist, 26 May 1839, in Randall, *Life of Thomas Jefferson*, 3:349.

57. For the "republican obsession with the problem of generational succession," see Onuf, *Mind of Thomas Jefferson*, 190–91. On the theme of "filial gratitude," the "parent's solicitude for his children," and the "importance of preparing the next generation to govern itself—and to provide, in turn, for succeeding generations," see ibid., 32, 174–76. For a recent convincing treatment of Jefferson's assumption of a "continuity between the Revolutionary generation of Americans and the latest one, down to our own," see Steele, *Jefferson and American Nationhood*, especially 46–52. For an interesting analysis of the interplay between public and private and what we may consider in strict dychotomic terms, see Allgor, *Parlor Politics*.

58. MacRae, "Body and Social Metaphor," 63.

59. TJ to William Short, 5 May 1816, *PTJ-RS* 10:10.

60. Hewes, "World Distribution of Certain Postural Habits," 86–87.

61. Bushman, *Refinement of America*, 64. For the departure from the more erect formality of earlier time, see ibid., 66. See also Annas, "Elegant Art of Movement."

62. On the practice of wearing stays for support, see Baumgarten, *What Clothes Reveal*, 121–22, 134.

63. Chesterfield, *Principles of Politeness*, 22.

64. Maclay, *Journal of William Maclay*, 272. I will return to the topic of Jefferson in his "dandy" phase.

65. On hair and wigs, see Haulman, *Politics of Fashion*, 64, 104, and n. 70, 250.

66. Thomas Jefferson Randolph in Hayes, *Jefferson in His Own Time*, 164. On wigs, see also http://www.monticello.org/site/research-and-collections/wigs. In his classic study on the life portraits of Jefferson, Fiske Kimball writes apropos Mather Brown's portrait that "the hair, his own, is powdered, with rolls over the ears." Kimball, "Life Portraits of Jefferson and Their Replicas," 501. Garry Wills writes instead that "Jefferson himself had dressed like a court dandy in Europe, as we know from the first portrait of him, by Mather Brown, in which he wears a wig and frilly lace in the highest French fashion." Wills, *Henry Adams and the Making of America*, 178. William Howard Adams agrees with Wills and points out that "The earliest portrait of Jefferson, painted by Mather Brown in 1786, . . . suggests a self-conscious dandy, with his overly ruffled jabot and tightly curled wig." W. H. Adams, *Paris Years of Thomas Jefferson*, 18. But I believe Brown showed a dandy preferring *not to* wear old-fashioned wigs. In Brown's portrait, we find other republican, if not downright democratic details—the untrimmed frock, for example, a type of coat adopted by English and French gentlemen but borrowed directly from the working classes. The frock had a practical, turned-down collar that could be buttoned up during inclement weather. Another element revealing republican priorities was the Goddess of Liberty, standing behind Jefferson. On the international success of the frock, see Cunnington and Cunnington, *Handbook of English Costume*, 16–18.

67. TJ to Thomas Jefferson Randolph, 6 May 1809, *PTJ-RS* 1:190. Frances Few wrote, circa 1808, that "he wears powder but it is evident that his hair is red." Few, "Diary of Frances Few," 350.

68. Dunlap cited in Burstein, *Jefferson's Secrets*, 303.

69. Thomas Jefferson Randolph in Hayes, *Jefferson in His Own Time*, 164. In his so-called autobiography, Jefferson wrote that "The tradition in my father's family was, that their ancestor came to this country from Wales, and from near the mountain of Snowdon, the highest in Great Britain." *Writings of TJ*, 1:1. See also the entries "Welsh Ancestry" (http://www.monticello.org/site/research-and-collections/welsh-ancestry#) and "Jefferson's Ancestry" (http://www.monticello.org/site/research-and-collections/jeffersons-ancestry#).

70. TJ to Joseph Delaplaine, 30 May 1813, *PTJ-RS* 6:148. To Horatio Spafford, Jefferson wrote that the medallion is "deemed the best which has been taken of me." TJ to Horatio G. Spafford, 21 February 1815, *PTJ-RS* 8:281. On the family's preference for Stuart's "medallion portrait," see Meschutt, "Gilbert Stuart's Portraits of Thomas Jefferson," 15. See also Bush, *Life Portraits of Thomas Jefferson*, 62.

71. On Saint-Mémin, see Bush, *Life Portraits of Thomas Jefferson*, 53. On Browere's plaster cast, see Meschutt, "'Perfect Likeness.'" On Houdon and Ceracchi, see Bush, *Life Portraits of Thomas Jefferson*, 15–17.

72. "Dress can be considered a form of performance in everyday life." Haulman, *Politics of Fashion*, n. 8, 228.

73. Few, "Diary of Frances Few," 350; Joseph Story to Samuel P. P. May, 30 May 1807, in Hayes, *Jefferson in His Own Time*, 43.

74. Maclay, *Journal of William Maclay*, 272; Robert Troup to Rufus King, 9 April 1802, *Life and Correspondence of Rufus King*, 4:103. See also H. Adams, *History of the United States*, 126–27, 546–66.

75. H. Adams, *History of the United States*, 127. On Jefferson's effort at democratizing American style, see Allgor, *Parlor Politics*, 4–47. Dumas Malone writes that Jefferson's behavior when receiving Anthony Merry may be "regarded as an act of bravado, or as a deliberate attempt to cut a pompous diplomat down to size." Malone, *Jefferson and His Time*, 4:380. On the whole episode, including Jefferson's "democratic" gesture and the Merrys' preexisting biases against "barbarous" Washington, see ibid., 378–84. In a letter to James Monroe (8 January 1804, *Works of TJ*, 10:67), Jefferson alleged that Mrs. Merry was "a virago, and in a short course of a few weeks has established a degree of dislike among all classes which one would have thought impossible in so short a time."

76. Brown, *Foul Bodies*, 137.

77. On the "Revolution of 1800" as a real revolution "in the principles of our government as that of 1776 was in its form," see TJ to Spencer Roane, 6 September 1819, *Works of TJ*, 12:136.

78. Rozbicki, "Barrier or a Bridge to American Identity," 434, 436.

79. TJ to Benjamin Smith Barton, 26 February 1815, *PTJ-RS* 8:285. On the embargo, see, for example, Spivak, *Jefferson's English Crisis*. Jefferson never doubted the doctrine that "the manners and spirit of a people" are the foundation "which preserve a republic in vigour." TJ, *Notes*, Query 19, *Works of TJ*, 4:86. Many documents demonstrate Jefferson's lifelong inclination to educate the people. An eloquent example is TJ to Uriah Forrest, with Enclosure (the so-called Forrest version of the famous letter to James Madison of 20 December 1787), 31 December 1787, *PTJ* 12:478: "Educate and inform the whole mass of the people, enable them to see that it is their interest to preserve peace and order, and they will preserve it."

80. TJ to Caesar Rodney, 16 March 1815, *PTJ-RS* 8:356.

81. Ségur's *Mémoires* are cited in W. H. Adams, *Paris Years of Thomas Jefferson*, 73–74. On Franklin's "provincial presence," see ibid. David Waldstreicher writes: "Jefferson's conspicuous refusal of finery as president was merely the tip of the iceberg. It was more than a symbol of republican simplicity: it was an example of material and political battles long waged and communicated through practices of dress." Waldstreicher, "Why Thomas Jefferson and African Americans Wore Their Politics on Their Sleeves," 82.

82. TJ to John Adams, 21 January 1812, *PTJ-RS* 4:428. In a letter to Jefferson dated 1 January 1812 (*PTJ-RS* 4:390–91), Adams had cracked a joke about "a Packett containing two Pieces of Homespun lately produced in this quarter by One who was

honoured in his youth with Some of your Attention and much of your kindness." Adams was alluding to John Quincy Adams's *Lectures on Rhetoric and Oratory, Delivered to the Classes of Senior and Junior Sophisters in Harvard University*, 2 vols. (1810; Sowerby #4659), but the books arrived only after Adams's letter reached Jefferson. As a consequence, Jefferson drafted his reply taking the reference to homespun literally. Jefferson's interest in merino sheep, carding machines, and looms is well known. See, for example, McEwan, *Thomas Jefferson*.

83. William Plumer to Jeremiah Smith, 9 December 1802, in Turner, *William Plumer of New Hampshire*, 94. Henry Tutwiler, the first student to earn a master's degree from the University of Virginia, saw Jefferson for the first time in the summer of 1825: "I was in the Proctor's office, when a tall, venerable gentleman, plainly dressed, entered the room, in a quiet, unobtrusive manner, and took a seat in my corner. . . . I thought that it was a plain country farmer, who had called to see the Proctor on business." Tutwiler in Hayes, *Jefferson in His Own Time*, 181. He also wrote that Jefferson had the habit of covering the four miles from Monticello to the campus on horseback, often unattended. John Bernard, a British actor who befriended Vice President Jefferson and later visited the president in Washington, provides an especially savory version of Jefferson going unrecognized. He claims that Jefferson himself told it. See Bernard in Hayes, *Jefferson in His Own Time*, 113–15. For other incidents in which people run into Jefferson failing to recognize him, see also Randall, *Life of Thomas Jefferson*, 3:232–34, 345. See also Stanton, *"Those Who Labor for My Happiness,"* 50. On Jefferson's refusal of having an attending servant, see ibid., 44. Stanton cites Nicholas Trist recalling a maxim Jefferson often referred to: "Never allow another to do for you what you can do for yourself."

84. Few, "Diary of Frances Few," 350.

85. See Ulrich, *Age of Homespun*. On religious restraint in New England and the refusal of British luxuries, see Bushman, *Refinement of America*, 193.

86. Isaac, *Transformation of Virginia*, 258–59. And see Virginia Nonimportation Resolutions, *PTJ* 1:29. See also Ragsdale, *Planter's Republic*, and Selby, *Revolution in Virginia*.

87. Joseph Story to Samuel P. P. May, 30 May 1807, in Hayes, *Jefferson in His Own Time*, 43; Brown, *Foul Bodies*, 186. On the "the embrace of rural wholesomeness as quintessentially American," see Brown, *Foul Bodies*, 203. On the late seventeenth- and early eighteenth-century American "attitude combining a desire for elegant taste and 'pre-genteel' practicality," see Rozbicki, "Barrier or a Bridge to American Identity," 438. On "improvisation," see ibid., 444.

88. TJ to John Page, 25 December 1762, *PTJ* 1:4. The most famous example of Jefferson's inclination to pitch hyperboles is the "Adam and Eve letter." Jefferson had declared himself "deeply wounded" by the blood shed by the French Revolution, "but rather than it should have failed, I would have seen half the earth desolated. Were there but an Adam and an Eve left in every country, and left free, it would be better than as it now is." TJ to William Short, 3 January 1793, *PTJ* 25:14. For an interpre-

tation of the "Adam and Eve letter" as a literal vindication of massacres and holocausts, see O'Brien, *Long Affair*, 148–50.

89. TJ to Thomas Adams, 1 June 1771, *PTJ* 1:71–72.

90. JMB 16. On Jefferson's several maxims, see ibid., 16–17. Diogenes Laertius cites Cleobulus in his *Lives*. See also Sowerby #31–33. "In all respects" is not Cleobulus's. Another interesting maxim is the one describing the wise man as conceived by the Stoics, according to Horace: "Altogether smooth and round in himself."

91. Haulman, *Politics of Fashion*, 8; TJ to John Bannister Jr., 15 October 1785, *PTJ* 8:636.

92. TJ to David Humphreys, 14 August 1787, *PTJ* 12:32. Paris was already Paris: see Darnton, *Forbidden Bestsellers of Pre-Revolutionary France*. The best study of Jefferson's Paris years is W. H. Adams, *Paris Years of Thomas Jefferson*. See also Rice, *Thomas Jefferson's Paris*. Adams reminds us that "the Paris that Jefferson entered was in the throes of dynamic modernization." W. H. Adams, *Paris Years of Thomas Jefferson*, 37. As early as 1764, Jefferson revealed a taste and a certain competence for fabrics and suits. See, for example, TJ to William Fleming, 20 March 1764, *PTJ* 1:16: "Tom: Randolph of Tuckahoe has a suit of Mecklenburgh Silk which he offered me for a suit of broadcloth."

93. Thomas Lee Shippen to William Shippen, 24 February–26 March 1788, *PTJ* 12:504.

94. W. H. Adams, *Paris Years of Thomas Jefferson*, 16; TJ to Eliza House Trist, 18 August 1785, *PTJ* 8:404. See also TJ to Charles Bellini, 30 September 1785, *PTJ* 8:569. In both letters, Jefferson praised European people as incapable of rudeness but ended with a still higher praise of American enduring happiness. As Jefferson said to Eliza Trist (18 August 1785, *PTJ* 8:404), "I am convinced they [the French] fall far short of effecting a happiness so temperate, so uniform and so lasting as is generally enjoyed with us." On the French liking Jefferson without reservations, see W. H. Adams, *Paris Years of Thomas Jefferson*, 184. On Jefferson's plainness, see ibid., 185–86. Countess de Flahaut, mistress of Gouverneur Morris, seemed to dislike Jefferson. Morris quotes her saying *"Cet homme est faux et emporté"* (false and hot-tempered). See Morris, *Diary and Letters*, 1:185.

95. Rush, *Autobiography*, 181.

96. Webster in Hayes, *Jefferson in His Own Time*, 94.

97. TJ to Philippe Létombe, 22 February 1801, *PTJ* 33:43. At Washington, Jefferson's servants were mostly whites, with the notable exception of John Freeman, one of his favorite domestics. As he wrote in 1804, "At Washington I prefer white servants, who, when they misbehave, can be exchanged." TJ to John Wayles Eppes, 7 August 1804, in Randolph, *Domestic Life of Thomas Jefferson*, 309. On the liveries of Jefferson's servants, see TJ, Statement of Account with Thomas Carpenter, *PTJ* 33:502–3; TJ, Statement of Account with Thomas Carpenter, *PTJ* 34:488–89; and *JMB* 1035, 1042. For extra information on Jefferson's slaves, servants, and domestics at the White House, see Stanton, *"Those Who Labor for My Happiness,"* 41–55.

98. Maclay, *Journal of William Maclay*, 272. Many comments exist on Jefferson's "small clothes," and we have already encountered some. However, the phrase does not necessarily mean outerwear that is small, but the "smalls" of the laundry, like underwear, hankies, cravats, and so on. It can be another way to refer to a type of clothing rather than to the size of jacket and trousers. Kathleen Brown made me aware of this last point, and I am indebted to her. For a useful collection of quotes on Jefferson's clothes, see http://www.monticello.org/site/research-and-collections /jeffersons-clothing#.

99. G. Wilson, "Jefferson and Creating an Image," 144–45, 146. See also Cunnington and Cunnington, *Handbook of English Costume*, 186, 192–97. Kate Haulman writes: "In the second half and especially the final third of the eighteenth century the silhouette of men's suits gradually grew slimmer, coats shorter, colors more subdued, and wigs less common." Haulman, *Politics of Fashion*, n. 53, 242. William Howard Adams writes that "the substantial London tailor's bills recorded in Jefferson's *Memorandum Books* . . . contradict Maclay's charge of ill-fitting clothes." W. H. Adams, *Paris Years of Thomas Jefferson*, 18.

100. On this "tone," see Maclay, *Journal of William Maclay*, 272.

101. See *JMB* 760. The point that most probably Maclay saw Jefferson in his French coats is made by G. Wilson, "Jefferson and Creating an Image," 145. I am deeply indebted to Wilson's essay. On the "well-bred Frenchman," see Randall, *Life of Thomas Jefferson*, 1:421. Many characterizations of Jefferson that outstrip the descriptive level and turn into an evaluation need to be deciphered and contextualized. Contentions that he was "stiff," "cold," "detached," "artificial," or that he wore "too small" clothes, have to be pitted against the person who made them. An interesting case of an "evaluative description," this time centered on "artificiality," is provided by Samuel Whitcomb Jr. Whitcomb's "artificiality" can be construed, however, as praise (qualified, indeed) of Jefferson's seductiveness, his cultivation and exoticism. Whitcomb was a New England book dealer, a working-class hero, an activist and reformer, not used to the company of Virginia high classes flaunting understatement and "simplicity" in their "habiliments": "His manners are much the most agreeable part of him. They are artificial, he shrugs his shoulders when talking, has much of the Frenchman, is rapid, varying, volatile, eloquent, amusing. . . . Mr. Madison appears less studied, brilliant and frank but more natural, candid and profound than Mr. Jefferson. Mr. Jefferson has more imagination and passion, quicker and richer conceptions. . . . Mr. Jefferson excites interest immediately on entering his presence." Whitcomb quoted in Peden, "Book Peddler Invades Monticello," 635. In fact, Whitcomb may have been taken aback by old Jefferson's studied cosmopolitanism (they met in 1824 while Whitcomb was trying to sell Jefferson a subscription to William Mitford's multivolume work *The History of Greece*), but he is also telling us that Jefferson's "artificiality" is agreeable, amusing, passionate, frank, rich, and imaginative.

102. Thomas Jefferson Randolph in Hayes, *Jefferson in His Own Time*, 163.

103. Ellen Wayles Randolph Coolidge to Henry S. Randall, in Randolph, *Domestic Life of Thomas Jefferson*, 392–93.

104. Isaac Jefferson in Bear, *Jefferson at Monticello*, 19–20.

105. See Bushman, *Refinement of America*, 70–71. For an interesting discussion of the problem of acting above one's station, see Hemphill, *Bowing to Necessities*, 18–19. On fugitive slaves stealing or buying finer clothes and trying to disappear into the free population, see Waldstreicher, "Reading the Runaways"; Prude, "To Look Upon the 'Lower Sort'"; White and White, "Slave Clothing and African-American Culture." The infamous South Carolina Slave Code of 1740 mandated, among other things, "that no owner or proprietor of any Negro slave, or other slave, (except livery men and boys,) shall permit or suffer such Negro or other slave, to have or wear any sort of apparel whatsoever, finer, other, or greater value than Negro cloth, duffels, kerseys, osnabrigs, blue linen, check linen or coarse garlix, or calicoes, checked cottons, or Scotch plaids, under the pain of forfeiting all and every such apparel and garment." See also Baumgarten, *What Clothes Reveal*, especially 106–39.

106. Tucker, *Life of Thomas Jefferson*, 2:506; A. J. Foster, *Jeffersonian America*, 10; Ticknor, *Life, Letters, and Journals*, 1:37. And see Isaac Jefferson in Bear, *Jefferson at Monticello*, 11, italics added.

107. On Jefferson staging blue and buff, see G. Wilson, "Jefferson and Creating an Image," 149–52.

108. Gray, *Thomas Jefferson in 1814*, 67; Few, "Diary of Frances Few," 350.

109. Plumer, *Memorandum of Proceedings in the United States Senate*, 193.

110. Bumstead, "Description of Jefferson," 310.

111. TJ to Christian Baehr, 19 August 1791, *PTJ* 21:39. On superfine French cloth, see also TJ to Christian Baehr, 14 August 1791, *PTJ* 22:39. Maybe the only partial refutation to the notion of Jefferson conveying messages through his clothes was his genuine, uncompromising preference for comfortable shoes, especially slippers. His slippers were old and down at the heel, as many testimonies tell us, because he used them up. The boots he wore in order to ride his horses were a matter of necessity, but slippers were an indulgence to himself, pure pleasure.

112. Ellen Wayles Randolph Coolidge to Henry S. Randall, in Randolph, *Domestic Life of Thomas Jefferson*, 392; Webster in Hayes, *Jefferson in His Own Time*, 93. On pantaloons, see also G. Wilson, "Jefferson and Creating an Image," 158–59.

113. Gaye Wilson writes: "The impetus [of wearing black] came from France and Britain, and by the second half of the 1790s, a survey of portraits and prints demonstrates that black had definitely taken hold as a color of preference among American men." G. Wilson, "Jefferson and Creating an Image," 159. On black, see ibid., 159–64. See also G. Wilson, "Recording History," and Hollander, *Seeing through Clothes*, 365–75. Abigail Adams recounts that when Jefferson arrived in Paris, he had to hastily assemble a mourning black outfit—which means that the color black, at the time, still signalized mourning. She tells an amusing story: "Poor Mr. Jefferson had to hie away for a Tailor to get a whole new black silk suit made up in two days; and at the

end of Eleven days should an other death happen, he will be obliged to have a new Suit of mourning of Cloth, because that is the Season when Silk must be cast of. We may groan and scold but these are expences which cannot be avoided. For Fashion is the Deity every one worships in this country and from the highest to the lowest you must submit." Abigail Adams to Mary Smith Cranch, 5 September 1784, *Adams Family Correspondence*, 5:443. Concerning Rembrandt Peale's 1800 portrait, Alfred Bush praises it as "the earliest and most penetrating likeness of Jefferson. . . . This portrait is unrivalled in having played a more significant iconographic role during Jefferson's lifetime than any other portrait. . . . No portrait of Jefferson, with the exception of the one painted in 1805 by Gilbert Stuart, which later eclipsed that of Peale in the public mind, seems to have been so frequently copied." Bush, *Life Portraits of Thomas Jefferson*, 39–40.

114. On Jefferson and the motive of virtue conducive to happiness, see, for example, TJ to Eliza House Trist, 18 August 1785, *PTJ* 8:403–5; TJ to Peter Carr, 6 August 1788, *PTJ* 13:470; TJ to Corrêa da Serra, 19 April 1814, *PTJ-RS* 7:301–2; and TJ to Amos J. Cook, 21 January 1816, *PTJ-RS* 9:374–75.

115. In his Notes on Ceremonial at New York (an account of the first public ball held on 7 June 1789 after Washington's arrival in New York), 10 June 1793, *PTJ* 26:248–49, Jefferson draws the picture of a republican and "simple" President Washington, a military hero who nonetheless wielded his good sense against gentlemen dancing with swords and abiding by aristocratic ceremonials: "the President [was] made to pass an evening which his good sense rendered a very miserable one to him." Biographies and comparative analyses have shown that many disagreements set Jefferson and Washington apart. But Washington was and remained, for Jefferson, both a model of republicanism and the perfect example of military elegance. He was "graceful" along the lines that Chastellux would have certainly favored: "his person," Jefferson wrote in 1813, "was fine, his stature exactly what one would wish, his deportment easy, erect, and noble; the best horseman of his age, and the most graceful figure that could be seen on horseback." TJ to Walter Jones, 2 January 1814, *PTJ-RS* 7:101. For the phrase "to find gendered meaning in war," see Friend and Glover, *Southern Manhood*, vii. On the "feminine silhouette" of men's dressings in the 1740s and 1750s, see Baumgarten, *What Clothes Reveal*, 226. On French revolutionaries inspiring lounging and relaxed antimilitary styles, see L. Hunt, *Politics, Culture, and Class*. We will see in part 2 Jefferson's attitude toward the feminine element and women's bodies concretely.

116. See Freeman, *Affairs of Honor*.

117. The best analysis of Jefferson's "escape" is Kranish, *Flight from Monticello*. On effeminacy as a disvalue, see, for example, Barker-Benfield, *Culture of Sensibility*, 141–49.

118. See the classic Mischel, "Convergences and Challenges in the Search for Consistency."

119. TJ to James Madison, 8 September 1793, *PTJ* 27:62.

120. TJ, Diary of Arnold's Invasion and Notes on Subsequent Events in 1781, *PTJ* 4:265. Jefferson sent this enclosure to Joseph Delaplaine on 26 July 1816 in reply to a request for factual details respecting Arnold's raid on Richmond and Tarleton's raid on Charlottesville. For more information, see ibid., 266–67. On Jefferson and military action, see Stuart, *Half-Way Pacifist*, and McDonald, *Thomas Jefferson's Military Academy*. On Jefferson's obsession with reputation, see Cogliano, *Thomas Jefferson*.

121. On "male softness," see Barker-Benfield, *Culture of Sensibility*, chap. 3.

122. Burstein, *Jefferson's Secrets*, 51, 52; Randall, *Life of Thomas Jefferson*, 3:232. Randall recounts of Thomas Jefferson Randolph spending a few days in Washington, at the president's house: "not long after his arrival, the latter [Jefferson] came into his room and desired him to unpack his trunks and spread out their contents. With the same careful scrutiny that a mother would have given, he examined every article of apparel. He then took out a pencil and paper and commenced making a list of additional things, saying, 'you will need this and this, when you get to Philadelphia.'" Ibid., 3:231.

123. On the lean body as a male ideal, see Glover, *Southern Sons*, 99–100.

124. TJ to Dr. Vine Utley, 21 March 1819, *Works of TJ*, 12:117. "He ate delicately and sparingly of light materials, and chose the lightest wines of French vintage." Randall, *Life of Thomas Jefferson*, 1:421. On Ellen Wayles Randolph Coolidge and Thomas Jefferson Randolph confirming Jefferson's frugality and quasi-vegetarianism, see Randall, *Life of Thomas Jefferson*, 3:675. Holmes, *Thomas Jefferson Treats Himself*, 69–71, argues that salads became a regular part of Jefferson's diet. See also Feirstein, *Real Men Don't Eat Quiche*. Feminist thinker Carol J. Adams asserts that "men who choose not to eat meat repudiate one of their masculine privileges" and thereby "challenge an essential part of the masculine role." C. J. Adams, *Sexual Politics of Meat*, 193. And see Brod and Kaufman, *Theorizing Masculinities*.

125. TJ to Abigail Adams, 25 September 1785, *PTJ* 8:548–49. On humans establishing their affinity with people who eat similarly and their difference from those who do not, see Eden, "Food, Assimilation, and the Malleability of the Human Body," 29. Trudy Eden claims that, by 1600, Europeans were by and large aware that "foods of a light or subtle substance—such as the flesh of young animals, young fowl, wine, leavened bread made of pure wheat, and fresh eggs and milk—produced refined bodies." Ibid., 33. She also refers to Norbert Elias's and Mikhail Bakhtin's equation that "refined foods made 'civilized' bodies and gross foods made 'grotesque' ones." See Elias, *Civilizing Process*, and Bakhtin, *Rabelais and His World*, 303–67. On the multiple social meanings achieved by eating, including establishing differences and similarities, see Lupton, *Food, the Body, and the Self*, 15–19.

126. Jefferson's efforts to attain some forms of equilibrium when dealing with the "other," instead of just eating and destroying, will be analyzed in part 2.

127. On Jefferson's "naturalistic" version of morality, see TJ to Peter Carr, 10 August 1787, *PTJ* 12:14–19, and TJ to Thomas Law, 13 June 1814, *PTJ-RS* 7:414. Other revealing documents on Jefferson's ethics are TJ to Maria Cosway, 12 October

1786, *PTJ* 10:443–55; TJ to Jean Baptiste Say, 1 February 1804, *Writings of TJ*, 11:2–3; TJ to James Fishback, 27 September 1809, *PTJ-RS* 1:563–66; and TJ to John Manners, 12 June 1817, *Works of TJ*, 12:65–68. On Jefferson's debt to the Scottish philosophers, see Wills, *Inventing America*, and M. White, *Philosophy of the American Revolution*. While Wills's treatment focused on Francis Hutcheson's sentimentalism, White saw a dominance of the realism of Lord Kames and Richard Price. See also Yarbrough, "Moral Sense, Character Formation, and Virtue," and especially Helo, *Thomas Jefferson's Ethics*.

128. Locke, *Some Thoughts Concerning Education*, 107. Jay Fliegelman has a powerful expression to address the absurdity of "becoming natural." He speaks of the eighteenth-century "oxymoronic project of discovering a natural rhetoric." Fliegelman, *Declaring Independence*, 79. A clear-cut meaning of the term "nature" and a formal definition are extremely difficult to grasp. Arthur Lovejoy, for instance, listed sixty-six meanings. He provided a clear example of an exasperating ambiguity. As far as Jefferson is concerned, the prospect does not become rosier. As Charles Miller writes, "little aware of the equivocality of 'nature,' Jefferson slipped unconsciously from one of its senses, including its antithetic senses, to another." Jefferson "seems never to have noticed the various roles that the word 'nature' played in his writings." On Jefferson and nature, see C. A. Miller, *Jefferson and Nature*, 6, 7. See also Lovejoy and Boas, *Primitivism and Related Ideas in Antiquity*, 447–56.

129. TJ to Maria Cosway, 24 April 1788, *PTJ* 13:104; TJ to William Wirt, 12 November 1816, *PTJ-RS* 10:523. For another famous praise of uncorrupted spontaneity, see TJ to Peter Carr, 10 August 1787, *PTJ* 12:15: "State a moral case to a ploughman and a professor. The former will decide it as well, & often better than the latter, because he has not been led astray by artificial rules." A twenty-seven-page essay, "Thoughts on English Prosody," which he intended as an appendix to a letter to Chastellux of October 1786 (see *PTJ* 10:498–99), is Jefferson's fullest piece of literary criticism. It has been reprinted many times, but see *Jefferson: Writings*, 593–622. See also Hayes, *Road to Monticello*, 304–8. On Jefferson on the canons of ancient architecture, see, for example, TJ to James Madison, 1 September 1785, *PTJ* 8:462, describing the Maison Carrée as "the best morsel of antient architecture now remaining." See also, on the "remains of Roman grandeur," TJ to Madame de Tessé, 20 March 1787, *PTJ* 11:226. And see TJ, Notes of a Tour into the Southern Parts of France, *PTJ* 11:415–62. By reading these notes, one gets the precise sense that Jefferson's notion of beauty, far from spontaneous, could only be translated into mathematical measures and structure. Among other things, he thought he could, via a comparative analysis, show why the sepulchral pyramid outside Vienna was imperfect, its ratios faulty. See ibid., 423–25.

130. Martha J. Randolph in Hayes, *Jefferson in His Own Time*, 117.

131. TJ to Maria Cosway, 12 October 1786, *PTJ* 10:447. On the theme of the "nature's nation," see R. N. Miller, "American Nationalism as a Theory of Nature,"

and P. Miller, *Nature's Nation*. See also Bak and Hölbling, *"Nature's Nation" Revisited*, and Nash, *Wilderness and the American Mind*.

132. Marx, *Machine in the Garden*, 110.

133. TJ, *Notes*, Query 6, *Works of TJ*, 3:440; Crèvecoeur, *Letters from an American Farmer*, 56. In Query 6, Jefferson offered a detailed catalog of the trees, plants, fruits, flowers, and vegetables, both native and produced on the American farms. Although the tone is generally detached and scientific, by compiling that list he put no fetters to his nationalistic pride. The poet Philip Freneau did the same. He declared the Nile "but a small rivulet and the Danube a ditch" when compared to the beautiful Mississippi River. Freneau, "Philosopher of the Forest," 228. Like several other settlers, Freneau liked to portray his new country as "naturally invincible." On Jefferson and the "virtual infinitude" of American nature, see C. A. Miller, *Jefferson and Nature*, 266.

134. TJ to the Osage nation, 16 July 1804, *Writings of TJ*, 16:406, italics added.

135. On the complex dynamics elicited by cosmopolitanism versus rootedness, and universalism versus particularism, see Nicolaisen and Spahn, *Cosmopolitanism and Nationhood*.

136. TJ to John Page, 7 October 1763, *PTJ* 1:11. On Jefferson's hyperboles, see above n. 88. On Rebecca Burwell, see Kukla, *Mr. Jefferson's Women*, 16–40. Burwell was at that time in Williamsburg, down the street from where Jefferson resided or at most a few miles away in Yorktown. And yet Jefferson did not visit her. This young man let his infatuation happen almost exclusively in the letters he wrote to Page and William Fleming. More than acting, he fictionalized and rationalized. Nonetheless, when Jefferson got news that Burwell was engaged to Jack Ambler, a "violent head ach" erupted. See TJ to William Fleming, 20 March 1764, *PTJ* 1:15–16.

137. Laing, *Divided Self*, 39.

138. Locke, *Some Thoughts Concerning Education*, 50; TJ, *Notes*, Query 18, *Works of TJ*, 4:82–83. See also Wagoner, *Jefferson and Education*. On the difference between Jefferson's and Franklin's views of education, see Zuckerman, "Founding Fathers." Zuckerman contends that Franklin was much more secular, democratic, and innovative, and certainly more antihierarchic. Historians agree that hesitancy was definitely not a trait of Jefferson's personality: "Like a Deistic mechanic," as Stephen Hodin puts it in a penetrating judgment, Jefferson "orchestrated the lives of mere mortals by fashioning a clockwork-like universe of men and machines at Monticello, where his 'overruling providence' is unquestioned." Hodin, "Mechanisms of Monticello," 415. Many examples of Jefferson's resolve can be provided, but let me insist on one. When devising his plan for the expatriation of enslaved Africans, Jefferson wrote to Jared Sparks that "The separation of infants from their mothers . . . would produce some scruples of humanity. But this would be straining at a gnat, and swallowing a camel." TJ to Jared Sparks, 4 February 1824, *Works of TJ*, 12:339.

139. J. Adams, *Discourses on Davila*, 91.

140. TJ to Thomas Jefferson Randolph, 24 November 1808, *Works of TJ*, 11:79–80.

141. Fliegelman, *Declaring Independence*, 137.

142. TJ to Peter Carr, 10 August 1787, *PTJ* 12:15. The entire passage goes as follows: "In the first place divest yourself of all bias in favour of novelty and singularity of opinion. Indulge them in any other subject rather than that of religion. It is too important, and the consequences of error may be too serious. On the other hand shake off all the fears and servile prejudices under which weak minds are servilely crouched. Fix reason firmly in her seat, and call to her tribunal every fact, every opinion. Question with boldness even the existence of a god; because, if there be one, he must more approve the homage of reason, than that of blindfolded fear. You will naturally examine first the religion of your own country. Read the bible then, as you would read Livy or Tacitus." In a letter to Henry Lee (8 May 1825, *Works of TJ*, 12:409), Jefferson stated clearly that "the object of the Declaration of Independence" was not "to find out new principles, or new arguments, never before thought of, not merely to say things which had never been said before." The goal was "to place before mankind the common sense of the subject, in terms so plain and firm as to command their assent. . . . Neither aiming at originality of principle or sentiment, not yet copied from any particular and previous writing," the Declaration "was intended to be an expression of the American mind."

143. TJ, First Inaugural Address, *PTJ* 33:149; TJ to Charles Yancey, 6 January 1816, *PTJ-RS* 9:331; TJ to William Taylor Barry, 2 July 1822, Library of Congress, Papers of Thomas Jefferson. On Franklin's motto, see TJ to Thomas Jefferson Randolph, 24 November 1808, *Works of TJ*, 11:81. On virtuosity not as the solitary voice but as a social adaptability, see Fliegelman, *Declaring Independence*, 66–69.

144. TJ to Robert Skipwith, 3 August 1771, *PTJ* 1:76; TJ to Peter Carr, 19 August 1785, *PTJ* 8:406–7.

145. TJ to Martha Jefferson, 14 June 1787, *PTJ* 11:472; Hamilton, Madison, and Jay, *The Federalist*, 170.

146. Hamilton, Madison, and Jay, *The Federalist*, 65. On character as "the interpenetration of habits," see J. Dewey, *Human Nature and Conduct*, 38. On the founders' attempts to establish a character, see Trees, *Founding Fathers*.

147. TJ to Stephen Girard, 10 July 1815, *PTJ-RS* 8:587, italics added; TJ, Declaration of Independence as Adopted by Congress, *PTJ* 1:431. On public and private as in continuity rather than in opposition, see Goodman, "Public Sphere and Private Life."

148. A. Smith, *Theory of Moral Sentiments*, 101; TJ to Thomas Jefferson Randolph, 24 November 1808, *Works of TJ*, 11:80; TJ, Opinion on the Treaties with France, 28 April 1793, *PTJ* 25:613; TJ to Peter Carr, 19 August 1785, *PTJ* 8:406.

149. TJ, *Notes*, Query 17, *Works of TJ*, 4:80–81. "The fear that a dull and plodding majority might stifle the moral or creative impulses of the individual, which figures so strongly in both Thoreau's and J. S. Mill's defenses of individual conscience and liberty, stands in stark contrast to Jefferson's solid faith in the decency and moral sense of ordinary men and women." Yarbrough, *American Virtues*, 190.

150. I have quoted snippets from the following texts: TJ, *Notes*, Query 18, *Works of TJ*, 4:83; TJ to John Holmes, 22 April 1820, *Works of TJ*, 12:159; TJ to Edward Carrington, 16 January 1787, *PTJ* 11:49; TJ, *Notes*, Query 17, *Works of TJ*, 4:81.

151. TJ to George Washington, 31 December 1792, *PTJ* 24:358; Chinard, *Thomas Jefferson*, 270. Jefferson had reservations about Hamilton's character, but he never pronounced him a "foreign bastard," like the late Arnold Rogow, author of *A Fatal Friendship: Alexander Hamilton and Aaron Burr* (1998), believed. Rogow stumbled upon one of those famous spurious Jefferson quotations. Joanne Freeman gives us the essential information on this episode: "In his first chapter's first paragraph, Rogow quotes Thomas Jefferson saying the following about Alexander Hamilton: 'It's monstrous that this country should be ruled by a foreign bastard!' (p. 4)—an exclamation that sent me scurrying to the footnotes. Rogow's source? *Alexander Hamilton: First American Business Man* by Robert Warshow (Garden City, NJ: Garden City Publishing, 1931), written in the era of many a creative 'Founder' biography, few of them footnoted. Rogow makes ample use of such questionable early (and late) twentieth-century works, a logical choice given that they were often more interested in the personalities of the 'Founders' than in historical fact." Freeman, "Review of Rogow." On Jefferson's spurious quotations, see http://www.monticello.org/site/jefferson/spurious-quotations.

152. TJ to Martha Jefferson, 28 March 1787, *PTJ* 11:250. See also Ricoeur, *Oneself as Another*.

153. TJ to Martha Jefferson, 11 December 1783, *PTJ* 6:380; TJ to James Madison, 9 June 1793, *PTJ* 26:240; TJ to James Madison, 17 April 1795, *PTJ* 28:339.

154. Abigail Adams to Cotton Tufts, 8 September 1784, *Adams Family Correspondence*, 5:458. Jefferson was taken ill in Annapolis in March (see TJ to James Madison, 16 March 1784, *PTJ* 7:30–31), and would go through ailments in Paris, from early November, or earlier, through the winter. Abigail Adams, however, described a man whose main apprehensions were courtier ostentations and parades. Her whole passage goes as follows: "His Hair too is an other affliction which he is tempted to cut off. He expects not to live above a Dozen years and he shall lose one of those in hair dressing. Their is not [there is not] a porter nor a washer woman but what has their hair powderd and drest every day." On this occasion, Jefferson may have simply cracked a joke, his real concern, more than his health, being the Parisian etiquette regarding hair dressing and his unwillingness to surrender to it.

155. On this last point, see Bear and Jones, *"Thomas Jefferson and His Health."* For the following sections, I am deeply indebted to Burstein, *Jefferson's Secrets*, and Holmes, *Thomas Jefferson Treats Himself.*

156. TJ to John F. Oliveira Fernandes, 16 December 1815, *PTJ-RS* 9:263; TJ to Dr. Vine Utley, 21 March 1819, *Works of TJ*, 12:117. See also https://www.monticello.org/site/research-and-collections/wine.

157. TJ to James Maury, 16 June 1815, *PTJ-RS* 8:544; TJ to Dr. Vine Utley, 21 March 1819, *Works of TJ*, 12:118.

158. TJ to Thomas Mann Randolph, 18 January 1796, *PTJ* 28:593.

159. TJ to Caspar Wistar, 21 June 1807, *Works of TJ*, 10:425.

160. See TJ, List of Inoculation, *PTJ* 35–34–35. See also TJ, Notes on Headaches, *PTJ* 27:824. For more information, see https://www.monticello.org/site/research-and-collections/inoculation.

161. TJ to Thomas Cooper, 7 October 1814, *PTJ-RS* 8:13. Jefferson praised one of his personal doctors, Thomas Watkins, precisely for "his experience and cautious practice for the restoration of my health." See TJ to James Madison, 28 January 1821, *Papers of James Madison*, Retirement Series, 2:238.

162. An interesting source of documents testifying to Jefferson's interest in medicine is Dorsey, *Jefferson–Dunglison Letters*. On surgery, medicine, and anatomy, see also Sowerby #854–1005.

163. On Jefferson's complete confidence in Dunglison and Watkins, see Burstein, *Jefferson's Secrets*, 19–30.

164. TJ to Caspar Wistar, 21 June 1807, *Works of TJ*, 10:425, 427; TJ to Henry Wheaton, 14 February 1812, *PTJ-RS* 4:495. On Jefferson's wariness of daring theories, see also, for example, TJ to Charles Thomson, 20 September 1787, *PTJ* 12:159; TJ to Reverend James Madison, 19 July 1788, *PTJ*, 13:379; TJ to Benjamin Rush, 17 August 1811, *PTJ-RS* 4:87. On Jefferson's praising medicine as a profession, see TJ to Benjamin Rush, 22 September 1809, *PTJ-RS* 1:559. For another interesting praise of the "followers of Esculapius," see TJ to David Campbell, 28 January 1810, *PTJ-RS* 2:187.

165. TJ to Caspar Wistar, 21 June 1807, *Works of TJ*, 10:428. On reading "with pleasure" medicine's "ingenious theories," see TJ to Benjamin Rush, 16 January 1811, *PTJ-RS* 3:304. On Jefferson's penchant for anatomy and the clinical practice, see also TJ to John Crawford, 2 January 1812, *PTJ-RS* 4:394–95, and TJ to John Brazier, 24 August 1819, *Writings of TJ*, 15:207–11.

166. TJ to James Currie, 28 January 1786, *PTJ* 9:239–40.

167. TJ to Thomas Sully, 8 January 1812, *PTJ-RS* 4:407; TJ to Elizabeth Trist, 10 May 1813, *PTJ-RS* 6:110. On Jefferson "scarcely able to walk from one room to another," see TJ to Nathaniel Macon, 21 February 1826, *Works of TJ*, 12:459. For a chronology and more detailed information on Jefferson's conditions, see https://www.monticello.org/site/research-and-collections/medicine.

168. TJ to Samuel Brown, 13 November 1813, *PTJ-RS* 6:615; TJ to Samuel Brown, 28 April 1814, *PTJ-RS* 7:325; TJ to John Adams, 5 July 1814, *PTJ-RS* 7:451; TJ to Horatio G. Spafford, 11 May 1819, *Writings of TJ*, 15:189; TJ to Maria Cosway, 27 December 1820, in Randolph, *Domestic Life of Thomas Jefferson*, 374. On the body as the machinery of a watch, see also TJ to Mann Page, 16 May 1796, *PTJ* 29:100.

169. TJ to John Adams, 1 June 1822, *Works of TJ*, 12:234–35; TJ to Lafayette, 28 October 1822, *Works of TJ*, 12:255. On the wrist injury, see https://www.monticello.org/site/research-and-collections/wrist-injury-1786.

170. To Benjamin Rush, 28 February 1803, *Works of TJ*, 9:453. On 20 December 1801 (*PTJ* 36:177–78), Jefferson wrote to Benjamin Rush and made a passing refer-

ence to a certain "flaw." On 12 March 1802, Rush asked for details about the flaw, but it took Jefferson almost a year to provide detailed information. On Jefferson trying to hide his "secret," see Randolph, *Domestic Life of Thomas Jefferson*, 367.

171. TJ to William Short, 31 October 1819, *Works of TJ*, 12:140. On Rush advising calomel and jalap, see Holmes, *Thomas Jefferson Treats Himself*, 34.

172. TJ to Robley Dunglison, 17 November 1825, University of Virginia. John Holmes (see *Thomas Jefferson Treats Himself*, 35–36) raises the suspicion of a possible opium addiction, another challenge to Jefferson's sense of independence and control.

173. TJ to William Short, 30 August 1806, Library of Congress, William Short Papers. And see TJ to William Eustis, 30 December 1801, *PTJ* 36:242. By 1822, Jefferson came to suspect that Sydenham's therapy could be better suitable, perhaps, to treat the early stages of the malady: "a couple of hours riding every day relieved me from a case tolerably manifest, altho but incipient." TJ to Spencer Roane, 18 July 1822, Library of Congress.

174. Jefferson's cause of death may have been a combination of several factors: exhaustion and dehydration from diarrhea, uremia from kidney damage, orthostatic old-age pneumonia, and prostatic cancer. For more information, see https://www .monticello.org/site/research-and-collections/jeffersons-cause-death. On Jefferson's hope to survive through his legacy, see TJ to James Madison, 17 February 1826, Library of Congress, Papers of James Madison: "Take care of me when dead, and be assured that I shall leave with you my last affections."

175. On Jefferson's last moments, see Randolph, *Domestic Life of Thomas Jefferson*, 428–29, and Randall, *Life of Thomas Jefferson*, 3:540–52.

176. Alexander Garrett to Evelina Bolling Garrett, 4 July 1826, University of Virginia, Papers of Alexander Garrett. Samples of Jefferson's hair are in many repositories, including the Academy of Natural Sciences in Philadelphia, the Library of Congress in Washington, D.C. (three specimens), and the Thomas Jefferson Foundation (thirteen specimens). They have various provenances, and it is very hard to tell whether these cuttings are what they claim to be. The three specimens now at the Library of Congress came in with the papers of Jefferson, stored in three separate envelopes. On one envelope, Martha Jefferson Randolph wrote: "My dear father Thomas Jefferson."

Passage

1. TJ to Roger Weightman, 24 June 1826, *Works of TJ*, 12:477. On the stadial theory, see Spahn, *Thomas Jefferson, Time, and History*, and Dierksheide, *Amelioration and Empire*. Jefferson was convinced that many travelers in America could get a visual representation of the fact that the gradual advance of civilization was already on its way: "Let a philosophic observer commence a journey from the savages of the Rocky Mountains, eastwardly towards our seacoast. These he would observe in the

earliest stage of association living under no law but that of nature, subsisting and covering themselves with the flesh and skins of wild beasts. He would next find those on our frontiers in the pastoral state, raising domestic animals to supply the defects of hunting. Then succeed our own semi-barbarous citizens, the pioneers of the advance of civilization, and so in his progress he would meet the gradual shades of improving man until he would reach his, as yet, most improved state in our seaport towns. This, in fact, is equivalent to a survey, in time, of the progress of man from the infancy of creation to the present day." TJ to William Ludlow, 6 September 1824, *Writings of TJ*, 16:74–75.

2. TJ to Edward Coles, 25 August 1814, *PTJ-RS* 7:604.

3. TJ to Benjamin Waterhouse, 3 March 1818, *Works of TJ*, 12:89–90. Jefferson made it very clear that he never intended "to go backwards instead of forwards to look for improvement, to believe that government, religion, morality & every other science were in the highest perfection in ages of the darkest ignorance, and that nothing can ever be devised more perfect than what was established by our forefathers." TJ to Elbridge Gerry, 26 January 1799, *PTJ* 30:647. See also TJ to Joseph Priestley, 27 January 1800, *PTJ* 31:341.

4. For Jefferson's three versions of the 1776 proposed drafts for the Virginia Constitution, not adopted, see *PTJ* 1:337–65. For the 1783 draft, see *PTJ* 6:294–308. In his so-called Bill to Abolish Entails, Jefferson introduced provisions affecting extant property relations. The bill was presented on 14 October 1776, while he sat as a member of the House of Delegates in Williamsburg. Entail, the custom of leaving family property only to direct descendants, as well as primogeniture, the practice of transferring property entirely to the oldest son, had the unwelcome effect of restricting inheritance and hence enforcing the status quo. Jefferson opposed concentration and, as Dumas Malone wryly noted, he "wanted land for the landless." Malone, *Jefferson and His Time*, 1:252. The bill on entail was effected immediately, while another bill on primogeniture was not brought about until nearly ten years later. Malone questioned the radicalism of Jefferson's bill: "Jefferson did not destroy the country gentry as a group with the blows of his mighty ax, and there is insufficient reason to believe that he wanted to, but he did remove legal vestiges of Old World aristocracy." Ibid., 1:254. For a clear synopsis of Jefferson and the question of entail and primogeniture, see ibid., 1:251–57, and Sloan, *Principle and Interest*, 70–76. Parting with Malone, Sloan writes that "there is little evidence that conditions in Virginia required Jefferson's reforms." Ibid., 71. In other words, entail and primogeniture were "a problem in Jefferson's mind, not in Virginia reality." Ibid., 76. See TJ, Bill to Enable Tenants in Fee Tail to Convey Their Lands in Fee Simple, *PTJ* 1:560–62.

Part 2: Others

1. Bumstead, "Description of Jefferson," 310.

2. TJ to Robert Mills, 3 March 1826, Copley Newspapers Incorporated, James S.

Copley Library. To Dr. Utley, Jefferson said that "I use spectacles at night, but not necessarily in the day, unless in reading small print." Unfortunately, however, "My hearing is distinct in particular conversation, but confused when several voices cross each other, which unfits me for the society of the table." TJ to Dr. Vine Utley, 21 March 1819, *Works of TJ*, 12:118.

3. Gray, *Thomas Jefferson in 1814*, 67; Bacon in Bear, *Jefferson at Monticello*, 71; Randall, *Life of Thomas Jefferson*, 1:34. See also Thomas Jefferson Randolph in Hayes, *Jefferson in His Own Time*, 164. On Jefferson's small eyes, see Webster in ibid., 93: "His eyes are small, very light."

4. For an excellent study of the association of whiteness with ideality and transparence, see DiPiero, "Missing Links." DiPiero writes: "Whiteness indexed specific culturally valorized characteristics while simultaneously producing itself as an empty category, one with no attributes but nevertheless capable of evaluating people and social practices." Ibid., 155.

5. Buffon, "Histoire naturelle de l'homme," 319, my translation. The entire passage reads as follows: *"Le climat le plus tempéré est depuis le 40e degré jusqu'au 50e; c'est aussi sous cette zone que se trouvent les hommes les plus beaux et les mieux faits, c'est sous ce climat qu'on doit prendre l'idée de la vraie couleur naturelle de l'homme, c'est là qu'on doit prendre le modèle ou l'unité à laquelle il faut rapporter toutes les autres nuances de couleur et de beauté; les deux extrêmes sont également éloignés du vrai et du beau: les pays policés situés sous cette zone sont la Géorgie, la Circassie, l'Ukraine, la Turquie d'Europe, la Hongrie, l'Allemagne méridionale, l'Italie, la Suisse, la France et la partie septentrionale de l'Espagne; tous ces peuples sont aussi les plus beaux et les mieux faits de toute la terre."* While studying the widespread eighteenth-century opinion that blackness was a degeneration from the original color, Winthrop Jordan made a reference to Oliver Goldsmith's *History of the Earth and Animated Nature* (1774), in which we read that "we may consider the European figure and colour as standards to which to refer all other varieties." Goldsmith cited in Jordan, *White over Black*, 248.

6. See DiPiero, "Missing Links," 169–70.

7. On prejudices about public baths and spas as fostering promiscuity and immorality, see Brown, *Foul Bodies*, 16–24, especially 24.

8. Brown, *Foul Bodies*, 13–14. For the assumption that "civilized people covered their skins," see ibid., 117. Jordan, *White over Black*, 241, insists on colonists' awareness about American Indians' "well-stocked cabinet of natural cosmetics."

9. Brown, *Foul Bodies*, 106. See also Calvert, "Function of Fashion."

10. See Brown, *Foul Bodies*, 108–9.

11. See Szwed, "Race and the Embodiment of Culture," 253–70.

12. Ibid., 257. For the argument that two peoples adopt some aspects of the other group's behavior, see ibid., 261.

13. *London Magazine*, 1746, quoted in Read, "British Recognition of American Speech," 329. On imitativeness, see TJ, *Notes*, Query 18, *Works of TJ*, 4:82–83.

14. Crèvecoeur, *Letters from an American Farmer*, 69, 68. On the "wilderness-

temptation," see Nash, *Wilderness and the American Mind*, 20, 29. On Euro-Americans "Africanizing" and England "Celticizing," see Szwed, "Race and the Embodiment of Culture," 262–63. Nancy Shoemaker writes that "whites adopted by Indians, either through captivity or by their own choice, looked like Indians to other whites." Shoemaker, *Strange Likeness*, 137.

15. Himself an environmentalist, Jefferson considered the climate of Virginia optimal: "When we consider how much climate contributes to the happiness of our condition, by the fine sensations it excites, and the productions it is the parent of, we have reason to value highly the accident of birth in such an one as that of Virginia." TJ to Martha Jefferson Randolph, 31 May 1791, *PTJ* 20:464. Jefferson linked the character of the American people to the latitude. In this way, he maintained that excessive warmth "unnerves and unmans both body and mind." See TJ to Chastellux, 2 September 1785, *PTJ* 8:467–70, especially 468. However, Jefferson's environmentalism took into account many other factors than just climate, including the soil and social and cultural influences. See C. A. Miller, *Jefferson and Nature*, 59–62. All in all, Jefferson believed that humans were created equal, with very similar biological needs, but they showed remarkable variations from one place to another, from one culture to another. On maize not being a human food, see Eden, "Food, Assimilation, and the Malleability of the Human Body," 37. On the fear of becoming contaminated by a savage land, see Finch, "'Civilized' Bodies and the 'Savage' Environment," 48, 49. And see Kupperman, "Fear of Hot Climates." While Buffon and Montesquieu had attributed the degeneration to the climate, the Dutch diplomat and geographer De Pauw, author of the famous *Recherches philosophiques sur les Américains* (1770), had insisted on the soil.

16. See Melish, "Emancipation and the Em-bodiment of 'Race,'" 224–25.

17. See C. D. Martin, *White African American Body*.

18. Rush, "Observations Intended to Favour a Supposition," 295. Voltaire, on the other hand, was convinced there was no transformation at play here. Albinos, "a very small and very rare nation," represented an inferior race: "nature has perhaps placed Albinos after the *nègres* and the Hottentots, and above the monkeys, like one of the gradations that descend from man to animal." Voltaire cited in Curran, *Anatomy of Blackness*, 144–45. Johann Friedrich Blumenbach, in his dissertation *De generis humani varietate nativa* (1775), was perhaps the first naturalist to claim that albinism (what he called *Leucaethiopia humana*) could be found in all varieties of human beings, no matter the "races."

19. TJ, *Notes*, Query 6, *Works of TJ*, 3:466–67. Jefferson, furthermore, speculated about a responsibility of the mother over the one of the father: "Whatever be the cause of the disease in the skin, or in its coloring matter, which produces this change, it seems more incident to the female than male sex." Ibid., 468.

20. TJ, *Notes*, Query 6, *Works of TJ*, 3:450–51; TJ, *Notes*, Query 14, *Works of TJ*, 4:58; TJ to John Adams, 27 May 1813, *A-JL* 324. In this same letter to Adams, Jefferson also wrote about Bernard Romans's *Concise Natural History of East and West*

Florida (1775): "Romans indeed takes a higher stand, and supposes a separate creation. On the same unscriptural ground, he had but to mount one step higher, to suppose no creation at all, but that all things have existed without beginning in time, as they now exist, and may for ever exist, producing and reproducing in a circle, without end." Ibid., 324. Jefferson did not seem to agree with such a "higher stand." On a common origin rather than a separate creation, see also TJ to Levett Harris, 18 April 1806, *Writings of TJ*, 11:101–3. On polygenesis, see Boulton, "American Paradox." Jefferson was not always so cautious in defining the source of the differences between whites and blacks. In *Notes*, Query 14, he did not rely on a "suspicion" but on a certainty when he wrote that "It is not their condition then, but nature, which has produced the distinction" (*Works of TJ*, 4:56). The role of conditions, education, and accidents in general seemed not to debase Jefferson's conviction that blacks were meant by nature to be inferior to whites. An interesting discussion of Jefferson's swerving between suspicion and certitude, as well as between environmentalism and the hypothesis of a congenital inferiority of blacks, can be found in J. C. Miller, *Wolf by the Ears*, 46–59.

21. Scholars have perfectly grasped the tension here implicit between Jefferson's Enlightenment principles and historical, factual realities into which he was immersed. Michael Zuckert, for example, has shown that the Declaration and other Jeffersonian texts seemingly addressing human rights and advocating an inclusive society without differences are not the best basis upon which to build a theory of universal egalitarianism. See Zuckert, "Self-Evident Truth," especially 326, and Zuckert, *Natural Rights Republic*, 41–55. On Jefferson's hope that, one day, the message of the Declaration could literally apply to everyone, see TJ to Roger Weightman, 24 June 1826, *Works of TJ*, 12:477.

22. Isaac, "Monticello Stories Old and New," 115. On the economic significance of the Virginia family, see Hodin, "Mechanisms of Monticello." On Jefferson's enlarged family, see Burstein, *Jefferson's Secrets*, 186. See also Jan Lewis, *Pursuit of Happiness*; Jan Lewis, "Blessings of Domestic Society"; and Stanton, *Free Some Day*.

23. TJ to Alexander Donald, 7 February 1788, *PTJ* 12:572; TJ to Martha Jefferson, 27 February 1809, *Family Letters*, 385. For similar examples, see also TJ to Mary Jefferson, 1 January 1799, *PTJ* 30:607; TJ to James Maury, 25 April 1812, *PTJ-RS* 4:669–71; TJ to Martha Jefferson, 15 January 1792, *PTJ* 23:44; and TJ to Martha Jefferson, 17 May 1798, *PTJ* 30:354.

24. William Byrd to Charles Boyle, Earl of Orrery, 5 July 1726, *Correspondence of the Three William Byrds*, 1:355; Brown, *Good Wives*, 267.

25. Isaac, *Transformation of Virginia*, 305.

26. See Hemphill, *Bowing to Necessities*, 67, and see n. 5, 244.

27. Glover, *Southern Sons*, 121.

28. Ibid., 57, 84, and see 41.

29. Ibid., 158. And see TJ to Chastellux, 2 September 1785, *PTJ* 8:467–70. Chappell and Richter write that "over the course of the eighteenth century, status became

increasingly defined by one's social and economic position, which could improve or decline." Chappell and Richter, "Wealth and Houses in Post Revolutionary Virginia," 4. For a discussion of sectional character stereotypes as part of an analysis of the emerging division of interests, see Greene, *Imperatives, Behaviors, and Identities*, 327–47.

30. TJ to Thomas Mann Randolph, 30 July 1821, Library of Congress, Papers of Thomas Jefferson. On Jefferson advising grandson Thomas Jefferson Randolph to learn a profession, see TJ to Thomas Jefferson Randolph, 3 January 1809, Massachusetts Historical Society, Coolidge Collection: "I do not know whether your father intends you for a profession, or to be a farmer. this last is the most honourable and happy of all. but farmers as well as professional men are apt to live beyond their income & thus to be reduced to bankruptcy. . . . under this possibility it is provident & comfortable to possess some resource within ourselves some means by which we can get a living if reduced by misfortune or imprudence to poverty. I know of none which you might look to with more expectation than Surgery. we have no good Surgeons in the country; so that emploiment would be certain." For the famous argument too often read as the proof of an anticommercial vision of rural self-sufficiency ("Those who labour in the earth are the chosen people of God" and "let our work-shops remain in Europe"), see TJ, *Notes*, Query 19, *Works of TJ*, 4:85–86. See also Marx, *Machine in the Garden*, especially 126–27. Jefferson's husbandman, Marx claimed, would be "the good shepherd of the old pastoral dressed in American homespun." But see Appleby, "Commercial Farming," and McCoy, *Elusive Republic*.

31. See F. L. Dewey, *Thomas Jefferson, Lawyer*. On the professions, see also TJ to William Duane, 16 September 1810, *PTJ-RS* 3:86–89, and TJ to William C. Rives, 18 September 1811, *PTJ-RS* 4:161–63.

32. On the distinction between patriarchy and paternalism, see Brown, *Good Wives*, 322, 462–63, n. 9. Brown convincingly argues that patriarchy and paternalism were parts of the same reality. For a compelling analysis of the fragility of male gentry identity in Virginia, see Lockridge, *On the Sources of Patriarchal Rage*. On the transformation from patriarchy to paternalism, see Schochet, *Patriarchalism in Political Thought*; Isaac, "Communication and Control"; and Fliegelman, *Prodigals and Pilgrims*.

33. Lockridge, *On the Sources of Patriarchal Rage*, 97.

34. TJ to Peter Carr, 19 August 1785, *PTJ* 8:406.

35. TJ, Autobiography, *Works of TJ*, 1:72; TJ to J.P.G. Muhlenberg, 31 January 1781, *PTJ* 4:487.

36. Marquis de Chastellux's portrayal of TJ, translation published in London in 1787, *PTJ* 7:586.

37. If Monticello, as Jefferson wrote, was "my essay in Architecture," he did publish this essay. See TJ to Benjamin Henry Latrobe, 10 October 1809, *PTJ-RS* 1:595.

38. McLaughlin, *Jefferson and Monticello*, 327, italics added. See also ibid., 321–23,

and McLaughlin, "Blind Side of Jefferson." And see http://www.monticello.org/site/house-and-gardens/blinds-and-shutters.

39. Bentham, *Panopticon*, 39. See Sowerby #2369, and TJ to Thomas Pinckney, 29 August 1792, *PTJ* 24:331. This, obviously, does not mean that Jefferson stood under the direct influence of Bentham. Jefferson began thinking and sketching about prisons as early as 1785, when Richmond's directors of public buildings asked his opinion about a state capital building, the governor's house, and a prison. See TJ to James Buchanan and William Hay, 13 August 1785, *PTJ* 8:366–68 and 26 January 1786, *PTJ* 9:220–22. See also TJ, Notes on Plan of a Prison, enclosed in TJ to James Wood, 31 March 1797, *PTJ* 29:337, and TJ to George Douglas, 21 December 1800, *PTJ* 32:334–35.

40. TJ to Littleton Waller Tazewell, 5 January 1805, *Jefferson: Writings*, 1152; TJ, Report of the Commissioners for the University of Virginia, Rockfish Gap, August 4, 1818, *Jefferson: Writings*, 458. See also TJ to Hugh L. White and Trustees of the Lottery for East Tennessee College, 6 May 1810, *PTJ-RS* 2:365.

41. Stanton, *"Those Who Labor for My Happiness,"* 78. See TJ to Caleb Lownes, 18 December 1793, *PTJ* 27:586. On the "Hobby of my old age," see TJ to Destutt de Tracy, 26 December 1820, *Works of TJ*, 12:183.

42. Stanton, *"Those Who Labor for My Happiness,"* 79; TJ to Démeunier, 29 April 1795, *PTJ* 28:341; TJ to James Lyle, 10 July 1795, *PTJ* 28: 405–6; TJ to William Short, 13 April 1800, *PTJ* 31:502. On the nailery, see also *JMB* 910, n. 89. Twenty years after his naileries, Jefferson devised a similar project, a textile factory. It employed "a few women, children & invalids who could do little in the farm." TJ to James Maury, 16 June 1815, *PTJ-RS* 8:544.

43. Bacon in Bear, *Jefferson at Monticello*, 98; Stanton, *"Those Who Labor for My Happiness,"* 84. Jefferson must have been aware of his power. According to Bacon, Jefferson exclaimed: "Ah, sir, we can't punish him. He has suffered enough already." Bacon in Bear, *Jefferson at Monticello*, 98. On the rod wasted and incentives, see Stanton, *"Those Who Labor for My Happiness,"* 79–80. On Jefferson's daily presence, especially from 1794 to 1797, as a "significant factor," see ibid., 82.

44. Epperson, "Panoptic Plantations," 59, 60. There are dozens of references to telescopes and other optical instruments in both Jefferson's correspondence and his Memorandum Books.

45. Besides Native Americans, African Americans, and women, other dimensions of corporeal "otherness" did not figure so preeminently in Jefferson's attempts at defining whiteness, maleness, and normality, especially his own. He was moderately attracted, for example, by physical disability, "freaks" in the language of the period. Although freaks and freak shows were popular entertainments, only one "encounter" appears in Jefferson's Memorandum Books. Upon his arrival in Philadelphia in 1798, he paid to see "Caleb Philips a dwarf." The Philadelphia *Porcupine's Gazette*, 16 January 1798, reported that the boy's name was Calvin, that he was seven

years old, that he stood twenty-six inches high, and that he weighed twelve pounds. See *JMB* 978.

46. TJ to John Adams, 8 April 1816, *A-JL* 467.

47. TJ to John Adams, 27 June 1813, *A-JL* 335. See also TJ to James Sullivan, 9 February 1797, *PTJ* 29:289–91; TJ to Joel Barlow, 3 May 1802, *PTJ* 37:400; TJ to Lafayette, 4 November 1823, *Works of TJ*, 12:323; and TJ to Henry Lee, 10 August 1824, *Writings of TJ*, 16:73–74.

48. On the murder, see Merrill, *Jefferson's Nephews*. See James Nelly to TJ, 18 October 1809, *PTJ-RS* 1:606 (informing Jefferson about the "suicide" of Meriwether Lewis). Jefferson never suspected homicide and attributed Meriwether's suicide to "hypochondriac affections": "it was a constitutional disposition in all the nearer branches of the family of his name, and was more immediately inherited by him from his father." TJ to Paul Allen, 18 August 1813, *PTJ-RS* 6:423.

49. TJ to John Banister, 15 October 1785, *PTJ* 8:636; TJ to Thomas Jefferson Randolph, 24 November 1808, *Works of TJ*, 11:83. For more details about the episode and an analysis of the "combustible spirit" of these two men, see Burstein, *Jefferson's Secrets*, 36, 70–71.

50. TJ to Thomas Mann Randolph, 23 June 1806, Yale University, Sterling Memorial Library.

51. On the "progress of society from it's rudest state to that it has now attained," see TJ to William Ludlow, 6 September 1824, *Writings of TJ*, 16:74–76.

52. TJ, First Inaugural Address, *PTJ* 33:149.

53. On Jefferson and religion, see Sanford, *Religious Life of Thomas Jefferson;* Sheridan, *Jefferson and Religion;* Gaustad, *Sworn on the Altar of God;* and Ragosta, *Religious Freedom.*

54. TJ to William Canby, 18 September 1813, *PTJ-RS* 6:508. On "diamonds in a dunghill," see TJ to John Adams, 12 October 1813, *A-JL* 383–86. On "our duties to others," see TJ, Syllabus of an Estimate of the Merit of the Doctrines of Jesus, enclosed in TJ to Benjamin Rush, 21 April 1803, *PTJ* 40:253. See also TJ to Joseph Priestley, 9 April 1803, *PTJ* 40:157–59. On the two version of Jefferson's Bible, see TJ, *Jefferson's Extracts from the Gospels.*

55. TJ to Ezra Styles Ely, 25 June 1819, *Jefferson's Extracts from the Gospels*, 387; TJ to François Adriaan Van der Kemp, 9 July 1820, Buffalo and Erie County Historical Society, Van der Kemp Papers, italics added. On Jefferson's binary between "primitive Christianity, in all the simplicity in which it came from the lips of Jesus," and "the subtleties of Commentators," see also TJ to John Davis, 18 January 1824, *Jefferson's Extracts from the Gospels*, 413.

56. TJ to Peter Carr, 10 August 1787, *PTJ* 12:16; TJ to Adams, 12 October 1813, *A-JL* 384. On Jefferson-the-politician wanting to break the same Gothic "long train of et ceteras" in order to modernize society, see TJ to James Madison, 6 September 1789, *PTJ* 15:396.

57. TJ to DeWitt Clinton, 19 March 1822, Columbia University, DeWitt Clinton Papers; TJ to Charles Clay, 29 January 1815, *PTJ-RS* 8:212.

58. The best study so far on Jefferson as a natural historian is Regis, *Describing Early America.*

59. TJ, *Notes*, Query 11, *Works of TJ*, 3:496, 497. On Native Americans (and other ethnic groups) as certainly not dead and their role in the colonization of North America, see Richter, *Before the Revolution*, and Taylor, *American Colonies.* On Jefferson and American Indians, see the excellent Wallace, *Jefferson and the Indians*, and Kornfeld, "Encountering 'the Other.'" Among the classics, see Pearce, *Savages of America*; Slotkin, *Regeneration through Violence*; Sheehan, *Seeds of Extinction*; and Berkhofer, *White Man's Indian.*

60. TJ, *Notes*, Query 6, *Works of TJ*, 3:440. Dana Nelson makes a convincing case about the fact that many whites have repeatedly identified Indianness not simply "as a mythological oppositional/negative contrast to 'white' identity, but as something more complex and flexible than that." Nelson, *National Manhood*, 61–101. On the need felt by Euro-Americans to identify with Native Americans, see Deloria, *Playing Indian.*

61. TJ to John Adams, 11 June 1812, *A-JL* 307.

62. TJ, *Notes*, Query 6, *Works of TJ*, 3:438–440. Buffon alleged that despite the fact that the "savage" of the New World is "about the same height" as the European, he is "feeble," has "small organs of generation," has "neither hair nor beard," and no "ardor" for the female. He is "less strong in body," albeit he runs faster; is "less sensitive"; "more timid and cowardly"; and has no "activity of mind." American Indians "love their parents and children but little." Their "heart is icy, their society cold, and their rule harsh." Buffon cited in TJ, *Notes*, Query 6, *Works of TJ*, 3:436–38, my translation. Jefferson took a critical stance even on Don Ulloa's hypothesis of Indians, from both South and North America, as constitutionally "cowardly and pusillanimous," whether or not they have been reduced to slavery. Don Ulloa, Jefferson was convinced, "had formed his opinion of them from hear-say." Cowardice, Jefferson concludes, "is the effect of subjugation and ill treatment." TJ, *Notes*, Query 6, *Works of TJ*, 3:439. And see Wallace, *Jefferson and the Indians*, 108–29. On Jefferson praising the Indian over the "enfeebled white" for an unmatched ability to go on foot for very long distances, see TJ to Peter Carr, 19 August 1785, *PTJ* 8:407.

63. TJ, *Notes*, Query 6, *Works of TJ*, 3:440, 443–44.

64. TJ to John Adams, 11 June 1812, *A-JL* 306–7.

65. TJ to John Adams, 11 June 1812, *A-JL* 307.

66. TJ, *Notes*, Query 11, *Works of TJ*, 3:495.

67. On American Indians being better than Europeans, see, for example, TJ, *Notes*, Query 11, *Works of TJ*, 3:495: "Insomuch that were it made a question, whether no law, as among the savage Americans, or too much law, as among the civilized Europeans, submits man to the greatest evil, one who has seen both conditions of

existence would pronounce it to be the last." On the violence implicit in the naturalization of Native Americans, see Kornfeld, "Encountering 'the Other,'" especially 291. On the way Jefferson exploited Native Americans to prove that American nature had turned into American history, see the excellent Holland, "Notes on the State of America."

68. TJ to John Adams, 20 April 1812, *A-JL* 299; TJ to Robert Fulton, 17 March 1810, *PTJ-RS* 2:301. On "Ignoro" and Jefferson on American Indian origins, see TJ to John Adams, 27 May 1813, *A-JL* 324. In his second inaugural address, Jefferson denounced that "the endeavors to enlighten them . . . are combated by the habits of their bodies, prejudice of their minds, ignorance, pride, and the influence of interested and crafty individuals among them. . . . These persons inculcate a sanctimonious reverence for the customs of their ancestors; that whatsoever they did, must be done through all time; that reason is a false guide, and to advance under its counsel . . . is perilous innovation; that their duty is to remain as their Creator made them, ignorance being safety, and knowledge full of danger." TJ, Second Inaugural Address, 4 March 1805, *Works of TJ*, 10:132–33. For a better assessment of the real reasons why Native Americans preferred to remain attached to their traditional way of life, see Wallace, *Jefferson and the Indians*, 297–300. See also Edmunds, *Shawnee Prophet*.

69. TJ to John Adams, 20 April 1812, *A-JL* 299.

70. TJ to Henry Dearborn, 14 February 1807, Historical Society of Pennsylvania, Daniel Parker Papers.

71. Wallace, *Jefferson and the Indians*, 62; TJ to Abner Nash, 12 August 1780, *PTJ* 3:544; TJ to Crèvecoeur, 26 August 1786, *PTJ* 10:301. On the war with the Cherokees, see also Wallace, *Jefferson and the Indians*, 54–60. On the war with the Shawnees, see ibid., 60–66. On how Native Americans became "red," see Shoemaker, *Strange Likeness*, 125–40. See also Shoemaker, "How Indians Got to Be Red."

72. TJ to Benjamin Hawkins, 13 August 1786, *PTJ* 10:240; TJ to Edmund Pendleton, 13 August 1776, *PTJ* 1:494; TJ to John Page, 5 August 1776, *PTJ* 1:485–86; TJ to George Rogers Clark, 1 January 1780, *PTJ* 3:259. See also TJ to George Rogers Clark, 29 January 1780, *PTJ* 3:273–78. In this letter Jefferson also insisted on "An evacuation of their Country and removal utterly out of interference with us" (276).

73. TJ to Kitchao Geboway, 27 February 1808, *Writings of TJ*, 16:426; TJ to the Chiefs of the Wyandots, Ottawas, Chippewas, Powtewatamies and Shawanese, 10 January 1809, *Writings of TJ*, 16:463. In *Nature's Man*, 144–51, I discuss many more examples of Jefferson's removal policy. On removal, see also, for example, TJ to William Claiborne, 24 May 1803, *PTJ* 40:422–24, and TJ to John Breckinridge, 12 August 1803, *PTJ* 41:184–86.

74. TJ to William Henry Harrison, 27 February 1803, *PTJ* 39:590.

75. See Keller, "Philanthropy Betrayed." Keller is right to argue that "removal was a new policy." After the Louisiana Purchase, when new land became available, Jef-

ferson "changed his mind" in the sense that he started to mull over the feasibility of the plan. See ibid., 41–42. As a policy, removal was new. However, the letters from 1776 and 1780 show that removal had always been on Jefferson's mind, at least as a hypothesis or in relation to particular groups. See also Wallace, *Jefferson and the Indians*, 224–26, 273–75.

76. TJ to Alexander von Humboldt, 6 December 1813, *PTJ-RS* 7:30. On intermixing and incorporation as the "natural course of things," see also TJ to Benjamin Hawkins, 18 February 1803, *PTJ* 39:546–49. Jefferson's case for "race mixing" was typical. "Several colonists were willing to allow, even advocate, intermarriage with the Indians—an unheard of proposition concerning Negroes." Jordan, *White over Black*, 163. With the black "race," as we will see better in the following sections, Jefferson had a totally different attitude. Despite the fact that he liked the dream of one people taking over the whole American continent, "speaking the same language, governed in similar forms, & by similar laws," he could not put up with the hypothesis that blacks could somehow become part of the game: "nor can we contemplate, with satisfaction, either blot or mixture on that surface." TJ to James Monroe, 24 November 1801, *PTJ* 35:719–20.

77. TJ to Handsome Lake, 3 November 1802, *PTJ* 38:628; TJ to Lydia Howard Huntley Sigourney, 18 July 1824, Saint Paul's School, Concord, N.H. On American Indians refusing to wear linen, see TJ to John Adams, 20 April 1812, *A-JL* 299. Bodies should look alike only because they would assume "civilized" outfits. But Jefferson declared not to look for uniformities other than exterior—manners, clothing, and styles. In *Notes*, he had written that uniformity of opinion, for example, is desirable "no more than of face and stature. Introduce the bed of Procustes then, and as there is danger that the large men may beat the small, make us all of a size, by lopping the former and stretching the latter. Difference of opinion is advantageous in religion. The several sects perform the office of a Censor morum over each other." TJ, *Notes*, Query 17, *Works of TJ*, 4:79–80. Faces, tempers, and talents should never look alike. See TJ to Charles Thomson, 29 January 1817, *PTJ-RS* 11:29. We must say that he was not particularly concerned about unity in the world of opinions because he was convinced that "It is error alone which needs the support of government. Truth can stand by itself." TJ, *Notes*, Query 17, *Works of TJ*, 4:79. In the Bill for Establishing Religious Freedom, *PTJ* 2:546, Jefferson had already expressed his conviction that "truth is great and will prevail if left to herself." In a letter to William Roscoe, 27 December 1820, *Writings of TJ*, 15:303, an old Jefferson said that "we are not afraid to follow truth wherever it may lead, nor to tolerate any error so long as reason is left free to combat it." On Jefferson trusting that reason will prevail if "left free to exert her force," see TJ to Diodati, 3 August 1789, *PTJ* 15:326.

78. TJ to the Miamis, Powtewatamies, Delawares, and Chippeways, 21 December 1808, *Writings of TJ*, 16:439–40; TJ to the Chiefs of the Upper Cherokees, 4 May 1808, *Writings of TJ*, 16:434. On Jefferson losing hope in a partial American Indian

assimilation as an unwelcome result of the latest wars ("My hopes . . . are damped by the transactions of the late war"), see TJ to Lydia Howard Huntley Sigourney, 18 July 1824, Saint Paul's School, Concord, N.H.

79. Jefferson's letters to the frontier leader George Rogers Clark have often been taken as "proof" that Jefferson was seized by an unqualified hatred against *all* Native Americans. Actually, he wrote the infamous letter to Clark advocating extermination *of the Shawnees* ("The same world will scarcely do for them and us") while serving as a beleaguered governor of Virginia and while settlers were actually being attacked. We should never take these desperate and unhappy expressions out of their context. See TJ to George Rogers Clark, 1 January 1780, *PTJ* 3:259.

80. On "After the injuries we have done them, they cannot love us," see TJ to Benjamin Hawkins, 13 August 1786, *PTJ* 10:240.

81. TJ to William Dunbar, 24 June 1799, *PTJ* 31:137.

82. TJ to William Linn, 2 April 1798, *PTJ* 30:238. On Jefferson's almost compulsive determination to collect Indian vocabularies, see also TJ to David Campbell, 14 March 1800, *PTJ* 31:433–34. About fifty American Indian vocabularies he had painfully collected for thirty years met a tragic fate in 1809. On the eve of retirement, Jefferson packed them in a trunk and shipped them by water from Washington to Monticello. But the trunk was stolen and its precious content dispersed. For details, see TJ to Benjamin Smith Barton, 21 September 1809, *PTJ-RS* 1:555–56.

83. TJ to John Sibley, 27 May 1805, *Writings of TJ*, 11:79, 80–81.

84. On these "amusing" hypotheses, see TJ to John Adams, 27 May 1813, *A-JL* 323–25. On "remounting thro' the gloom of ages," see TJ to John Pickering, 26 February 1823, privately owned, available through Founders Early Access, http://rotunda.upress.virginia.edu/founders/FOEA.html.

85. TJ, *Notes*, Query 14, *Works of TJ*, 4:49. Articles and books attempting various "defenses" of Jefferson's character, including the rebuff of his "alleged" racism, appear regularly. The truth is that Jefferson may or may not have been a "racist," depending on the notion of racism one embraces. For sure, he kept despising the very blackness of African Americans. And he did so coherently and consistently. According to common sense, this is tantamount to racism.

86. TJ, *Notes*, Query 14, *Works of TJ*, 4:49–50.

87. On albinos sporting "cadaverous" white, see TJ, *Notes*, Query 6, *Works of TJ*, 3:467. Nowadays philosophers would claim that Jefferson made the logical error of deriving evaluative statements from factual premises. The problem was enunciated by the Scottish philosopher David Hume in his *Treatise of Human Nature* (1738–40).

88. TJ, *Notes*, Query 14, *Works of TJ*, 4:50–51. Many European philosophers had insisted that blacks, whether enslaved or free, had an extremely offensive odor. See M. M. Smith, *How Race is Made*, 14, and Jordan, *White over Black*, 245–65, passim.

89. TJ, *Notes*, Query 14, *Works of TJ*, 4:50. This was a peculiar idea expressed by Buffon, that the orangutan, or *pithecos* of the Greeks or *simia* of the Latins, was "an ape as tall and as strong as man, and equally ardent for women as for its own

females; an ape who knows how to bear arms, to attack his enemies with stones, and to defend himself with clubs." Buffon, *Natural History*, 8:40. Buffon and his contemporaries often did not differentiate orangutans and chimpanzees from monkeys—the first two are great apes and have no tail. On European and American discussions of the link between human beings (Africans, in particular) and apes, see Wokler, "Tyson and Buffon on the Orang-utan"; Wokler, "Ape Debates in Enlightenment Anthropology"; Mizelle, "Man Cannot Behold It without Contemplating Himself"; Bellhouse, "Candide Shoots the Monkey Lovers"; and Spencer, "Link Which Unites Man with Brutes." See also Jordan, *White over Black*, 228–34.

90. TJ, *Notes*, Query 14, *Works of TJ*, 4:51–53, *passim*. Eighteenth-century pseudo-anthropology restated over again the theme of Africans lacking superior faculties, including aesthetic taste. Immanuel Kant, for example, wrote that "the Negroes of Africa have by nature no feeling that rises above the trifling. Mr. [David] Hume challenges anyone to cite a single example in which a Negro has shown talents, and asserts that among the hundreds of thousands of blacks who are transported elsewhere from their countries, although many of them have even been set free, still not a single one was ever found who presented anything great in art or science or any other praiseworthy quality." Kant, *Observations on the Feeling of the Beautiful and Sublime*, 110–11. Kant refers to a celebrated and infamous footnote the Scottish philosopher appended to his essay "Of National Characters." Hume's essay appeared in 1748; a first version of the footnote was added in 1753–54, while a revised version of the same note was published posthumously in 1777. Here is the first version: "I am apt to suspect the Negroes and in general all other species of men (for there are four or five different kinds) to be naturally inferior to the whites. There never was a civilized nation of any other complexion than white, nor even any individual eminent either in action or speculation. No ingenious manufacturers amongst them, no arts, no sciences." Hume, *Essays and Treatises on Several Subjects* (1758), n. 125. Here is the revised, final version: "I am apt to suspect the negroes to be naturally inferior to the whites. There scarcely ever was a civilized nation of that complexion, nor even any individual eminent either in action or speculation. No ingenious manufactures amongst them, no arts, no sciences." Hume, *Essays and Treatises on Several Subjects* (1777), 1:550. On Hume and race, see Valls, "'Lousy Empirical Scientist,'" and Eze, "Hume, Race, and Human Nature." For an interesting assessment of the prevailing ideas about blacks' intellectual capacities, see Jordan, *White over Black*, 187–190. For the link between Africans and apes, see ibid., 228–34.

91. TJ, *Notes*, Query 14, *Works of TJ*, 4:57–58, *passim*. On Jefferson trusting he had always expressed his "doubts" with great hesitation, see also TJ to Henri Grégoire, 25 February 1809, *Works of TJ*, 11:99–100. In a letter to Joel Barlow, 8 October 1809, *PTJ-RS* 1:588–89, Jefferson took a dim view on Henri Grégoire's book, *De la littérature des nègres* (1808). Abbé Grégoire was a Catholic priest, supporter of universal suffrage, abolitionist, and advocate of racial equality. But Jefferson was clearly unconvinced by Grégoire's favorable assessment of the intellectual capacity of

blacks. On *De la littérature des nègres*, see Sowerby #1398. Jefferson also owned *Lettre aux philanthropes, sur les malheurs, les droits et les réclamations des gens de couleur de Saint-Domingue* (1790). See Sowerby #1388.

92. TJ, *Notes*, Query 14, *Works of TJ*, 4:54, 58.

93. TJ, *Notes*, Query 14, *Works of TJ*, 4:51, 53, 58–59. In a letter to Edward Coles, 25 August 1814, *PTJ-RS* 7:604, Jefferson similarly lamented that "amalgamation with the other color produces a degradation to which no lover of his country, no lover of excellence in the human character can innocently consent." On emancipated slaves staining the blood of whites, see the discussion in Jordan, *White over Black*, 542–45. Buffon as well had declared blacks "almost equally wild, and as ugly as these apes." Buffon, *Natural History*, 8:41. In Jefferson's manuscript of *Notes*, Jefferson had originally written: "but love is with them only an eager desire, not a tender delicate excitement, not a delicious foment of the soul." TJ, *Notes on the State of Virginia*, 288, n. 8. Not surprisingly, the rigidity and determinism of such an "eager desire" stood in iconic opposition to any "modern" ideal of gentility, softness, tenderness, or flexibility.

94. TJ, *Notes*, Query 14, *Works of TJ*, 4:53, 56, 57. Over the years, Jefferson did not amend his "suspicions" about African Americans' natural inferiority, nor, after *Notes*, did he devote much time and energy to fresh research. Despite scattered claims about "wishes" to see "proofs" that nature "has given to our black brethren, talents equal to those of the other colours of men, and that the appearance of a want of them is owing merely to the degraded condition of their existence both in Africa and America" (TJ to Benjamin Banneker, 30 August 1791, *PTJ* 22:97–98), Jefferson did not change his opinion. For an analogous wish, see TJ to Condorcet, 30 August 1791, *PTJ* 22:99. As president first and Sage of Monticello later, he identified much more urgent problems on the national agenda than deepening or recanting his personal "scientific" hypotheses about blacks. National debt, crises with Britain, commerce, territorial expansion, Barbary wars, North-South rivalry, a new university, to name just a few, were for him more pressing. In 1809, three years after astronomer and mathematician Benjamin Banneker died, Jefferson wrote to Joel Barlow alleging that this black man could not have made the calculations contained in his celebrated almanacs without assistance: "I have a long letter from Banneker which shews him to have had a mind of very common stature indeed." TJ to Joel Barlow, 8 October 1809, *PTJ-RS* 1:588–89.

95. Stanton, *"Those Who Labor for My Happiness,"* 57.

96. Fanon, *Black Skin, White Masks,* 189. On "the blackest traitor," see Draft of a Letter to Officers Retired from Service, enclosed to Baron Steuben, 1 January 1781, *PTJ* 4:291; on "the blackest slanders," see TJ to Abigail Adams, 25 September 1785, *PTJ* 8:548; on "hic niger est," see TJ to James Madison, 28 August 1789, *PTJ* 15:367. On the association between dark complexion and dirt, see Brown, *Foul Bodies,* 340. Eighteenth-century aesthetic theory supported the notion that colors degenerated as they approached black. William Hogarth wrote that colors "absolutely lose their

beauty by degrees as they approach nearer to black, the representative of darkness."
Hogarth, *Analysis of Beauty*, 116. Edmund Burke, for his part, argued that "Black will
always have something melancholy in it, because the sensory will always find the
change to it from other colours too violent." Burke, *Philosophical Enquiry*, 135.

97. On old Jefferson bolstering his lifelong commitment "to feed & clothe them
well, protect them from ill usage," see TJ to Edward Coles, 25 August 1814, *PTJ-RS*
7:604.

98. See Staples, "Useful, Ornamental or Necessary in This Province," 59. On
clothing the "other" in a rather stingy way, see Stanton, *"Those Who Labor for My
Happiness,"* 61. In *White over Black*, Jordan insisted on the fact of black slaves' nakedness as a way to sustain the difference between the two races. Africans, to begin
with, had different standards from Europeans as to which parts of the body had to be
covered. But they were also kept by their masters in an "atmosphere of semi-nudity."
Sexual prissiness mingled perfectly with a deliberate effort to debase these people.
On Southern plantations, slaves usually wore long shirts or simple trousers made of
"negro cloth." "More surprising, it was apparently common practice for partially or
fully matured Negro boys to wait upon dinner tables wearing only a shirt not always
long enough to conceal their private parts." Jordan, *White over Black*, 161. There is no
record suggesting that Jefferson ever humiliated slaves in this way.

99. TJ to Jeremiah A. Goodman, 23 December 1814, *PTJ-RS* 8:158; TJ to Jeremiah A. Goodman, 6 January 1815, *PTJ-RS* 8:185; TJ to Thomas Jefferson Randolph,
4 February 1826, College of William and Mary, Jefferson Papers, Tucker-Coleman
Collection; TJ to Edmund Bacon, Memorandums, 13 May 1807, Yale University, Sterling Memorial Library. In his reminiscences, Israel Jefferson (born Israel Gillette)
wrote that each time the president returned home for a brief period, everyone was
excited: "It was a time looked forward to with great interest by his servants, or when
he came home many of them, especially the leading ones, were sure to receive pre-
sents from his hands." Israel Jefferson in Brodie, *Thomas Jefferson*, 477–78.

100. Breen captures that, as a general principle, the act of choosing "could be
liberating, even empowering, for it allowed them [people from every walk of life]
to determine for themselves what the process of self-fashioning was all about. . . .
It should not come as a surprise that for such men and women choice in the consumer marketplace gradually merged with a discourse of rights." Breen, *Marketplace
of Revolution*, 151.

101. TJ to John Taylor, 29 December 1794, *PTJ* 28:232, 233.

102. TJ to Thomas Mann Randolph, 9 May 1798, *PTJ* 30:341; TJ to Thomas Mann
Randolph, 20 March 1802, *PTJ* 37:96; TJ to Stevens Thomson Mason, 27 October
1799, *PTJ* 31:222. On the tax on slaves, see also TJ to James Monroe, 21 May 1798,
PTJ 30:360–61.

103. TJ to Joel Yancey, 17 January 1819, Massachusetts Historical Society, Coolidge
Collection. Jefferson did not buy or sell slaves for mere commercial reasons. However, it has been calculated that in his lifetime he sold more than 110 people, mainly

for financial reasons. Seventy-one were sold from his Goochland and Bedford County plantations in three sales in the 1780s and 1790s. For more details, see http://www.monticello.org/site/plantation-and-slavery/property.

104. TJ to Joel Yancey, 17 January 1819, Massachusetts Historical Society, Coolidge Collection. On Jefferson's economic gaze on black women, see also, for instance, TJ to John Jordan, 21 December 1805, Massachusetts Historical Society, Coolidge Collection, and TJ to John Wayles Eppes, 30 June 1820, University of Virginia.

105. Martha J. Trist Burke, Reminiscences of Monticello, Thomas Jefferson Library, Thomas Jefferson Foundation. Burke entered this account in 1889, many years after she "saw" the interior of the cabin. But since her mother, Virginia Jefferson Randolph Trist, corroborated the reminiscence, we can hazard the conclusion that this was more than a fantasy: "I described the Cabin to my mother years afterwards, & asked her where it was? she was surprised & said 'why that is the exact description of mammy's [Priscilla's] Cabin, which you have not seen since you were two 1/2 years old.'" John Hemmings (Hemings), Priscilla's husband, was a skilled cabinetmaker who worked as Monticello's head joiner after 1809. Many years earlier, when Jefferson famously entered another cabin during his tour of the South of France, he only noticed misery and wretchedness. To peep into people's dwellings was for Jefferson the best method to ascertain their prosperity: "you must ferret the people out of their hovels as I have done, look into their kettles, eat their bread, loll on their beds under pretence of resting yourself, but in fact to find if they are soft." TJ to Lafayette, 11 April 1787, *PTJ* 11:285. We will never know if the experience of peeping into the coziness and dignity of the Hemings's cabin would have provided Jefferson with an extra reason to empathize with African Americans, and maybe force him to revise his racial prejudices more quickly, or if he would have simply concluded that his slaves were better off in comparison to French peasants.

106. On the liberating power of style, see White and White, *Stylin'*; P. D. Morgan, *Slave Counterpoint*; and P. K. Hunt, "Struggle to Achieve Individual Expression." On slaves developing "a sense of style in the clothes they made for themselves," see Fox-Genovese, *Within the Plantation Household*, 183.

107. De Volney and the Duc de La Rochefoucauld-Liancourt quoted in Stanton, *"Those Who Labor for My Happiness,"* respectively, 306, n. 18, and 8; Henry S. Randall to James Parton, 1 June 1868, in Gordon-Reed, *Thomas Jefferson and Sally Hemings*, 254. Thomas Jefferson Randolph thought the Carr brothers were the fathers.

108. Isaac Jefferson in Bear, *Jefferson at Monticello*, 4. For Thomas Jefferson Randolph, see Henry S. Randall to James Parton, 1 June 1868, in Gordon-Reed, *Thomas Jefferson and Sally Hemings*, 254.

109. TJ to Francis Calley Gray, 4 March 1815, *PTJ-RS* 8:310–11. On mathematics as Jefferson's favorite study, see TJ to Benjamin Rush, 17 August 1811, *PTJ-RS* 4:87.

110. Jefferson owned more than 600 enslaved people. So far 87 have been identified. See http://slavery.monticello.org/mulberry-row/people. Jupiter (1743–1800) spent his entire life as Jefferson's trusted personal servant. When this man died,

probably poisoned by a substance given to him by an African American doctor, Jefferson somehow felt the blow. He wrote to Thomas Mann Randolph: "I am sorry for him as well as sensible he leaves a void in my [domestic] administration which I cannot fill up." TJ to Thomas Mann Randolph, 4 February 1800, *PTJ* 31:360. A few days later, he also wrote to his daughter Maria: "you have perhaps heard of the loss of Jupiter. with all his defects, he leaves a void in my domestic arrangements which cannot be filled." TJ to Mary Jefferson Eppes, 12 February 1800, *PTJ* 31:368. Jefferson was always rather laconic when he had to record or make comments on someone's death, no matter how close the person. But taking what he said about Jupiter as a sign of closeness and friendship requires a dose of imagination.

111. Rothman, *Notorious in the Neighborhood*, 42, 44. And see ibid. 42–43 for more examples. See also P. D. Morgan, "Interracial Sex."

112. Suggestive on the many daily acts of slave resistance, despite a focus on the Old South, is Camp, *Closer to Freedom*. See also Scott, *Weapons of the Weak*, and Scott, *Domination and the Arts of Resistance*.

113. Tim Matthewson says that as long as Jefferson realized that the Haitian Revolution could work as an invitation to rebellion and a refuge for blacks, he developed "an overriding loyalty to the planters of Virginia." Matthewson, "Jefferson and the Nonrecognition of Haiti," 23. Despite his love for universal freedom, Jefferson refused to recognize the new black republic in Haiti/St. Domingue, even by means of embargo bills with a pro-French quality and public denigration. In particular, "he was aware of the reaction of southern slaveholders against Saint Domingue-Haiti." Ibid., 22. For a convincing appraisal of Jefferson's complex attitudes toward St. Domingue, see Burstein and Isenberg, *Madison and Jefferson*, 258–61, 374–80. Burstein and Isenberg contend that Jefferson kept swerving between prudence and aggressive diplomacy, but they agree with Matthewson in the conclusion that "Madison and Jefferson were not the sort to risk alienating the majority in the South" (379).

114. TJ, Autobiography, *Works of TJ*, 1:77. On deportation, see also, for example, TJ to James Monroe, 24 November 1801, *PTJ* 35:718–21; TJ to Edward Coles, 25 August 1814, *PTJ-RS* 7:603–5; and the famous "Wolf by the ear" letter, TJ to John Holmes, 22 April 1820, *Works of TJ*, 12:158–60. Jefferson, of course, was not the first to insist on deporting blacks somewhere else. "Plans" about removal, or "colonization," date back to the early 1770s. However, after the summer of 1800, these speculations took on a sense of an urgent policy. See the range of discussion in Jordan, *White over Black*, 546–69.

115. TJ to Rufus King, 13 July 1802, *PTJ* 38:54–55. Jefferson had already brought up the issue of Sierra Leone as the ideal destination in a letter to James Monroe, 3 June 1802, *PTJ* 37:531–33.

116. TJ to William Short, 18 January 1826, *Works of TJ*, 12:434. "Freed negroes and persons of colour" is taken from TJ to James Monroe, 3 June 1802, *PTJ* 37:532.

117. On women's bodies as the radical other, see Karlsen, *Devil in the Shape of a*

Woman, and Gubar, "Female Monster." "Weaker sex" was the phrase that Jefferson favored over others.

118. Hemphill, *Bowing to Necessities,* 47, 49. On the "combination of intimacy with inequality," see ibid., 48. On women's behavior as unconstructed, see ibid., 59. On women soliciting, see TJ to George Washington, 4 December 1788, *PTJ* 14:330.

119. Brown, *Foul Bodies,* 141; TJ to Martha Jefferson, 22 December 1783, *PTJ* 6:417. "Male disgust for the female body was the hobbyhorse not only of British authors but of Anglo-Americans, too." Brown, *Foul Bodies,* 142.

120. I take the suggestion that love is never "pure" from Scharff, *Women Jefferson Loved,* xx. See also Kukla, *Mr. Jefferson's Women.* The sole biography that takes Jefferson's relation to women as a central theme is Brodie, *Thomas Jefferson.*

121. On the strictures suffered by women in the 1790s, see Kierner, *Beyond the Household,* 102–38.

122. "From the very beginning, women played a central role in the expansive world of goods, and after 1764 it became absolutely essential to enlist their enthusiastic participations in the boycotts." Breen, *Marketplace of Revolution,* 25. On women's power, see Zagarri, *Revolutionary Backlash;* Kolp and Snyder, "Women and the Political Culture of Eighteenth-Century Virginia"; and J. M. Lewis, "Women and Economic Freedom." Kierner, *Beyond the Household,* has brilliantly shown that women were neither frail nor leisured but participated in the public sphere. On consumption as "powerful" and political, see A. S. Martin, *Buying into the World of Goods,* 9.

123. On widows' power, see Conger, *Widows' Might.*

124. On the need for men to constantly reinforce their authority within the household, see Rotundo, *American Manhood,* 2–3, 10–12. See also Jan Lewis, "Republican Wife."

125. Hemphill, *Bowing to Necessities,* 108.

126. See Wilentz, *Rise of American Democracy;* Smolenski, "From Men of Property to Just Men"; and Zuckerman, "Endangered Deference, Imperiled Patriarchy."

127. TJ to George Washington, 4 December 1788, *PTJ* 14:330.

128. For an analysis of these misogynist quotations, see Lockridge, *On the Sources of Patriarchal Rage.* Lockridge interprets Jefferson's rage against women in terms of a conflict against his mother: "Jefferson was confessing a frustration with and hatred of his mother's control of [economic] resources." Ibid., 75. Interesting as Lockridge's interpretation certainly is, many readers may find "rage" a too modern notion to make sense of Jefferson's conflicts.

129. Jefferson's misogyny almost disappeared, but when he started the Memorandum Book for the year 1770 he inscribed these lines on the inside of the front cover: "Faemina [*sic*] nulla bona est; sed si bona contigit ullae [*sic*] / Nescio quo fato res mala facta bona est [No woman is good; but if a good one has befallen anyone I know not by what fate an evil thing has become a good one]." *JMB* 154.

130. TJ to Madame de Tessé, 20 March 1787, *PTJ* 11:226.

131. TJ to Abigail Adams, 21 June 1785, *PTJ* 8:239. Abigail could not force Jefferson to dismiss his prejudices but, as Jon Kukla writes, "If anyone ever presented a serious feminist challenge to Jefferson's general disregard for women, that person was Abigail Adams." Kukla, *Mr. Jefferson's Women*, 152. Probably the most flirtatious letter Jefferson sent to Abigail Adams is the one dated 25 September 1785, *PTJ* 8:547–49. Besides other innuendos (like a Mars with "his faulchion not drawn, but ready to be drawn"), Jefferson called Abigail a "Venus."

132. TJ to James Madison, 16 December 1786, *PTJ* 10:604.

133. TJ to John T. Mason, 18 August 1814, *PTJ-RS* 7:569.

134. TJ to Thomas Cooper, 2 November 1822, *Works of TJ*, 12:270–71.

135. Rush, *Benjamin Rush's Lectures on the Mind*, 686, 687. On the more recent medical "discoveries" certifying the difference between men and women, see Haller and Haller, *Physician and Sexuality*, 24 ff. On the eighteenth-century "scientific" conceptions of a woman, see also Jordanova, *Sexual Visions*, and Stafford, *Body Criticism*.

136. Burstein, "Jefferson's Rationalizations," 189. On women as playthings, see Lasch, *Women and the Common Life*, 67–89. On republican wives and mothers, see Kerber, "Republican Mother"; Jan Lewis, "Blessings of Domestic Society"; and Isaac, "First Monticello." See also Brown, *Good Wives*. On women caring for the education of children should the father die, see TJ to Nathaniel Burwell, 14 March 1818, *Works of TJ*, 12:90–93.

137. TJ to John Jay, 8 October 1787, *PTJ* 12:217.

138. TJ to John Banister, 15 October 1785, *PTJ* 8:636; TJ to Anne Willing Bingham, 11 May 1788, *PTJ* 13:152.

139. For an interesting discussion of Jefferson's conviction that French women and, at the other end of the spectrum, American Indian women could never enjoy republican happiness and "equality," see Steele, *Thomas Jefferson and American Nationhood*, 53–90. As Steele argues, Jefferson believed that by forcing women to do fieldwork or, conversely, by letting them waste their time pursuing the buzz of society, both American Indian and French social models subverted "natural" gender roles. Only republican America placed women, at least white women, in their proper role of republican domesticity.

140. Anne Willing Bingham to TJ, 1 June 1787, *PTJ* 11:393. Jefferson had already written to Bingham from Paris, 7 February 1787 (*PTJ* 11:122–24), praising the "tranquil pleasures of America" as "preferable to the empty bustle of Paris."

141. Haulman, *Politics of Fashion*, 49.

142. TJ to Abigail Adams, 30 August 1787, *PTJ* 12:65–66.

143. TJ to Albert Gallatin, 13 January 1807, *Works of TJ*, 10:339. See also TJ to George Washington, 4 December 1788, *PTJ* 14:330. Very recently, David A. Paterson has reconstructed the specific context in which the president made his famous comment to Gallatin. Furthermore, Paterson makes the convincing case that Jefferson expressed his perplexity in reaction to Gallatin's proposal to appoint a specific woman to a specific job. Her name was Rebecca Long, and the "public office" in

question was that of lighthouse-keeper. See Paterson, "Jefferson's Mystery Woman Identified."

144. TJ to Samuel Kercheval, 5 September 1816, *PTJ-RS* 10:368.

145. TJ to John Pleasants, 19 April 1824, *Works of TJ*, 12:353.

146. TJ, *Notes*, Query 6, *Works of TJ*, 3:440–41.

147. TJ to Anne Willing Bingham, 11 May 1788, *PTJ* 13:151–52.

148. TJ to Angelica Schuyler Church, 21 September 1788, *PTJ* 13:623; TJ to Martha Jefferson Randolph, 4 April 1790, *PTJ* 16:300. See also TJ to Martha Jefferson Randolph, 17 July 1790, *PTJ* 17:215: "Be you, my dear, the link of love, union, and peace for the whole family. The world will give you the more credit for it in proportion to the difficulty of the task. And your own happiness will be the greater as you percieve that you promote that of others."

149. Kierner, *Martha Jefferson Randolph*, 89. On "performances of domesticity," see ibid., 113. On Martha and the Parisian excesses at the threshold of revolution, see ibid., 39.

150. On Martha's desire to convert, see Kierner, *Martha Jefferson Randolph*, 64–65. And see Jefferson's reaction in TJ to John Jay, 19 November 1788, *PTJ* 14:215–16. See also Randolph, *Domestic Life of Thomas Jefferson*, 146.

151. Marie Jacinthe de Botidoux to Martha Jefferson, Saturday morning [1789], editors' translation, privately owned, Thomas Jefferson Foundation.

152. Marie Jacinthe de Botidoux to Martha Jefferson Randolph, 21 June 1801, editors' translation, privately owned, Thomas Jefferson Foundation. On Patsy, "a wild and playful girl," see Kierner, *Martha Jefferson Randolph*, 56. See also Marie Jacinthe de Botidoux to Martha Jefferson Randolph, 31 October 1798, Botidoux letters, University of Virginia.

153. On Jefferson's "perfect knowlege," see TJ to Martha Jefferson, 28 March 1787, *PTJ* 11:251.

154. TJ to Martha Jefferson, 28 March 1787, *PTJ* 11:250.

155. TJ to Martha Jefferson, 22 December 1783, *PTJ* 6:417. Many similar examples of moral blackmails may be provided. On 28 November 1783 (*PTJ* 6:360), he had written to Martha: "If you love me then, strive to be good under every situation and to all living creatures, and to acquire those accomplishments which I have put in your power, and which will go far towards ensuring you the warmest love of your affectionate father."

156. TJ to Mary Jefferson, 20 September 1785, *PTJ* 8:533.

157. TJ to Martha Jefferson, 11 December 1783, *PTJ* 6:380.

158. TJ to Nathaniel Burwell, 14 March 1818, *Works of TJ*, 12:92, italics added.

159. TJ to Nathaniel Burwell, 14 March 1818, *Works of TJ*, 12:92–93.

160. See Guillaumin, "Constructed Body," especially 47–48. And see the classic Young, "Throwing Like a Girl."

161. TJ to Ann C. Bankhead, 26 May 1811, *PTJ-RS* 3:633.

162. TJ to William Drayton, 30 July 1787, *PTJ* 11:647–48. For the following concluding sections, I am deeply indebted to Kathleen Brown and Annette Gordon-Reed.

163. On class and status tensions within the female gender, see, for example, D. G. White, *Ar'n't I a Woman;* Fox-Genovese, *Within the Plantation Household;* J. L. Morgan, *Laboring Women;* and Sweet, *Bodies Politic.* It is clear that some women served as foils for others.

164. Few scholars have tried to provide real traits to the figure of Sally Hemings. Lucia Stanton's and Annette Gordon-Reed's books and essays represent the most successful remedies so far. On Sally Hemings as a real person, see also the essays in Lewis and Onuf, *Sally Hemings and Thomas Jefferson,* and Kukla, *Mr. Jefferson's Women,* 115–41. A handy summary of the literature on the debate is provided by Kukla, *Mr. Jefferson's Women,* n. 2, 248–49. Callender's articles appeared in the *Richmond Recorder* on 1, 22, 29 September, 5 November, and 1 December 1802. Some key passages of these "reports" are reprinted in Lewis and Onuf, *Sally Hemings and Thomas Jefferson,* 259–61. I will not be chiming in in the debate. Personally, I believe the evidence supporting the sexual affair is overwhelming, but this is beyond the point. I find it very depressing, however, the notion that Jefferson scholars should be categorized as "revisionists" or "defenders." Scholars, especially historians, should share the goal of giving all protagonists likely traits and a plausible personality.

165. Jefferson owned Tissot's collected works in French and a single volume titled *Advice to the People in General, with Regard to Their Health* (1768), an English translation of Tissot's *Avis au peuple sur la santé* (1761). See Sowerby #889–890. Anne C. Vila has described *De la santé* as "a medical cautionary tale for those who pursued cerebral stimulation with excessive zeal." Vila, *Enlightenment and Pathology,* 95. See also Burstein, *Jefferson's Secrets,* 34–38.

166. Gordon-Reed, *Hemingses of Monticello,* 272; Isaac Jefferson commenting on Sally Hemings's hair in Bear, *Jefferson at Monticello,* 4. For an interesting discussion of light-skinned Hemings blushing, see Gordon-Reed, *Hemingses of Monticello,* 271–72.

167. Jefferson mentioned Sally Hemings directly in a letter to his son-in-law John Wayles Eppes ("Maria's maid" had just given birth to a daughter, Thenia, who died in infancy) and indirectly when, in 1802, measles spread among some of the slave children and he wanted to give reassurance that everything was under control. See TJ to John Wayles Eppes, 21 December 1799, *PTJ* 31:274; TJ to Maria Jefferson Eppes, 1 July 1802, *PTJ* 38:4–5; and TJ to Martha Jefferson Randolph, 2 July 1802, *PTJ* 38:13.

168. Abigail Adams to TJ, 27 June 1787, *PTJ* 11:503. Many letters exchanged by the Eppeses and Jefferson during the months of the planning are lost.

169. Abigail Adams to TJ, 6 July 1787, *PTJ* 11:551.

170. Gordon-Reed, *Thomas Jefferson and Sally Hemings,* 164. For more information on Heming's education in France, see ibid., 160–66. It is also possible that

she may have lived with Jefferson's daughters at their convent school. See http://
www.monticello.org/site/plantation-and-slavery/appendix-h-sally-hemings-and-her
-children.

171. Marie Jacinthe de Botidoux to Martha Jefferson, November 1789–January
1790, Botidoux letters, University of Virginia; Maria Jefferson to Kitty Church, *PTJ*
16:xxxi and facing 52. In *Hemingses of Monticello*, 230, Gordon-Reed writes apropos
Botidoux's letter to Martha: "After Patsy returned to America, Botidoux wrote to her
and asked her to say hello to 'Mlle [Mademoiselle] Sale [Sally]' for her. In rigidly hierarchical ancien régime France, the honorifics monsieur, madame, and mademoiselle were strictly reserved for those of high standing, and they were guarded jeal-
ously. One cannot say it 'never' happened, but members of the French upper class
did not refer to *serviteurs* by any of those titles; 'Sally' should have sufficed. Patsy
Jefferson was a 'mademoiselle' in that world. Botidoux, for purposes of the letter,
put Hemings on a par with her. The young French woman was evidently making
a bow to her American friend's sensibilities, which indicates that Patsy Jefferson's
behavior toward Hemings signaled to outsiders that she was something more than
just a normal servant in the Jefferson household."

172. Isaac Jefferson in Bear, *Jefferson at Monticello*, 4; Henry S. Randall to James
Parton, 1 June 1868, in Gordon-Reed, *Thomas Jefferson and Sally Hemings*, 254.

173. I took these negative judgments from Callender's articles in the *Richmond
Recorder*; from a letter from Thomas Gibbons to Jonathan Dayton, 20 December
1802, William L. Clements Library, University of Michigan, copy at the Thomas Jefferson Library, Thomas Jefferson Foundation; and from Garry Wills's 1974 review in
the New York Review of Books of Fawn Brodies's *Thomas Jefferson* ("Uncle Thomas's
Cabin").

174. Jordan, "Hemings and Jefferson: Redux," 48. For a discussion of the fact that
individuals in general have always chosen as their mates "people who looked something like themselves," see Gordon-Reed, *Hemingses of Monticello*, 334.

175. Gordon-Reed, *Hemingses of Monticello*, 363. On the question of the eighteenth-
century lack of an African American identity, see ibid., 336–37.

176. Annette Gordon-Reed and Clarence Walker are even more radical, claiming
that Sally Hemings may have not defined herself principally as a black. See Gordon-
Reed, *Thomas Jefferson and Sally Hemings*, 165, and Walker, *Mongrel Nation*, 48–50.
Madison Hemings claimed that her mother "refused to return with him," and that
consequently Jefferson "promised her extraordinary privileges, and made a solemn
pledge that her children should be freed at the age of twenty-one years." Madison
Hemings in Gordon-Reed, *Thomas Jefferson and Sally Hemings*, 246.

177. On the "extraordinary privileges," see Madison Hemings in Gordon-Reed,
Thomas Jefferson and Sally Hemings, 246. On Thomas Jefferson Randolph, see
Henry S. Randall to James Parton, 1 June 1868, in ibid., 254. Edmund Bacon wrote
that women servants at Monticello, especially when Jefferson was president, "had
very little to do." Bacon in Bear, *Jefferson at Monticello*, 100. For further information

about Sally Hemings's residences, see http://www.monticello.org/site/plantation
-and-slavery/appendix-h-sally-hemings-and-her-children. On the best-case scenario,
see the discussion in Brodie, *Thomas Jefferson*, 352–53.

178. Possibly, in Paris Jefferson bought Hemings items he knew she could never
get once back in Virginia. But the amounts are never considerable. He spent, for example, 96 livres for Sally's clothes on 6 April 1789 and 72 on the 16th. But, on the
17th, he spent 64 livres for stockings for himself. On the 18th, 600 livres were paid
"on account for Encyclopedies for Dr. Franklin, F. Hopkinson, J. Madison & myself."
On the 19th, he spent 274 livres for linen for Patsy. On 11 May, silk for Patsy cost
229 livres, and on 17 May, 106 livres were employed for Patsy's shoes. *JMB* 729–30,
733. Jefferson's Farm Book documents, for example, that Sally received, for the year
1794, 10½ yards of Irish linen instead of rough osnaburg, but so had Jupiter, James,
Peter, Critta, and Betsy. TJ, *Farm Book*, 41. Clothing charts for the following years do
not show any startling difference among Jefferson's slaves, whether shoes, blankets,
stockings, or other necessities. These data seem to back up what Thomas Jefferson
Randolph said, that Sally Hemings "was treated, dressed, etc., exactly like the rest [of
the slaves]." Henry S. Randall to James Parton, 1 June 1868, in Gordon-Reed, *Thomas
Jefferson and Sally Hemings*, 255. On Sally Hemings counting on nurses, see Gordon-
Reed, *Hemingses of Monticello*, 518. On Hemings not entering the market with the
Jeffersons, see ibid., 608.

179. TJ to Mary Jefferson, 11 April 1790, *PTJ* 16:331.

Bibliography

Adams, Carol J. *The Sexual Politics of Meat: A Feminist-Vegetarian Critical Theory.* New York, 1990.

Adams, Henry. *History of the United States of America during the Administrations of Thomas Jefferson.* Ed. Earl N. Harbert. New York, 1986.

Adams, John. *The Adams-Jefferson Letters.* Ed. Lester J. Cappon. 2 vols. 1959. Reprint, Chapel Hill, N.C., 1987.

————. *Discourses on Davila: A Series of Papers on Political History.* 1790–91. Reprint, Boston, 1805.

Adams, William Howard. *The Paris Years of Thomas Jefferson.* New Haven, Conn., 1997.

Allgor, Catherine. *Parlor Politics: In Which the Ladies of Washington Help Build a City and a Government.* Charlottesville, Va., 2000.

Annas, Alicia M. "The Elegant Art of Movement." In *An Elegant Art: Fashion and Fantasy in the Eighteenth Century: Los Angeles County Museum of Art Collection of Costumes and Textiles,* 35–60. Organized by Edward Maeder. Essays by Edward Maeder et al. Los Angeles–New York, 1983.

Appleby, Joyce. "Commercial Farming and the 'Agrarian Myth' in the Early Republic." *Journal of American History* 68 (1982): 833–49.

Bak, Hans, and Walter W. Hölbling, eds. *"Nature's Nation" Revisited: American Concepts of Nature from Wonder to Ecological Crisis.* Amsterdam, 2003.

Bakhtin, Mikhail. *Rabelais and His World.* Trans. Hélène Iswolsky. Bloomington, Ind., 1984.

Barker-Benfield, G. J. *The Culture of Sensibility: Sex and Society in Eighteenth-Century Britain.* Chicago, 1992.

Baumgarten, Linda. *What Clothes Reveal: The Language of Clothing in Colonial and Federal America.* Williamsburg, Va., 2002.

Bear, James A., Jr., ed. *Jefferson at Monticello: Recollections of a Monticello Slave and of a Monticello Overseer.* Charlottesville, Va., 1967.

Bear, James A., Jr., and Gordon Jones, M.D. "Thomas Jefferson and His Health." Unpublished ms. Thomas Jefferson Foundation, 1979.

Beeman, Richard R. The Varieties of Political Experience in Eighteenth-Century America. Philadelphia, 2004.

Bellhouse, Mary L. "Candide Shoots the Monkey Lovers: Representing Black Men in Eighteenth-Century French Visual Culture." Political Theory 34 (2006): 741–84.

Benthall, Jonathan, and Ted Polhemus, eds. The Body as a Medium of Expression. London, 1975.

Bentham, Jeremy. Panopticon: or, the Inspection-House. 1791. In The Works of Jeremy Bentham, Published Under the Superintendence of his Executor, John Bowring. Vol. 4. Edinburgh, 1843.

Berkhofer, Robert F., Jr. The White Man's Indian: Images of the American Indian, from Columbus to the Present. New York, 1979.

Boulton, Alexander O. "The American Paradox: Jeffersonian Equality and Racial Science." American Quarterly 47 (1995): 467–92.

Breen, Timothy H. "Horses and Gentlemen: The Cultural Significance of Gambling among the Gentry of Virginia." William and Mary Quarterly 34 (1977): 239–57.

———. The Marketplace of Revolution: How Consumer Politics Shaped American Independence. New York, 2004.

———. Tobacco Culture: The Mentality of the Great Tidewater Planters on the Eve of Revolution. 1985. 2nd ed. with a new preface. Princeton, N.J., 2001.

Brod, Harry, and Michael Kaufman, eds. Theorizing Masculinities. Thousand Oaks, Calif., 1994.

Brodie, Fawn M. Thomas Jefferson: An Intimate History. 1974. Intro. Annette Gordon-Reed. Reprint, New York, 2010.

Brown, Kathleen M. Foul Bodies: Cleanliness in Early America. New Haven, Conn., 2009.

———. Good Wives, Nasty Wenches, and Anxious Patriarchs: Gender, Race, and Power in Colonial Virginia. Chapel Hill, N.C., 1996.

Buffon, Georges-Louis Leclerc, Comte de. "Histoire naturelle de l'homme." In Oeuvres Complètes de Buffon, avec des extraits de Daubenton, et la classification de Cuvier. 5 vols. Paris, 1837–41. Vol. 3, Mammifères, 1839.

———. Natural History, General and Particular. Ed. William Smellie. 2nd ed. 9 vols. London, 1785.

Bumstead, S. A. "A Description of Jefferson." Virginia Magazine of History and Biography 24 (1916): 309–11.

Burke, Edmund. A Philosophical Enquiry into the Origin of Our Ideas of the Sublime and Beautiful. 1757. Ed. Adam Phillips. Reprint, Oxford, 1998.

Burstein, Andrew. "Jefferson's Rationalizations." William and Mary Quarterly 57 (2000): 183–97.

———. Jefferson's Secrets: Death and Desire at Monticello. New York, 2005.

————. *Sentimental Democracy: The Evolution of America's Romantic Self-Image.* New York, 1999.

Burstein, Andrew, and Nancy Isenberg. *Madison and Jefferson.* New York, 2010.

Bush, Alfred L. *The Life Portraits of Thomas Jefferson.* Rev. ed. Charlottesville, Va., Thomas Jefferson Memorial Foundation, 1987.

Bushman, Richard L. *The Refinement of America: Persons, Houses, Cities.* New York, 1992.

Butterfield, Lyman Henry, et al., eds. *Adams Family Correspondence.* 12 vols. Cambridge, Mass., 1963–2015.

Byrd, William. *The Correspondence of the Three William Byrds of Westover, Virginia, 1684–1776.* Ed. Marion Tinling. Foreword by Louis B. Wright. 2 vols. Charlottesville, Va., 1977.

Calvert, Karin. "The Function of Fashion in Eighteenth-Century America." In *Of Consuming Interests,* ed. Cary Carson, Ronald Hoffman, and Peter J. Albert, 252–83. Charlottesville, Va., 1994.

Camp, Stephanie M. H. *Closer to Freedom: Enslaved Women and Everyday Resistance in the Plantation South.* Chapel Hill, N.C., 2004.

Campbell, Julie A. *The Horse in Virginia: An Illustrated History.* Charlottesville, Va., 2010.

Chappell, Edward A., and Julie Richter. "Wealth and Houses in Post Revolutionary Virginia." *Perspectives in Vernacular Architecture* 7 (1997): 3–22.

Chesterfield, Philip Dormer Stanhope, 4th Earl of. *Lord Chesterfield's Letters.* 1774. Ed. David Roberts. Oxford, 1992.

————. *Principles of Politeness, and of Knowing the World . . . Methodised and Digested under Distinct Heads . . . a New Edition, Carefully Revised and Corrected by James Ansell.* Antwerp, 1804.

Chinard, Gilbert. *Thomas Jefferson: The Apostle of Americanism.* Boston, 1929.

Clagett, Martin Richard. *Scientific Jefferson: Revealed.* Charlottesville, Va., 2009.

Cogliano, Francis D. *Emperor of Liberty: Thomas Jefferson's Foreign Policy.* New Haven, Conn., 2014.

————. *Thomas Jefferson: Reputation and Legacy.* Charlottesville, Va., 2006.

Cohen, I. Bernard. *Science and the Founding Fathers: Science in the Political Thought of Jefferson, Franklin, Adams, and Madison.* New York, 1995.

Conger, Vivian Bruce. *The Widows' Might: Widowhood and Gender in Early British America.* New York, 2009.

Crèvecoeur, Hector St. John. *Letters from an American Farmer.* 1782. Reprint, with prefatory note by W. P. Trent and introduction by Ludwig Lewisohn, New York, 1904.

Cripe, Helen. *Thomas Jefferson and Music.* Charlottesville, Va., 1974.

Cunnington, Cecil Willett, and Phillis Cunnington. *Handbook of English Costume in the Eighteenth Century.* London, 1964.

Curran, Andrew S. *The Anatomy of Blackness: Science and Slavery in an Age of Enlightenment.* Baltimore, 2011.

Darnton, Robert. *The Forbidden Bestsellers of Pre-Revolutionary France.* New York, 1995.

Deloria, Philip Joseph. *Playing Indian.* New Haven, Conn., 1998.

Dewey, Frank L. *Thomas Jefferson, Lawyer.* Charlottesville, Va., 1986.

Dewey, John. *Human Nature and Conduct: An Introduction to Social Psychology.* New York, 1922.

Dierksheide, Christa. *Amelioration and Empire: Progress and Slavery in the Plantation Americas.* Charlottesville, Va., 2014.

DiPiero, Thomas. "Missing Links: Whiteness and the Color of Reason in the Eighteenth Century." *Eighteenth Century* 40 (1999): 155–74.

Dorsey, John M., ed. *Jefferson–Dunglison Letters.* Charlottesville, Va., 1960.

Eden, Trudy. "Food, Assimilation, and the Malleability of the Human Body in Early Virginia." In *A Centre of Wonders: The Body in Early America,* ed. Janet Moore Lindman and Michele Lise Tarter, 29–42. Ithaca, N.Y., 2001.

Edmunds, David. R. *The Shawnee Prophet.* Lincoln, Neb., 1983.

Elias, Norbert. *The Civilizing Process.* Trans. Edmund Jephcott. Oxford, 1994.

Ellis, Joseph J. *American Sphinx: The Character of Thomas Jefferson.* New York, 1997.

Epperson, Terrence W. "Panoptic Plantations: The Garden Sights of Thomas Jefferson and George Mason." In *Lines That Divide: Historical Archaeologies of Race, Class, and Gender,* ed. James A. Delle, Stephen A. Mrozowski, and Robert Paynter, 58–77. Knoxville, Tenn., 2000.

Eze, Emmanuel Chukwudi. "Hume, Race, and Human Nature." *Journal of the History of Ideas* 61 (2000): 691–98.

Fanon, Frantz. *Black Skin, White Masks.* Trans. Charles Lam Markmann. New York, 1967.

Feirstein, Bruce. *Real Men Don't Eat Quiche.* New York, 1982.

Few, Frances. "The Diary of Frances Few, 1808–1809." Ed. Noble E. Cunningham, Jr. *Journal of Southern History* 29 (1963): 345–61.

Fiering, Norman S. "Irresistible Compassion: An Aspect of Eighteenth-Century Sympathy and Humanitarianism." *Journal of the History of Ideas* 37 (1976): 195–218.

Finch, Martha L. "'Civilized' Bodies and the 'Savage' Environment of Early New Plymouth." In *A Centre of Wonders: The Body in Early America,* ed. Janet Moore Lindman and Michele Lise Tarter, 43–59. Ithaca, N.Y., 2001.

Fliegelman, Jay. *Declaring Independence: Jefferson, Natural Language, and the Culture of Performance.* Stanford, Calif., 1993.

———. *Prodigals and Pilgrims: The American Revolution against Patriarchal Authority, 1750–1800.* Cambridge, 1982.

Foster, Augustus John, Sir. *Jeffersonian America: Notes on the United States of America,*

Collected in the Years 1805–6–7 and 11–12. Ed. Richard Beale Davis. 1954. Reprint, Westport, Conn., 1980.

Foster, Thomas A. *Sex and the Founding Fathers: The American Quest for a Relatable Past.* Philadelphia, 2014.

Fox-Genovese, Elizabeth. *Within the Plantation Household: Black and White Women of the Old South.* Chapel Hill, N.C., 1988.

Freeman, Joanne B. *Affairs of Honor: National Politics in the New Republic.* New Haven, Conn., 2001.

———. "Review of Rogow, Arnold A., *A Fatal Friendship: Alexander Hamilton and Aaron Burr.*" H-SHEAR, H-Net Reviews. September 2000.

Freneau, Philip. "The Philosopher of the Forest." No. 10. *Prose of Philip Freneau.* Ed. Philip M. Marsh. New Brunswick, N.J., 1955.

Friend, Craig Thompson, and Lorri Glover, eds. *Southern Manhood: Perspectives on Masculinity in the Old South.* Athens, Ga., 2004.

Gadsden, Christopher Edwards. *An Essay on the Life of the Right Reverend Theodore Dehon, D. D.* Charleston, S.C. 1833.

Gallagher, Shaun. *How the Body Shapes the Mind.* 2005. Reprint, Oxford, 2011.

Gaulmier, Jean. *Un grand témoin de la révolution et de l'empire, Volney.* Paris, 1959.

Gaustad, Edwin S. *Sworn on the Altar of God: A Religious Biography of Thomas Jefferson.* Grand Rapids, Mich., 1996.

Gilligan, Carol. *In a Different Voice: Psychological Theory and Women's Development.* 1982. Reprint, Cambridge, Mass., 1993.

Gilreath, James A., and Douglas L. Wilson, eds. *Thomas Jefferson's Library: A Catalog with Entries in His Own Order.* Washington, D.C., 1989.

Glover, Lorri. *Southern Sons: Becoming Men in the New Nation.* Baltimore, 2007.

Goodman, Dana. "Public Sphere and Private Life: Toward a Synthesis of Current Historiographical Approaches to the Old Regime." *History and Theory* 31 (1992): 1–20.

Gordon-Reed, Annette. *The Hemingses of Monticello: An American Family.* New York, 2008.

———. *Thomas Jefferson and Sally Hemings: An American Controversy.* Charlottesville, Va., 1997.

Gray, Francis Calley. *Thomas Jefferson in 1814, Being an Account of a Visit to Monticello, Virginia.* Boston, 1924.

Greene, Jack P. *Imperatives, Behaviors, and Identities: Essays in Early American Cultural History.* Charlottesville, Va., 1992.

Gubar, Susan. "The Female Monster." *Signs* 3 (1977): 380–94.

Guillaumin, Colette. "The Constructed Body." In *Reading the Social Body,* ed. Catherine B. Burroughs and Jeffrey David Ehrenreich, 40-60. Iowa City, 1993.

Gustafson, Sandra M. *Eloquence Is Power: Oratory and Performance in Early America.* Chapel Hill, N.C., 2000.

Hall, Stephen S. *Size Matters: How Height Affects the Health, Happiness, and Success of Boys—and the Men They Become.* Boston, 2006.

Haller, John S., Jr., and Robin M. Haller. *The Physician and Sexuality in Victorian America.* 1974. Reprint, Carbondale, Ill., 1995.

Hamilton, Alexander, James Madison, and John Jay *The Federalist.* Intro. Cass R. Sunstein. Cambridge, Mass., 2009.

Haulman, Kate. *The Politics of Fashion in Eighteenth-Century America.* Chapel Hill, N.C., 2011.

Hayes, Kevin J. *The Road to Monticello: The Life and Mind of Thomas Jefferson.* Oxford, 2008.

————, ed. *Jefferson in His Own Time: A Biographical Chronicle of His Life, Drawn from Recollections, Interviews, and Memoirs by Family, Friends, and Associates.* Iowa City, 2012.

Helo, Ari. *Thomas Jefferson's Ethics and the Politics of Human Progress: The Morality of a Slaveholder.* New York, 2014.

Hemphill, Dallett C. *Bowing to Necessities: A History of Manners in America, 1620–1860.* New York, 1999.

Hewes, Gordon. "World Distribution of Certain Postural Habits." In *The Body Reader: Social Aspects of the Human Body,* ed. Ted Polhemus, 81–87. New York, 1978.

Hodin, Stephen B. "The Mechanisms of Monticello: Saving Labor in Jefferson's America." *Journal of the Early Republic* 26 (2006): 377–418.

Hogarth, William. *The Analysis of Beauty: Written with a View of Fixing the Fluctuating Ideas of Taste.* 1753. Reprint, London, 1772.

Holland, Catherine A. "Notes on the State of America: Jeffersonian Democracy and the Production of a National Past." *Political Theory* 29 (2001): 190–216.

Hollander, Anne. *Seeing through Clothes.* 1978. Reprint, Berkeley, Calif., 1993.

Holmes, John M. *Thomas Jefferson Treats Himself: Herbs, Physicke, and Nutrition in Early America.* Fort Valley, Va., 1997.

Hume, David. *Essays and Treatises on Several Subjects. A New Edition.* London, 1758.

————. *Essays and Treatises on Several Subjects. In Two Volumes.* London, 1777.

Hunt, Lynn. *Politics, Culture, and Class in the French Revolution.* Berkeley, Calif., 1984.

Hunt, Patricia K. "The Struggle to Achieve Individual Expression through Clothing and Adornment: African American Women under and after Slavery." In *Discovering the Women in Slavery: Emancipating Perspectives on the American Past,* ed. Patricia Morton, 227–40. Athens, Ga., 1996.

Isaac, Rhys. "Communication and Control." In *Rites of Power: Symbolism, Ritual, and Politics since the Middle Ages,* ed. Sean Wilentz, 275–302. Philadelphia, 1985.

————. "The First Monticello." In *Jeffersonian Legacies,* ed. Peter S. Onuf, 77–108. Charlottesville, Va., 1993.

————. "Monticello Stories Old and New." In *Sally Hemings and Thomas Jefferson,* ed. Jan Lewis and Peter S. Onuf, 114–26. Charlottesville, Va., 1999.

———. *The Transformation of Virginia, 1740–1790.* 1982. Reprint, New York, 1988.

James, William. "What Is an Emotion?" *Mind* 9 (1884): 188–205.

Jefferson, Thomas. *Catalogue of the Library of Thomas Jefferson; Compiled with Annotations by E. Millicent Sowerby.* 5 vols. Washington, D.C., 1952–59.

———. *Family Letters of Thomas Jefferson.* Ed. Edwin Morris Betts and James Adam Bear Jr. Columbia, Mo., 1966.

———. *Jefferson's Extracts from the Gospels: "The Philosophy of Jesus" and "The Life and Morals of Jesus."* Ed. Dickinson W. Adams. In *The Papers of Thomas Jefferson.* 2nd Series. Princeton, N.J., 1983.

———. *Jefferson's Literary Commonplace Book.* Ed. Douglas L. Wilson. Princeton, N.J., 1989.

———. *Jefferson's Memorandum Books: Accounts with Legal Records and Miscellany, 1767–1826.* Ed. James A. Bear Jr. and Lucia C. Stanton. 2 vols. In *The Papers of Thomas Jefferson.* 2nd Series. Princeton, N.J., 1997.

———. *Notes on the State of Virginia.* Ed. William Peden. 1954. Reprint, Chapel Hill, N.C., 1982.

———. *The Papers of Thomas Jefferson.* Ed. Julian Boyd et al. 42 vols. to date, plus 13 vols. to date in the *Retirement Series.* Princeton, N.J., 1950–.

———. *Thomas Jefferson: Writings.* Ed. Merrill D. Peterson. New York, 1984.

———. *Thomas Jefferson's Farm Book: with Commentary and Relevant Extracts from Other Writings.* Ed. Edwin Morris Betts. 1953. Reprint, Charlottesville, Va., 1976.

———. *The Works of Thomas Jefferson.* Ed. Paul Leicester Ford. 12 vols. New York, 1904–5.

———. *The Writings of Thomas Jefferson.* Ed. Andrew A. Lipscomb and Albert Ellery Bergh. 20 vols. Washington, D.C., 1907.

Jordan, Winthrop D. "Hemings and Jefferson: Redux." In *Sally Hemings and Thomas Jefferson,* ed. Jan Lewis and Peter S. Onuf, 35–51. Charlottesville, Va., 1999.

———. *White over Black: American Attitudes toward the Negro, 1550–1812.* 1968. 2nd ed. Chapel Hill, N.C., 2012.

Jordanova, Ludmilla. *Sexual Visions: Images of Gender in Science and Medicine between the Eighteenth and Twentieth Centuries.* Madison, Wis., 1989.

Judge, Timothy A., and Daniel M. Cable. "The Effect of Physical Height on Workplace Success and Income: Preliminary Test of a Theoretical Model." *Journal of Applied Psychology* 89 (2004): 428–41.

Kant, Immanuel. *Observations on the Feeling of the Beautiful and Sublime.* 1764. Trans. John T. Goldthwait. Reprint, Berkeley, Calif., 1960.

Karlsen, Carol. *The Devil in the Shape of a Woman.* New York, 1987.

Keller, Christian B. "Philanthropy Betrayed: Thomas Jefferson, the Louisiana Purchase, and the Origins of Federal Indian Removal Policy." *Proceedings of the American Philosophical Society* 144 (2000): 39–66.

Kelso, Ruth. *The Doctrine of the English Gentleman in the Sixteenth Century.* 1929. Reprint, Gloucester, Mass, 1964.

Kerber, Linda K. "The Republican Mother: Women and the Enlightenment—An American Perspective." *American Quarterly* 28 (1976): 187–205.

Kierner, Cynthia A. *Beyond the Household: Women's Place in the Early South, 1700–1835.* Ithaca, N.Y., 1998.

———. *Martha Jefferson Randolph, Daughter of Monticello: Her Life and Times.* Chapel Hill, N.C., 2012.

Kimball, Fiske. "The Life Portraits of Jefferson and Their Replicas." *Proceedings of the American Philosophical Society* 88 (1944): 497–534.

King, Rufus. *The Life and Correspondence of Rufus King: Comprising His Letters, Private and Official, His Public Documents, and His Speeches.* Ed. Charles R. King. 6 vols. New York, 1894–1900.

Kolp, John G., and Terri L. Snyder. "Women and the Political Culture of Eighteenth-Century Virginia: Gender, Property Law, and Voting Rights." In *The Many Legalities of Early America,* ed. Christopher L. Tomlins and Bruce H. Mann, 272–92. Chapel Hill, N.C., 2001.

Kopelson, Heather Miyano. *Faithful Bodies: Performing Religion and Race in the Puritan Atlantic.* New York, 2014.

Kornfeld, Eve. "Encountering 'the Other': American Intellectuals and Indians in the 1790s." *William and Mary Quarterly* 52 (1995): 287–314.

Kranish, Michael. *Flight from Monticello: Thomas Jefferson at War.* Oxford, 2010.

Kukla, Jon. *Mr. Jefferson's Women.* New York, 2007.

Kupperman, Karen Ordahl. "Fear of Hot Climates in the Anglo-American Colonial Experience." *William and Mary Quarterly* 41 (1984): 213–40.

Laing, Ronald David. *The Divided Self: An Existential Study in Sanity and Madness.* 1960. Reprint, Harmondsworth, England, 1973.

Lasch, Christopher. *Women and the Common Life: Love, Marriage, and Feminism.* New York, 1997.

Lewis, Jan. "'The Blessings of Domestic Society': Thomas Jefferson's Family and the Transformation of American Politics." In *Jeffersonian Legacies,* ed. Peter S. Onuf, 109–46. Charlottesville, Va., 1993.

———. "Domestic Tranquillity and the Management of Emotion among the Gentry of Pre-Revolutionary Virginia." *William and Mary Quarterly* 39 (1982): 135–49.

———. *The Pursuit of Happiness: Family and Values in Jefferson's Virginia.* Cambridge, 1983.

———. "The Republican Wife: Virtue and Seduction in the Early Republic." *William and Mary Quarterly* 44 (1987): 689–721.

Lewis, Jan, and Peter S. Onuf, eds. *Sally Hemings and Thomas Jefferson: History, Memory, and Civic Culture.* Charlottesville, Va., 1999.

Lewis, Johanna Miller. "Women and Economic Freedom in the North Carolina Backcountry." In *Women and Freedom in Early America,* ed. Larry D. Eldridge, 191–210. New York, 1997.

Lindman, Janet Moore, and Michele Lise Tarter, eds. *A Centre of Wonders: The Body in Early America*. Ithaca, N.Y., 2001.

Locke, John. *Some Thoughts Concerning Education* and *Of the Conduct of the Understanding*. Ed. Ruth W. Grant and Nathan Tarcov. Indianapolis, 1996.

Lockridge, Kenneth A. *On the Sources of Patriarchal Rage: The Commonplace Books of William Byrd and Thomas Jefferson and the Gendering of Power in the Eighteenth Century*. New York, 1992.

Lovejoy, Arthur O., and George Boas. *Primitivism and Related Ideas in Antiquity*. 1935. Reprint, Baltimore, 1997.

Lupton, Deborah. *Food, the Body, and the Self*. Thousand Oaks, Calif., 1996.

Maclay, William. *Journal of William Maclay, United States Senator from Pennsylvania, 1789–1791*. Ed. Edgar S. Maclay. New York, 1890.

MacRae, Donald G. "The Body and Social Metaphor." In *The Body as a Medium of Expression*, ed. Jonathan Benthall and Ted Polhemus, 59–73. London, 1975.

Madison, James. *The Papers of James Madison*. Retirement Series. Vol. 2, *1 February 1820–26 February 1823*. Ed. David B. Mattern, J. C. A. Stagg, Mary Parke Johnson, and Anne Mandeville Colony. Charlottesville, Va., 2013.

Malone, Dumas. *Jefferson and His Time*. 6 vols. Boston, 1948–81. Reprint, Charlottesville, Va., 2005.

Martin, Ann Smart. *Buying into the World of Goods: Early Consumers in Backcountry Virginia*. Baltimore, 2008.

Martin, Charles D. *The White African American Body: A Cultural and Literary Exploration*. New Brunswick, N.J., 2002.

Marx, Leo. *The Machine in the Garden: Technology and the Pastoral Ideal in America*. New York, 1964.

Mason, John Edward. *Gentlefolk in the Making*. 1935. Reprint, New York, 1971.

Matthewson, Tim. "Jefferson and the Nonrecognition of Haiti." *Proceedings of the American Philosophical Society* 140 (1996): 22–48.

McCoy, Drew R. *The Elusive Republic: Political Economy in Jeffersonian America*. Chapel Hill, N.C., 1980.

McDonald, Robert M. S., ed. *Thomas Jefferson's Military Academy: Founding West Point*. Charlottesville, Va., 2004.

McEwan, Barbara. *Thomas Jefferson: Farmer*. 1991. Reprint, Jefferson, N.C., 2012.

McLaughlin, Jack. "The Blind Side of Jefferson." *Early American Life* 20 (1989): 30–33.

———. "Jefferson, Poe, and Ossian." *Eighteenth-Century Studies* 26 (1993): 627–34.

———. *Jefferson and Monticello: The Biography of a Builder*. New York, 1988.

Meacham, Jon. *Thomas Jefferson: The Art of Power*. New York, 2012.

Melish, Joanne Pope. "Emancipation and the Em-bodiment of 'Race.'" In *A Centre of Wonders: The Body in Early America, ed.* Janet Moore Lindman and Michele Lise Tarter, 223–36. Ithaca, N.Y., 2001.

Merleau-Ponty, Maurice. *Phenomenology of Perception*. 1945. Trans. Colin Smith. Reprint, New York, 2002.

Merrill, Boynton. *Jefferson's Nephews: A Frontier Tragedy*. 1976. Reprint, Lincoln, Neb., 2004.

Meschutt, David. "Gilbert Stuart's Portraits of Thomas Jefferson." *American Art Journal* 13 (1981): 2–16.

———. "'A Perfect Likeness': John H. I. Browere's Life Mask of Thomas Jefferson." *American Art Journal* 21 (1989): 4–25.

Miller, Charles A. *Jefferson and Nature: An Interpretation*. Baltimore, 1988.

Miller, John Chester. *The Wolf by the Ears: Thomas Jefferson and Slavery*. New York, 1977.

Miller, Perry. *Nature's Nation*. Cambridge, Mass., 1967.

Miller, Ralph N. "American Nationalism as a Theory of Nature." *William and Mary Quarterly* 12 (1955): 74–95.

Mischel, Walter. "Convergences and Challenges in the Search for Consistency." *American Psychologist* 39 (1984): 351–64.

Mizelle, Brett. "'Man Cannot Behold It without Contemplating Himself': Monkeys, Apes and Human Identity in the Early American Republic." *Pennsylvania History* 66 (*Supplemental Issue*) (1999): 144–73.

Morgan, Jennifer L. *Laboring Women: Reproduction and Gender in New World Slavery*. Philadelphia, 2004.

Morgan, Philip D. "Interracial Sex in the Chesapeake and the British Atlantic World, c. 1700–1820." In *Sally Hemings and Thomas Jefferson*, ed. Jan Lewis and Peter S. Onuf, 52–84. Charlottesville, Va., 1999.

———. *Slave Counterpoint: Black Culture in the Eighteenth-Century Chesapeake and Lowcountry*. Chapel Hill, N.C., 1998.

Morris, Gouverneur. *The Diary and Letters of Gouverneur Morris, Minister of the United States to France . . . etc*. Ed. Anne Cary Morris. 2 vols. New York, 1888.

Mullan, John. *Sentiment and Sociability: The Language of Feeling in the Eighteenth Century*. New York, 1988.

Nash, Roderick F. *Wilderness and the American Mind*. 1967. Reprint, New Haven, Conn., 2014.

Nelson, Dana D. *National Manhood: Capitalist Citizenship and the Imagined Fraternity of White Men*. Durham, N.C., 1988.

Newman, Simon P. *Parades and the Politics of the Streets: Festive Culture in the Early American Republic*. Philadelphia, 1997.

Nicolaisen, Peter, and Hannah Spahn, eds. *Cosmopolitanism and Nationhood in the Age of Jefferson*. Heidelberg, Germany, 2013.

O'Brien, Conor Cruise. *The Long Affair: Thomas Jefferson and the French Revolution, 1785–1800*. Chicago, 1996.

Onuf, Peter S., ed. *Jeffersonian Legacies*. Charlottesville, Va., 1993.

————. *Jefferson's Empire: The Language of American Nationhood.* Charlottesville, Va., 2000.

————. *The Mind of Thomas Jefferson.* Charlottesville, Va., 2007.

Parton, James. *Life of Thomas Jefferson, Third President of the United States.* Boston, 1874.

Pasley, Jeffrey L., Andrew W. Robertson, and David Waldstreicher, eds. *Beyond the Founders: New Approaches to the Political History of the Early American Republic.* Chapel Hill, N.C., 2004.

Paterson, David E. "Jefferson's Mystery Woman Identified." *Common-place.org.* 15, no. 4 (Summer 2015). http://common-place.org/book/jeffersons-mystery-woman -identified/.

Pearce, Roy Harvey. *The Savages of America: A Study of the Indian and the Idea of Civilization.* Baltimore, 1953.

Peden, William. "A Book Peddler Invades Monticello." *William and Mary Quarterly* 6 (1949): 631–36.

Plumer, William. *William Plumer's Memorandum of Proceedings in the United States Senate, 1803–1807.* Ed. Everett Somerville Brown. 1923. Reprint, New York, 1969.

Polhemus, Ted. "Social Bodies." In *The Body as a Medium of Expression,* ed. Jonathan Benthall and Ted Polhemus, 13–35. London, 1975.

Prude, Jonathan. "To Look Upon the 'Lower Sort': Runaway Ads and the Appearance of Unfree Laborers in America, 1750–1800." *Journal of American History* 78 (1991): 124–59.

Ragosta, John A. *Religious Freedom: Jefferson's Legacy, America's Creed.* Charlottesville, Va., 2013.

Ragsdale, Bruce A. *A Planter's Republic: The Search for Economic Independence in Revolutionary Virginia.* Madison, Wis., 1996.

Randall, Henry S. *The Life of Thomas Jefferson.* 3 vols. New York, 1858.

Randolph, Sarah N. *The Domestic Life of Thomas Jefferson.* 1871. Reprint, Charlottesville, Va., 1978.

Read, Allen Walker. "British Recognition of American Speech in the Eighteenth Century." *Dialect Notes* 6 (1933): 313–34.

Regis, Pamela. *Describing Early America: Bartram, Jefferson, Crèvecoeur, and the Influence of Natural History.* 1992. Reprint, Philadelphia, 1999.

Reinhold, Meyer. "Classical World." In *Thomas Jefferson: A Reference Biography,* ed. Merrill D. Peterson, 135–56. New York, 1986.

Rice, Howard C. *Thomas Jefferson's Paris.* Princeton, N.J., 1976.

Richter, Daniel K. *Before the Revolution: America's Ancient Pasts.* Cambridge, Mass., 2011.

Ricoeur, Paul. *Oneself as Another.* Trans. Kathleen Blamey. Chicago, 1992.

Roberts, Julian V., and C. Peter Herman. "The Psychology of Height: An Empirical

Review." In *Physical Appearance, Stigma, and Social Behavior*, ed. C. Peter Herman, Mark P. Zanna, and E. Tory Higgins, 113–40. Hillsdale, N.J., 1986.

Rothman, Joshua D. *Notorious in the Neighborhood: Sex and Families across the Color Line in Virginia, 1787–1861.* Chapel Hill, N.C., 2003.

Rotundo, E. Anthony. *American Manhood: Transformations in Masculinity from the Revolution to the Modern Era.* New York, 1993.

Rousseau, G. S. "Nerves, Spirits, and Fibres: Towards Defining the Origins of Sensibility." In *Studies in the Eighteenth Century.* Vol. 3, *Papers Presented at the Third David Nichol Smith Memorial Seminar, Canberra*, ed. R. F. Brissenden and J. C. Eade, 137–57. Toronto, 1976.

Rozbicki, Michal J. "A Barrier or a Bridge to American Identity?: The Uses of European Taste among Eighteenth-Century Plantation Gentry in British America." *Amerikastudien/American Studies* 42 (1997): 433–49.

Rush, Benjamin. *The Autobiography of Benjamin Rush; His "Travels through life" together with his Commonplace Book for 1789–1813.* Ed. George W. Corne. *Memoirs of the American Philosophical Society*, Vol. 25. Princeton, N.J., 1948.

———. *Benjamin Rush's Lectures on the Mind (Memoirs of the American Philosophical Society 144).* Ed. Eric T. Carlson, Jeffrey L. Wollock, and Patricia S. Noel. Philadelphia, 1981.

———. "Observations Intended to Favour a Supposition That the Black Color (As It Is Called) of the Negroes Is Derived from the Leprosy." *Transactions of the American Philosophical Society* 4 (1799): 289–97.

Sanford, Charles B. *The Religious Life of Thomas Jefferson.* Charlottesville, Va., 1984.

———. *Thomas Jefferson and His Library: A Study of His Literary Interests and of the Religious Attitudes Revealed by Relevant Titles in His Library.* Hamden, Conn., 1977.

Scharff, Virginia. *The Women Jefferson Loved.* New York, 2010.

Schlesinger, Arthur M. *Learning How to Behave: A Historical Study of American Etiquette Books.* 1946. Reprint, New York, 1968.

Schochet, Gordon J. *Patriarchalism in Political Thought: The Authoritarian Family and Political Speculation and Attitudes Especially in Seventeenth-Century England.* New York, 1975

Scott, James C. *Domination and the Arts of Resistance: Hidden Transcripts.* New Haven, Conn., 1990.

———. *Weapons of the Weak: Everyday Forms of Peasant Resistance.* New Haven, Conn., 1985.

Selby, John E. *The Revolution in Virginia, 1775–1783.* 1988. Reprint, Williamsburg, Va., Charlottesville, Va., 2007.

Shammas, Carole. "The Space Problem in Early United States Cities." *William and Mary Quarterly* 57 (2000): 505–42.

Sheehan, Bernard W. *Seeds of Extinction: Jeffersonian Philanthropy and the American Indian.* Chapel Hill, N.C., 1973.

Sheridan, Eugene R. *Jefferson and Religion.* Charlottesville, Va., 1998.

Shoemaker, Nancy. "How Indians Got to Be Red." *American Historical Review* 102 (1997): 625–44.

———. *A Strange Likeness: Becoming Red and White in Eighteenth-Century North America.* New York, 2004.

Sloan, Herbert E. *Principle and Interest: Thomas Jefferson and the Problem of Debt.* New York, 1995.

Slotkin, Richard. *Regeneration through Violence: The Mythology of American Frontier, 1600–1860.* 1973. Reprint, Norman, Okla., 2000.

Smith, Adam. *The Theory of Moral Sentiments.* 1759. In *The Essential Adam Smith,* ed. Robert L. Heilbroner and Laurence J. Malone. New York, 1987.

Smith, Mark M. *How Race Is Made: Slavery, Segregation, and the Senses.* Chapel Hill, N.C., 2006.

Smith, Samuel Harrison. *Memoir of the Life, Character, and Writings of Thomas Jefferson: Delivered in the Capitol before the Columbian Institute on the Sixth of January, 1827.* Washington, D.C., 1827.

Smith-Rosenberg, Carroll. *This Violent Empire: The Birth of an American National Identity.* Chapel Hill, N.C., 2010.

Smolenski, John. "From Men of Property to Just Men: Deference, Masculinity, and the Evolution of Political Discourse in Early America." *Early American Studies: An Interdisciplinary Journal* 3 (2005): 253–85.

Solnit, Rebecca. *Wanderlust: A History of Walking.* New York, 2000.

Spahn, Hannah. *Thomas Jefferson, Time, and History.* Charlottesville, Va., 2011.

Spencer, Jane. "'The Link Which Unites Man with Brutes': Enlightenment Feminism, Women and Animals." *Intellectual History Review* 22 (2012): 427–44.

Spivak, Burton. *Jefferson's English Crisis: Commerce, Embargo, and the Republican Revolution.* Charlottesville, Va., 1979.

Stafford, Barbara Maria. *Body Criticism: Imaging the Unseen in Enlightenment Art and Medicine.* Cambridge, Mass., 1991.

Stanton, Lucia C. *Free Some Day: The African-American Families of Monticello.* Charlottesville, Va., 2000.

———. *"Those Who Labor for My Happiness": Slavery at Thomas Jefferson's Monticello.* Charlottesville, Va., 2012.

Staples, Kathleen. "'Useful, Ornamental or Necessary in This Province': The Textile Inventory of John Dart, 1754." *Journal of Early Southern Decorative Arts* 29 (2003): 39–82.

Steele, Brian. *Thomas Jefferson and American Nationhood.* Cambridge, 2012.

Stuart, Reginald C. *The Half-Way Pacifist: Thomas Jefferson's View of War.* Toronto, 1978.

Sweet, John Wood. *Bodies Politic: Negotiating Race in the American North, 1730–1830.* Baltimore, 2003.

Szwed, John F. "Race and the Embodiment of Culture." In *The Body as a Medium of Expression,* ed. Jonathan Benthall and Ted Polhemus, 253–70. London, 1975.

Taylor, Alan. *American Colonies.* New York, 2001.

Ticknor, George. *Life, Letters, and Journals of George Ticknor.* 2 vols. Boston, 1876.

Trees, Andrew S. *The Founding Fathers and the Politics of Character.* Princeton, N.J., 2004.

Tucker, George. *The life of Thomas Jefferson, Third President of the United States: With parts of His Correspondence Never Before Published, and Notices of His Opinions on Questions of Civil Government, National Policy, and Constitutional Law.* 2 vols. Philadelphia, 1837.

Turner, Lynn W., ed. *William Plumer of New Hampshire, 1759–1850.* Chapel Hill, N.C., 1962.

Ulrich, Laurel T. *The Age of Homespun: Objects and Stories in the Creation of an American Myth.* New York, 2001.

Valls, Andrew. "'A Lousy Empirical Scientist': Reconsidering Hume's Racism." In *Race and Racism in Modern Philosophy,* ed. Andrew Valls, 127–49. Ithaca, N.Y., 2005.

Valsania, Maurizio. "Beyond Particularism: Thomas Jefferson's Republican Community." In *Cosmopolitanism and Nationhood in the Age of Jefferson,* ed. Peter Nicolaisen and Hannah Spahn, 93–111. Heidelberg, Germany, 2013.

———. *Nature's Man: Thomas Jefferson's Philosophical Anthropology.* Charlottesville, Va., 2013.

Vila, Anne C. *Enlightenment and Pathology: Sensibility in the Literature and Medicine of Eighteenth-Century France.* Baltimore, 1998.

Wagoner, Jennings L. *Jefferson and Education.* Chapel Hill, N.C., 2004.

Waldstreicher, David. *In the Midst of Perpetual Fetes: The Making of American Nationalism, 1776–1820.* Chapel Hill, N.C., 1997.

———. "Reading the Runaways: Self-Fashioning, Print Culture, and Confidence in Slavery in the Eighteenth-Century Mid-Atlantic." *William and Mary Quarterly* 56 (1999): 243–72.

———. "Why Thomas Jefferson and African Americans Wore Their Politics on Their Sleeves: Dress and Mobilization between American Revolutions." In *Beyond the Founders,* ed. Jeffrey L. Pasley, Andrew W. Robertson, and David Waldstreicher, 79–103. Chapel Hill, N.C., 2004.

Walker, Clarence Earl. *Mongrel Nation: The America Begotten by Thomas Jefferson and Sally Hemings.* Charlottesville, Va., 2009.

Wallace, Anthony F. C. *Jefferson and the Indians: The Tragic Fate of the First Americans.* Cambridge, Mass., 1999.

White, Deborah G. *Ar'n't I a Woman?: Female Slaves in the Plantation South.* 1985. Reprint, New York, 1999.

White, Morton. *The Philosophy of the American Revolution.* New York, 1978.

White, Shane, and Graham White. "Slave Clothing and African-American Culture in the Eighteenth and Nineteenth Centuries." *Past and Present* 148 (1995): 149–86.

————. *Stylin': African American Expressive Culture from Its Beginnings to the Zoot Suit.* Ithaca, N.Y., 1998.

Wiencek, Henry. *Master of the Mountain: Thomas Jefferson and His Slaves.* New York, 2012.

Wilentz, Sean. *The Rise of American Democracy: Jefferson to Lincoln.* New York, 2005.

Wills, Garry. *Henry Adams and the Making of America.* Boston, 2005.

————. *Inventing America: Jefferson's Declaration of Independence.* Garden City, N.Y., 1978.

————. "Uncle Thomas's Cabin." Review of *Thomas Jefferson: An Intimate History,* by Fawn M. Brodie. *New York Review of Books,* 18 April 1974, 216–27.

Wilson, Douglas L. *Jefferson's Books.* Charlottesville, Va., 1996.

————. "Thomas Jefferson's Early Notebooks." *William and Mary Quarterly* 42 (1985): 433–52.

Wilson, Gaye. "Recording History: The Thomas Sully Portrait of Thomas Jefferson." In *Light and Liberty: Thomas Jefferson and the Power of Knowledge,* ed. Robert M. S. McDonald, 187–206. Charlottesville, Va., 2012.

————. "Thomas Jefferson and Creating an Image for a New Nation." In *Cosmopolitanism and Nationhood in the Age of Jefferson,* ed. Peter Nicolaisen and Hannah Spahn, 137–67. Heidelberg, Germany, 2013.

Wokler, Robert. "The Ape Debates in Enlightenment Anthropology." *Studies on Voltaire and the Eighteenth Century* 192 (1980): 1164–75.

————. "Tyson and Buffon on the Orang-utan." *Studies on Voltaire and the Eighteenth Century* 155 (1976): 2301–19.

Yarbrough, Jean M. *American Virtues: Thomas Jefferson on the Character of a Free People.* Lawrence, Kans., 1998.

————. "The Moral Sense, Character Formation, and Virtue." In *Reason and Republicanism: Thomas Jefferson's Legacy of Liberty,* ed. Gary L. McDowell and Sharon L. Noble, 271–303. Lanham, Md., 1997.

Young, Iris Marion. "Throwing Like a Girl: A Phenomenology of Feminine Body Comportment Motility and Spatiality." In *Throwing Like a Girl and Other Essays in Feminist Philosophy and Social Theory,* 141–59. Bloomington, Ind., 1990.

Zagarri, Rosemarie. *Revolutionary Backlash: Women and Politics in the Early American Republic.* Philadelphia, 2007.

Zuckerman, Michael. "Endangered Deference, Imperiled Patriarchy: Tales from the Marchlands." *Early American Studies* 3 (2005): 232–52.

————. "Founding Fathers: Franklin, Jefferson, and the Educability of Americans." In *"The Good Education of Youth": Worlds of Learning in the Age of Franklin,* ed. John H. Pollack, 37–53. New Castle, Del., 2009.

Zuckert, Michael P. *The Natural Rights Republic: Studies in the Foundation of the American Political Tradition.* Notre Dame, Ind., 1996.

————. "Self-Evident Truth and the Declaration of Independence." *Review of Politics* 49 (1987): 319–39.

Index

Italicized page numbers refer to illustrations.

Recent Books in the Jeffersonian America Series

Maurizio Valsania
Nature's Man: Thomas Jefferson's Philosophical Anthropology

John Ragosta
Religious Freedom: Jefferson's Legacy, America's Creed

Robert M. S. McDonald, editor
Sons of the Father: George Washington and His Protégés

Simon P. Newman and Peter S. Onuf, editors
Paine and Jefferson in the Age of Revolutions

Daniel Peart
Era of Experimentation: American Political Practices in the Early Republic

Margaret Sumner
Collegiate Republic: Cultivating an Ideal Society in Early America

Christa Dierksheide
Amelioration and Empire: Progress and Slavery in the Plantation Americas

John A. Ruddiman
Becoming Men of Some Consequence: Youth and Military Service in the Revolutionary War

Jonathan J. Den Hartog
Patriotism and Piety: Federalist Politics and Religious Struggle in the New American Nation

Patrick Griffin, Robert G. Ingram, Peter S. Onuf, and Brian Schoen, editors
Between Sovereignty and Anarchy: The Politics of Violence in the American Revolutionary Era

Armin Mattes
Citizens of a Common Intellectual Homeland: The Transatlantic Origins of American Democracy and Nationhood

Julia Gaffield, editor
The Haitian Declaration of Independence: Creation, Context, and Legacy

Robert M. S. McDonald
Confounding Father: Thomas Jefferson's Image in His Own Time

Adam Jortner
Blood from the Sky: Miracles and Politics in the Early American Republic

Spencer W. McBride
Pulpit and Nation: Clergymen and the Politics of Revolutionary America

Maurizio Valsania
Jefferson's Body: A Corporeal Biography